Fada

Fada

Boredom and Belonging in Niger

ADELINE MASQUELIER

The University of Chicago Press
Chicago and London

The University of Chicago Press, Chicago 60637
The University of Chicago Press, Ltd., London
© 2019 by The University of Chicago
Published 2019
Printed in the United States of America

28 27 26 25 24 23 22 21 20 19   1 2 3 4 5

ISBN-13: 978-0-226-62420-4 (cloth)
ISBN-13: 978-0-226-62434-1 (paper)
ISBN-13: 978-0-226-62448-8 (e-book)
DOI: https://doi.org/10.7208/chicago/9780226624488.001.0001

Library of Congress Cataloging-in-Publication Data

Names: Masquelier, Adeline Marie, 1960– author.
Title: Fada : boredom and belonging in Niger / Adeline Masquelier.
Description: Chicago ; London : The University of Chicago Press, 2019. |
    Includes bibliographical references and index.
Identifiers: LCCN 2018051058 | ISBN 9780226624204 (cloth : alk. paper) |
    ISBN 9780226624341 (pbk : alk. paper) | ISBN 9780226624488 (ebk)
Subjects: LCSH: Young men—Niger—Social conditions. | Young
    men—Niger—Social life and customs. | City dwellers—Niger. |
    Masculinity—Niger.
Classification: LCC HV1441.N55 M37 2019 | DDC 305.242/1096626—dc23
LC record available at https://lccn.loc.gov/2018051058

The remedy for unpredictability, for the chaotic uncertainty of the future, is contained in the faculty to make and keep promises. . . . [B]inding oneself through promises serves to set up in the ocean of uncertainty, which the future is by definition, islands of security without which not even continuity, let alone durability of any kind, would be possible in the relationships between men.

Hannah Arendt, *The Human Condition*

CONTENTS

Introduction

Hausa speakers in Niger have an expression to capture the sense of immobility and powerlessness they associate with the failure to secure decent, stable livelihoods: *zaman kashin wando*, which translates literally as "the sitting that kills the pants." Figuratively speaking, to "kill one's pants" is to wear them out. In the past, manual labor frayed, ripped, and distressed garments, but in the absence of jobs it is now stasis that wears out a person's trousers. "*Zaman kashin wando, c'est la misère quoi!* [it's simply destitution/misery]" is how a young man, sitting with friends in a street of Niamey, Niger's capital city, pithily put it. By evoking simultaneously the material poverty and the mental distress he and his friends suffered as they just sat, waiting for elusive jobs, his comment captures the dual sense of deprivation and dislocation that characterizes the experience of many young men in urban Niger whose prospects for employment are limited.

In the past three decades, the labor market's ability to absorb emerging cohorts of job seekers has been undercut by economic reforms implemented in the name of fiscal responsibility.[1] Far from spurring economic growth and encouraging foreign investments, these reforms have plunged the country into economic insecurity, worsening many people's lives and shattering expectations of upward mobility. The state has shrunk social services and now dispenses minimal and largely inadequate education, healthcare, and security. Pressured to rely on cheap, flexible, disposable labor,[2] it has stopped acting as a job provider. Permanent positions in the civil service are scarce. Youths who sought upward mobility through schooling can no longer expect to be automatically recruited by the state, as was once the case. The private sector, insufficiently diversified, offers few opportunities for recent graduates. Though the mining sector has expanded and revenues from extractive industries have risen, unemployment, specifically youth unemployment, remains one of Niger's biggest challenges.

If educational credentials no longer offer guarantees of financial stability, they have nevertheless created aspirations that prevent youth, especially young men, from taking jobs they consider debasing. *Sai da dogon hannu*, unless someone with a "long arm" intervenes on their behalf, they will not find proper work. Every year large numbers of *jeunes diplômés* (young graduates) thus join existing cohorts of unemployed rather than take what some of them call *un travail de Vietnamien*, marginal, backbreaking, poorly paid, shamingly low-status labor. Because they lack the resources to marry and provide for dependents, they are unable to transition into adulthood. Their nonliterate counterparts, who navigate the so-called informal economy or end up working low-level, irregular jobs, are not much better off; the means of support they cobble up through a combination of hustling, hawking, and economic ingenuity are limited, and they lead lives of considerable precarity.

The enforced inactivity associated with joblessness weighs on those who, because they lack sustainable livelihoods, must put the future on hold. In a neoliberal world boasting of forward momentum and global potentialities, such inactivity is, in fact, the ultimate form of displacement.[3] The image of idle young men who fray their pants by *just* sitting captures the misery of an existence that has them burdened by immediate needs yet unable to plot a way out. It is a reminder that insecurity inscribes itself on the body and "registers on the senses" (Allison 2013:14) as a sense of being out of place, disconnected. According to Pierre Bourdieu (1977), bodily hexis is "political mythology realized" (93). It is through the body as the "site of incorporated history" (Thompson 1991:13) that social and ethical values become naturalized. In the case at hand, young men's economic marginalization is turned into an embodied disposition through the act of sitting. By producing signs of wear on garments, *zaman kashin wando* makes visible the damaging impact of social immobility on aspiring selfhoods. No matter how jobless young men pretend—through dress and other projects of self-fashioning—to follow expected life courses, their enforced idleness "kills their pants," defeating any efforts to project an appearance of prosperity against all odds. Granted, the deterioration young men invoke by deprecatingly referring to themselves as *masu kashin wando* (those who wear out their pants) is metaphorical. Their frustrated fantasies of middle-class consumerism—and their anguished wait for jobs that do not materialize—are real, however.

When asked what they were up to, young men I met in the streets of

Niamey and Dogondoutchi, a provincial town located some 270 kilometers east of the capital, often quipped that they were "just sitting." As they waited for the right job—or a job *tout court*—they spent their waking hours socializing and drinking tea. In urban neighborhoods throughout Niger young men routinely congregate in the street, seemingly unaware of the surrounding hustle and bustle. Their quotidian gatherings, which range from informal conversation spots to relatively structured organizations with governing boards and well-defined missions, are known as *fadas*—after the chief's or the emir's court. Though they can be occasionally found during the daytime (especially on weekends) under the shade afforded by a large tree, a straw shelter, or a mud wall, it is in the early evening that *fadas* truly come alive. At night, when other residents have retreated to their homes, the streets teem with clusters of young men who play cards, smoke water pipes, and chat or listen to the radio while waiting for the tea to brew.

Originally a Hausa term, *fada* has slipped into the Zarma language (spoken as a first or second language by a majority of Niamey residents), where it also designates conversation groups and "tea circles."[4] In urban Niger the fada is a place where young men excluded from the arena of work and wages forge new expressions of sociability and new spaces of belonging. Today the fada is an integral part of the transient infrastructure of urban Niger. Its presence bears witness to the collapse of what educated Nigériens call *l'État providence* (the welfare state) and the reconfiguration of modes of living and struggling at the margins of society. Fadas in Niamey, Dosso, Zinder, and elsewhere are filled with disaffected young men who seem to be "stuck," unable to progress into adulthood. Seemingly idle and with no places to go, they spend much of their waking hours at the fada. Elders complain that they are "sitting idly" (*zaman banza*) when they don't accuse them of being parasites who live off their parents for years (*zaman cin tuwo*, being there only to eat). "Sitting" here expresses in condensed form a sense of disaffection at the nexus of distinctly gendered experiences of juniority, contingency, and sociality. Aside from being part of the vocabulary of victimhood deployed by young men to describe the period of suspension between youth and adulthood, it conjures fixity, boredom, a sense of depletion, and a general inability to move forward. As is the case elsewhere on the continent (Archambault 2017; Mains 2012), the language of stasis captures young men's failure to meet social expectations measured against the universal telos of development.

Though seemingly benign, the discourse of idleness is often fraught with moral implications: to be idle is to be lazy. It is also to be weak and potentially susceptible to moral decay, or worse. Rather than seeing idleness as a by-product of structural inequality, many elders associate it with thievery and delinquency. Stably employed members of the younger generation themselves occasionally voice the opinion that *zaman banza* leads to alcoholism, drug addiction, and overall decadence. Claiming Niger needed youth who worked and took responsibility, a Nigérien activist recently said in an interview that young people "cannot build the country by continuing to sit around the shisha" (Aboubacar 2016, my translation). As observers such as this young activist see it, idleness is self-inflicted: the legions of unemployed who spend their time at the fada are slackers. They need to pull themselves up by their bootstraps; otherwise, sooner or later, they may find themselves on the wrong side of the law.

When it does not blame jobless youth for their lack of productivity, the discourse of idleness is steeped in the language of contingency, making space for certain narratives while excluding others. Among other things, it privileges the notion that young men's inability to attain mainstream ideals of masculinity is symptomatic of a wider crisis—a perspective that has inspired numerous studies of youth in the Global South. To fully understand what the fada as a collectivity does and how it enables young men to carve provisional spaces of existential possibility in the face of severely narrowed futures, I argue, we must separate the signs of crisis as explanatory models from the lived experience of un(der)employed young men who struggle in contexts of poverty and privation. The concept of crisis frequently mobilized to make events legible and give them historical significance is fraught, Janet Roitman (2014) has warned. Once an event is explained as "crisis," its singularity is abstracted by a generic logic that acquires the status of historical truth. Arguing that crisis is a "transcendental placeholder," not an observable event, Roitman invites us to scrutinize how it is used to designate revelatory moments (3). Responding to Roitman's invitation, this book, rather than framing youth in "crisis," considers how *samari*, young unmarried men on the cusp of adulthood, overcome insecurity and boredom by fashioning new spaces of belonging.

We have seen how *zama* (sitting) can be used to evoke the hardship of poverty and unemployment as in *zaman kashin wando*. *Zama* also has a range of other meanings associated with life and, specifically, the business of living, being, and becoming. In short, existing. In his *Dictionary of the Hausa Language*, R. C. Abraham (1946) offers the following translation for the noun *zama*: "state of being seated, remaining, dwelling" (964). For my present purposes, allow me to single out "dwelling." To dwell, according to Martin Heidegger (1977), is not merely to be inside a particular place.

Rather it is to *belong* to it, to have a sense of familiarity with that place. Put differently, to dwell is to be at home. For Heidegger, an important implication of having a place in which to dwell is that it leads us to spare and preserve that place—to nurture it and be, in turn, nurtured by it. The sense of homeliness that dwelling implies can also be experienced as a source of ease and comfort. Where one dwells, there is no need to put up a front for the outside world; one can be oneself. At another level, focusing on the lived experience of young men rather than on the so-called crisis they face also means recognizing the diversity of their urban experiences. Not all young men who dwell at the fada are jobless and "unoccupied." Some of them attend school, others are university students or civil servants, and yet others earn livelihoods as shoeshiners, motorcycle washers, itinerant tailors, street vendors, and so on. Whether they peddle, hustle, sit in classrooms, or simply sit and wait, many of them have a somber outlook on the state's capacity to take care of the younger generation. The government, they frequently complain, has let them down. In the absence of direct pathways to sustainable livelihoods, what they share despite their divergent life trajectories is a distinct sense of having been robbed of the predictable future.

This book sets out to describe Nigérien young men's experience of dwelling at the fada. Against the backdrop of economic volatility and material constraints, it explores the daily micropolitics through which forms of being-in-the-world and spaces of belonging are elaborated at the fada. My account focuses largely on samari (singular: *saurayi*), many of whom hope to secure decent jobs but are excluded from stable, salaried employment. As a vernacular expression of sociality largely fashioned by samari for samari, the fada is the place where they hang out and where they most feel at home. It is where they retreat when the world outside (elders, the government, and those who "hog" jobs) becomes too inhospitable and where they seek solace in moments of vulnerability—after a romantic setback, for instance. In short, it is *un entre-soi*, a "between us" space, as geographer Florence Boyer (2014:12) put it—a small bubble of intimacy built on a shared bond of trust and loyalty. The fada is also a space of experimentation that escapes communitarian prescriptions by charting new paths to recognition. It invites young men to be "themselves" (and open up to others without fear of being judged) while allowing for the emergence of alternative identities, imaginaries, and aspirations. In sum, the fada is a steady hub amid a volatile world. Through its "insistent materiality" (Chalfin 2014:93), it makes visible how disenfranchised samari lay claim to public space, crafting new codes and customs, new modes of inhabiting the world, and new expressions of belonging in the process. By considering the fada as a site of bricolage that allows for both pragmatism and acts of imagination, this book examines how young men in urban Niger, many of whom live precariously, engage in the quest for visibility and recognition in the absence of conventional avenues to self-realization.

In focusing on samari's aspirational projects, I seek to answer Joel Robbins's (2013) call for an "anthropology of the good" that overcomes the discipline's reliance on a metanarrative of suffering. This requires that we attend to the way people imagine life in a world that often exceeds the one they actually live in. Taking seriously people's imaginings of the good, Robbins insists, is not an invitation to assume they are always striving to do good. Rather it entails giving "these aspirational and idealizing aspects of the lives of others a place in our accounts" (458). From this perspective, disenfranchised samari can be reduced neither to victims, denied opportunities to secure sustainable livelihoods, nor to thugs who prey on more vulnerable others. Instead they are striving subjects who experiment, aspire, make mistakes, and exercise practical judgment on a routine basis. Let me stress here that the fada is not just a place for *fadantchés* (members of the fada) to hang out and pass time; it is also, I argue, a way of living. In this book, I discuss the performances young men engage in, the aesthetics they embrace, and the narratives they deploy as they tentatively stitch together fragments of the good life they aspire to. I focus on the patterns of relationality and the norms of conviviality as well as the codes of civility that shape life at the fada. Though many youth groups supply logistical assistance and mentorship that facilitate access to employment, I aim to show that the fada is more than a simple career training workshop. As an infrastructure of support, it provides the tools and techniques for repairing crippled selfhoods and giving bored, disoriented samari a sense of purpose while shaping them into responsible, discerning persons. Put differently, it constitutes a forum for testing and introspection where fadantchés can experiment with models of life while also reflecting on their actions and imagining alternatives. As such, it can be described as a "moral laboratory" (Mattingly 2014). At the intersection between moral experimentation and transformative experience, moral laboratories afford a privileged perspective on life such that habitual ways of seeing and living in the world can be actively questioned. They allow for possible futures within the ordinary, at times dispiriting, present. "At the fada, we do a lot of thinking and talking. You take a look at your life, so far, and where you want to go. The folks at the fada help you. Even when they point to your shortcomings," a saurayi explained.[5] As a form of "experiment in hope and possibility" (14), the fada empowers young men to create spaces for living that are also testing grounds for how life might be lived.

The Time of Youth

A vast, landlocked country whose economy depends heavily on agriculture and uranium exports, Niger is routinely described by foreign analysts as plagued by political instability, recurrent droughts, and chronic food insecurity. A decade or so after independence from France in 1960, Niger enjoyed a period of relative prosperity thanks to uranium revenues. With the collapse of the uranium market in the early 1980s, however, affluence abruptly ended. Unable to support its newly expanded infrastructure, Niger has experienced financial woes ever since, a predicament that neoliberal policies mandated by international lenders to ensure economic restructuring have only exacerbated. Although higher revenues are expected to fill government coffers—Niger, one of the world's largest uranium producers, recently became an oil producer, and it is expanding gold mining— the country's fiscal situation remains tenuous. In 2009 Niger struck a major deal with France on opening Imouraren, the largest open pit uranium mine in Africa. With the downturn in global uranium prices caused by the Fukushima nuclear disaster, however, the French dropped their plan for Imouraren, denting the country's economic prospects. Taking advantage of Libyan borders left unpatrolled after the Libyan state collapsed in 2011, the desert town of Agadez, a former tourist destination, became a major hub of migration of Africans to Europe. Local residents welcomed the economic activity after war and insecurity had driven tourists away. But after the Nigérien government, pressured by the European Union to intervene, passed a law targeting human traffickers in 2015 and some smugglers were arrested, the economic spurt surrounding migration dried to a trickle. Meanwhile, responding to attacks perpetrated by Boko Haram in eastern Niger and other sources of insecurity along the Malian and Libyan borders, the government has scaled up defense and security forces, reducing the financing of other projects.

For the majority of Nigériens, the politics of uranium extraction and the criminalization of migrant smuggling have made little difference. The UN's Human Development Index[6] routinely ranks Niger as the poorest country on earth. Well over half the country's population lives below the poverty line. Niger, where an average of seven children are born to every woman, also has the world's highest natality rate and highest population growth rate. With roughly half its population under fifteen, it is the world's youngest country. These demographics have real consequences for the cohorts of young people seeking to enter the workforce. While Niger's population has doubled over the last ten years, employment has failed to keep pace. There are simply not enough jobs for the thousands of youths entering the formal labor market every year. In urban areas, the problem of youth un(der)employment is especially acute. Many young men, wishing to escape the drudgery of subsistence farming, migrate to the city. But urban life offers no guarantee of financial security. I met young migrants in Niamey who, in the absence of supportive kin, struggled on their meager, erratic income. Had it not been for the fada, they might have gone hungry at times.

Given the country's limited resources, demographers warn that the current population explosion is unsustainable. Some of them describe Niger's youth as a "ticking time bomb," based on the "youth bulge" model, which identifies male youth as a historically volatile population. In other words, they see the abundance of young men without jobs as a threat to the country's security. Echoing alarmist discourses warning that the expansion of youth cohorts in Muslim majority countries provides recruits for terrorism, they argue that unemployment among the younger generation has turned Niger into a promising recruiting ground for extremist organizations such as Boko Haram. Ironically, samari often describe themselves as a ticking time bomb to underscore the urgency of addressing unemployment among the young. The state, their choice of language implies, ignores them at its own peril.

Before the World Bank and other international lenders imposed severe limitations on state spending as part of the implementation of structural adjustment programs, formal education was widely advertised as the ticket to a better life. Today, however, having a high school or university degree rarely translates into financial security. "The government brags, 'we created this, we created that.' What they created is poverty! You see samari with their *bac* [*baccalauréat*, high school diploma] who are stuck having to polish other people's shoes," an unemployed saurayi told me. Although still the largest employer in the nation, the state has stopped recruiting massively. In the past three decades, cohorts of irregular workers have been hired to fill the void left by the retirement of *titulaires* (permanent employees). *Contractuels* (workers in contract jobs) and *civicards* (volunteers of the civic service) now make up over two-thirds of the state's administration, including schools. Every year fresh university graduates apply for permanent positions in the civil service knowing they have few chances of being hired unless they have "connections." Consequently, many *jeunes diplômés* are either jobless or trapped in low-level, temporary jobs that provide limited financial security. They widely resent what they see as the government's blatant disregard for their predicament.

Given how restricted the private sector is, the overwhelming majority of unschooled young men and school leavers are pushed into the oversaturated informal economy where competition for resources is fierce, gains are generally minimal, and livelihood strategies are often marked by transience. I know self-employed men who have sold fruit or served tea for over a decade, but many samari I met rarely seemed to keep the same job for long unless they worked as skilled artisans. To capture at once the plight of the informally employed and that of graduates who seem to be "going nowhere," I use the term *un(der)employment*.

Many aspiring artisans and would-be technicians blame Nigérien leaders for not doing more to create opportunities (in the form of vocational training and financial assistance) for the younger generation. Yet it is youth who sought upward mobility through education who are the government's most vocal critics; they feel particularly victimized by economic policies aimed at shrinking the public sector. Some young men told me they took on poorly paid work "to avoid dying of hunger." They claimed they were driven by their grumbling bellies and could not make long-term plans to extract themselves from poverty. As far as they were concerned, life in Niger was reduced to a perpetual search for nourishment, and until this changed, the country could not advance. That the national drive to achieve food self-sufficiency—an ambitious target promoted in the early 2010s with the slogan *Les Nigériens Nourrissent Les Nigériens*—has so far failed highlights the challenges facing individual Nigériens. "One day, we will end up eating our diplomas," Zakari, a former sociology student, said. Aside from conjuring what another saurayi characterized as *la vision ventriste des Nigériens*, that is, his fellow Nigériens' inability to plan beyond their next meal, Zakari's comment hints at the anxiety permeating young people's attempts to imagine what lies ahead for them. Like his peers, Zakari attended school thinking he was acquiring skills that would ensure his professional future. When I met him in 2007, he was jobless. Like others who had joined the ranks of *diplômés-chômeurs* (unemployed graduates), he was forced to depend on his parents for subsistence.

Not only has schooling failed to guarantee livelihoods but it has created aspirations that make it difficult for youth, especially young men, to consider alternative income-earning strategies.[7] More than one saurayi told me they attended school with the expectation that their education would entitle them to a job "behind a desk" (i.e., in the Nigérien administration). Instead, their educational credentials seem to have diminished their employability. Whereas their nonliterate counterparts work as farmers, auto mechanics, tailors, carpenters, *kabu-kabu* (motorcycle taxi) drivers, or petty traders, young graduates expect to find jobs matching their qualifications. Rather than take what they call "shit jobs" (they use the English term), low-paying, labor-intensive occupations that will earmark them, many of them remain unemployed. Others take temporary positions as *contractuels*, waiting for something better to materialize. Yet others, desperate to improve their situation, leave their native communities in search of greener pastures. On foreign soil (where no one they know can see them engaging in menial labor) they realize marginal profits peddling imported goods or working as night watchmen, freight loaders, or masons.

With excess time on their hands, un(der)employed young men, throughout Niger, have joined fadas that meet under sheds, in entrance porches, or on simple benches in the street. Membership in these organizations cuts across social divides, educational backgrounds, and religious affiliations, affirming the spirit of egalitarianism and comradeship that drives these largely urban projects. They unite young men from the same neighborhood or who met in school. As members of fadas with evocative names such as L'Internationale des Chômeurs (The Internationale of the Unemployed), Money Kash, Lune de Miel (Honeymoon), or Brooklyn Boys, samari meet ostensibly to listen to popular music, play card games, and enjoy each other's company. They share resources, exchange information on career opportunities, and develop new friendships.

Above all the fada is a space of and for conversation in which humor alternates with pathos, and dreams coexist with existential angst. "We talk about everything; the good stuff, the bad stuff," a fadantché explained. Dire pronouncements about upcoming elections or a possible currency devaluation may follow lighthearted banter about a fada member's new motorbike or cell phone or the latest exploits of their favorite soccer player. At the fada young men find refuge from formal social constraints: they talk freely about the torments of love or tense relations with parents and need not hide their anxieties about the future or the resentment they feel for being abandoned by the government. At times, they huddle together around a large boom box blasting the jams of their favorite rap artists. At other times the exchange of words and tea enmeshes the participants in a tight web of solidarity and friendship, hinting that conversational sociability is a critical means of carving spaces of belonging in urban Niger.

Being Young in Urban Niger

In the past decades, owing to shifting demographics and rising rates of urbanization, the urban youth population has grown rapidly in the Global South. This has made youth a salient category for addressing issues of agency, generation, and social reproduction. There is by now a robust literature on urban youth, the creativity they deploy, the risks they take, and the livelihoods they craft in the face of significant challenges (Hecht 2008; Newell 2012; Sommers 2012). In Africa and elsewhere young people's responses to disaffection and disillusion have ranged from religious engagement to social banditry to excessive consumption. In appropriating cultural resources to overcome poverty, boredom, and exclusion, urban youth often break away from social (and religious) conventions, defying authority and heightening generational tensions. The licit or illicit itineraries they follow serve not only to map out possible futures but also to question society at large. A focus on urban youth thus provides a privileged vantage point for understanding broader transformations in the social fabric of cities. Cities, Karen Hansen (2008:13) writes, are not just places—settings for human activity: they are also ways of life. The carving of space along gender, class, age, and generational differences shapes the geography of urban environments, resulting in social configurations that often exclude people, especially young people.

Historically, scholarly representations of youth relied uncritically on stereotypical portrayals of young people as either victims or rebels. Whether they were viewed as vulnerable subjects, victimized by war, poverty, and disease, or as disruptive agents, they were largely relegated to the margins through their classification as a second-rate constituency—a subculture (Sharp 2002). Overcoming these blind spots has required focusing on children as legitimate social actors (Stephens 1995). As scholars have recently shown, a focus on youth provides a useful perspective on the dynamics of intergenerational reproduction and change (Cole and Durham 2007; Honwana and De Boeck 2005). By virtue of their structural liminality and through their position as relational beings, young people are uniquely situated to develop new perspectives—"fresh contacts" (Mannheim 1952). As a result, they can become significant actors in the struggle to define and speak for their generation.

In trying to remedy the limitations of earlier approaches to the "problem" of youth, however, anthropologists occasionally overcompensate. Deborah Durham (2008) has noted how pervasive the conception of youthful agency as "fundamentally oppositional" (165) is in the anthropological literature. Our views of adolescence, she argues, have been so thoroughly influenced by classic psychosocial models of human develop-ment and romanticized narratives of identity crisis that, in our accounts, youthful agency is almost always equated with rebellion, autonomy, and individualization. While we should certainly view youth as social actors, as Sharon Stephens urged us to, we must also situate them within the wider fields of power in which they are enmeshed. This means attending to the ways in which particular relations of subordination produce a "capacity for action" (Mahmood 2005:18) while also recognizing that agency is not nec-essarily antithetical to dependency, as I show in chapter 7.

Nigérien society is divided into young people and elders, but since the notions of juniority and seniority are situational, this means different things in different contexts, enabling people to claim (and perform) par-ticular age statuses as well as the entitlements and entailments associated with them. Male children are now circumcised at birth. At seven, they are considered *yara* (boys) and old enough to be sent away from home. Af-ter puberty, boys become samari (though they are still occasionally called *yara*). It is around that time that gender norms governing conduct take on their full implications. Samari are given separate sleeping quarters (called *ghettos* or *bunkers*), and their access to the houses of other men is restricted. Since adulthood is a matter of providing for a dependent, samari become fully adult upon marrying their first wife. In contrast '*yammata* (girls, never married young women) become women (*mata*) when they give birth to their first child. Social norms dictate that female sexuality be regulated within the bounds of marriage (roughly half of adolescent girls are mar-ried before the age of sixteen). Consequently, Nigérien females' experience of youth is much shorter than young men's. This means that women's ac-cess to social adulthood is not hampered to the same extent as men's by the austerity and joblessness they must navigate, though, of course, their ability to realize their visions of middle-class domesticity has often been substantially compromised.

That age or seniority is situational has important consequences in daily life. I once witnessed a mother fret about her youngest daughter's upcom-ing wedding because neither one of her older daughters had yet married. She felt the youngest of her daughters should not be the first to thread the path to adulthood. Back in his village at the end of the school year, a schoolteacher was initially rebuffed by local men for wanting to attend their meeting. Since he had yet to marry, he was technically a youth. The men eventually agreed that as the most knowledgeable man in the village (and the only one to attend school), he could not be excluded. Formal knowledge is highly valued in Niger, and teachers are accorded special status. Thus male teachers are called "Monsieur" by almost everyone, including senior men, signaling how class is entangled with age status. In chapter 6 I tackle the situationality of age and youth through a discussion of dress practices. In the way they give form (and substance) to identities, clothes are complexly implicated in the performance of age status. By dressing a certain way, young men can "play" at being adult (or youth). In an age of disappearing futures, the performance of age and seniority can be weighty, informed as it is by a pragmatic knowledge of life's exigencies.

Lacking the prospect of secure livelihoods, many young men delay the markers of transition to adulthood: marriage, parenting, and the formation of households. Hence the paradox: on the one hand, the overwhelming presence of samari in Nigérien cities and towns is difficult to ignore. Whether employed or not, sitting at the fada or contributing to the urban fabric in some other fashion, young men are seemingly everywhere. As Scott Youngstedt (2013:177) observes, Niamey today is a city of young people. Half its population is under fourteen years of age, and an additional quarter of it is between fifteen and twenty-four years old. On the other hand, young men are literally out of place—denied participation in the world of regular work and wages. Cast aside by the strictures of neoliberal policies and the structures of gerontocratic power, they turn to the street in their quest for dignified selfhoods.

In the anthropological literature, young men excluded from education, salaried jobs, and social adulthood are said to be in limbo or to linger in a state of "waithood" (Honwana 2012). Having become superfluous to the workings of capital, they must be rescued from social invisibility by our analyses. A problem is that life stages across time and space can no longer be described as unfolding in ways that would grant young people reliable pathways to seniority. The concept of youth, in this context, is notoriously difficult to pin down. Rather than constituting the transitional phase leading to adulthood, youth is often an indefinitely expandable life stage, affected by political instability, economic decline, and shrinking aspirations. In the absence of predictable life stages, scholars write about "social navigations" (Vigh 2006), "youthscapes" (Maira and Soep 2005), and "vital conjectures" (Johnson-Hanks 2002). Durham (2004) has usefully characterized youth as a "social shifter" (589) to highlight its indexical and relational nature, that is, the ways in which it is repositioned socially (and spatially) and claimed by people of widely varying age. While models of society often construct youth as symbolically pointing the way to the future, young people are increasingly unable to make something of the "utopic potential" (Comaroff and Comaroff 2005:24) typically associated with liberal conceptions of youngsters.

In Africa, Brad Weiss (2004) observes, it is the very capacity to shape the future that is currently caught up in a baffling conjecture, hindering self-fashioning projects as well as social reproduction. The chronic uncertainty that characterizes life under neoliberal capitalism has given rise, Jane Guyer (2007) contends, to a temporal frame in which the near future has been evacuated and replaced with a combination of "enforced presentism" and "fantasy futurism" (410). Stripped of their capacity to imagine a tangible future for themselves, people are caught between everyday survivalism, on the one hand, and a distant apocalyptic horizon, on the other. Based on the futurities produced by religion and economics, Guyer's bipolar model of temporality resonates with other attempts to capture the subjective experience of time in contexts of deep uncertainty (Comaroff and Comaroff 2000). Achille Mbembe (2002) thus writes of a future horizon overwhelmed by the urgency of the present and by mundane short-term calculations in which life becomes a "game of chance, a lottery" (271). The poor, it seems, are stuck in a dystopian present and find relief only by imagining the future through the lens of millennialism.

This situation is not confined to the Global South. As automation replaces jobs and certain types of labor are rendered irrelevant to the needs of global capital, growing numbers of people in the Global North find themselves cast aside—displaced from an increasingly competitive marketplace and from social networks once nurtured by professional engagements and consumer practices. Their lives, devoid of productivity and progression, slow down considerably, and boredom sets in. Given the scale of the problem, one can predict that idleness, its temporalities, and its affects will become topics of considerable interest to scholars documenting the experience of downward mobility and disenfranchisement. In a world where socioeconomic success is measured in terms of productivity, understanding inactivity (and the boredom that comes with it) may require new concepts and new methods. Here perhaps is a lesson to be learned from the Global South. By exploring the mechanisms un(der)employed young Nigérien men have devised to confront boredom, I hope to call attention to a social experiment under way in a part of the world long considered irrelevant to the centers of power and capitalist production. For the conditions to which the fada is a response—persistently high unemployment, intensifying informalization, and so on—are no longer specific to what once used to be known as the "Third World" but are, in fact, increasingly relevant to what is happening in the Global North.

The fada provides a counterpoint to isolation and boredom by endowing daily action with a purposeful quality. As a refuge from the harsh realities of the economic downturn, it transforms idleness into leisure, thanks in part to the way that "teatime" (during which tea is prepared and consumed) and other routines punctuate the boredom un(der)employed young men experience. Inactivity, this book aims to demonstrate, is a form of production. As an institution focused on the management of temporality through both the scheduling of concrete activities and the lived experience of social time, the fada fills the emptiness young men feel in the absence of regular occupations. By establishing temporal regimes, routinized programs, and highly codified moral prescriptions, samari are making life meaningful, valuable, and virtuous while also giving a sense of direction to their futures. This is not to say, of course, that these coping strategies necessarily bring about desired outcomes.

Searching for Respect

In Niger, where manhood is predicated on a particular nexus of rights and responsibilities vis-à-vis one's dependents, it is by marrying that male adolescents effectively become men. By founding a household, a man acquires "wealth in people" (Guyer 1995) and becomes a respectable person, that is, a person who receives social recognition from others, including peers and elders. Put differently, a man builds himself up through his capacity to provide for dependents. By the same token, those who cannot secure a livelihood are doomed to social immobility. They cannot hope to attract a wife until they have better prospects. Regardless of their actual age, they won't be seen as *cikakku mutane*, full persons, until they marry; a wife is said to complement her husband, while marriage is a sign of social maturity. *Ils ne sont pas considérés* (they are not respected), is how a *kabu-kabu* driver put it, implying samari were not awarded the social recognition married men typically received.

Respect, Hildred Geertz (1961) wrote, is "a matter of etiquette, the roles of proper behavior in specific situations" (19). In Niger, the principle of seniority governing how people relate to one another operates at all levels. This means that a fifteen-year-old can lord over a ten-year-old and a ten-year-old over a six-year-old. The fact that seniority dictates appropriate behavior between people should not blind us to the multiple ways that samari are disparaged because of their youth, however. More than simply a matter of "proper behavior in specific situations" (though it is that too), respect provides a measure of young men's success in carving a *proper place* for themselves. In the end, it is not (or not just) age so much as their ability to follow their plotted life trajectory that typically confers social recognition and allows them to carry themselves with confidence.

A number of samari I came to know complained that men younger than they were afforded more consideration because of their status as *masu gida* (household heads). "No one listens to us," a saurayi explained. "When someone greets you and you are married, they can ask 'how is your wife?' If you have no wife, they ask how you are. That's all. It reminds me I'm a *petit*," is how Bassirou, a fruit vendor, described the stigma of youth he experienced on a quotidian basis. Greeting someone can be a lengthy procedure in Niger. Whereas the daily greetings a household head typically receives acknowledge his "wealth in people," those Bassirou received were short, succinct, and seemingly less considerate. They were a painful reminder that he had no dependents whose well-being his acquaintances could inquire about as a matter of courtesy.

It is tempting to trivialize the humiliation Bassirou felt on the basis that his greeters did what they were supposed to do. A recognition of the embeddedness of the ethical in small acts of everyday life nevertheless alerts us to the ways in which our capacity to hurt others can take on trivial, seemingly benign expressions (Das 2012). For Bassirou, it was precisely the appropriateness of the greetings, the fact that they befitted his status as "social cadet" (Argenti 2002), that made them sting. By being perfunctorily asked about his own health—and nothing more—Bassirou felt belittled. The greetings hinted at his dependence on his family's goodwill for shelter and food. Intentional or not, they were an implicit condemnation of his inability to realize the life course he was expected to pursue. The fact that he attributed his incapacity to move up the generational ladder to the greed of elders—those very elders whose condescending greetings he had to endure—only added to his resentment.

Aside from gaining access to leadership positions, married men can draw support from kin and other webs of social connections in ways that single men cannot. Ibrahim, a twenty-seven-year-old saurayi who lived with his large family in a multigenerational compound headed by one of his uncles, explained: "If you are married and you need money, they will loan it to you because you have responsibilities. But no one helps you if you're wifeless." Ibrahim operated a *chap chap*, selling credit to cell phone owners. He dreamed of opening his own shop where he could sell fancy mobile phones. Looking for capital to purchase inventory, he had turned to family members for assistance, but no one would loan him money. "They know samari spend all their money on clothes and other things they don't approve of," he offered as a justification for both the lack of support his business scheme had generated and his thwarted ambitions to become a successful business owner. Many young men invoke a lack of capital as the principal reason why they just sit, waiting for the government to intervene. They speak of wanting to set up a tailor's workshop or earning a living as a *kabu-kabu* driver but not having the money to buy the sewing machine or motorbike they would need to set themselves in business. Ibrahim's story captures the predicament of samari whose juniority, equated with irresponsibility, is typically invoked by elders to deny them access to resources and preserve the status quo.

Worldly and educated as they may be, samari lack the wisdom of household heads—which is why the word of a married man weighs more than that of his single counterpart regardless of their ages. In a country where roughly 95 percent of people identify as Muslims, the consequences of being stuck in youth extend well beyond earthly life. Since unmarried Muslim youths are said to receive fewer divine rewards than married men for their five daily prayers, wifelessness can potentially compromise their chances of entering paradise. According to a young taxi driver, "even the Prophet [Muhammad] said he pitied single men. If they die before they marry, they will not go to heaven." In the way that their words and deeds are unfavorably compared with those of married men, male youths are routinely reminded of their inferior status.

The predicament of young men trapped in social immaturity extends beyond Niger. Across Africa male youth struggle to come to terms with unfulfilled personhood in conditions of anomie, economic hardship, and political instability (see Sommers 2012). In his study of social marginalization in East Harlem, Philippe Bourgois (1996) has documented how street culture, and particularly selling crack, offers young Latino men an alternative avenue to personal dignity that minimum-wage jobs cannot provide. In fact, the crack economy emerged out of young men's search for respect. Socialized not to accept public subordination, young men found that dealing crack was a morally acceptable compromise that fit with the street-centered dignity of rejecting legitimate work for low wages. For young Nigérien men who are routinely reminded of their juniority, the search for respect typically entails joining a fada. As a prime locus of masculine self-fashioning, the fada constitutes a sanctuary from life's daily indignities. In this respect, it is not unlike the boxing gym that Loïc Wacquant (2004), in his ethnography of pugilism on Chicago's South Side, depicted as "a lair. Where you come to seek refuge, to rest from the harsh, cruel light and looks you get from people outside your world" (238). Samari go to the fada to unburden themselves among like-minded others and bracket momentarily the miseries they experience in their efforts to secure livelihoods. Just as boxing enables poor African American men to regain pride, honor, and social approval, so weight lifting was, until recently, a critical component of many samari's quest for self-esteem at the fada (see chapter 5).

A Brief History of Fadas

Young men often connect the emergence of fadas with the beginnings of democracy in the early 1990s. The transition to democracy, they argue, was a time of loitering, debates, and tea drinking in the streets of Niamey. "The fada appeared with democracy. In fact, it began right after three students were killed," a saurayi told me, referring to the peaceful student march of February 9, 1990, that ended in a deadly shooting. University students were protesting a new round of austerity measures. Following the killing of three students by the Nigérien army, former students told me, youth started assembling in the street and drinking tea. According to a civil servant who was attending university at the time, "After the killings on the Kennedy Bridge, we began striking to pressure the government to listen to our demands. There were no classes to attend so we were bored and took to sitting in the streets. That's how the tea drinking started." Amid the new freedom and transparency that characterized talk about politics during the National Conference (held in 1991 at the instigation of students, teachers, and trade unions), students formed informal discussion groups throughout Niamey. They sat together in the street in plain view of everyone until late into the night. With the class boycott, they had plenty of time on their hands: they listened to music, played cards, and engaged in lengthy discussions about the world in which they lived. They also brought portable furnaces and small teapots to make tea. This is, according to former students, how the fadas were born. The sight of assembled young people freely discussing politics—an impossibility during the military regime of Seyni Kountché (1974–87) characterized by severe political censure—signaled a new era. As a prime instance of how ordinary citizens reclaim the right of self-expression, previously usurped by the state, the fadas radically reconfigured the spaces of sociality as well as the logic of political participation in the urban landscape. They exemplified what Jean-François Bayart has called "le politique par le bas," that is, politics from below (Bayart, Mbembe, and Toulabor 2008).

The narrative tracing the birth of fadas to the political turmoil that paved the way for democracy in Niger relies on a somewhat romanticized version of history and of the place of youth in it. Yet it also points to the critical role that fadas, as spaces of discussion, played in the formation of democratic subjectivities and to the ways in which, with the subsequent emergence of private radio stations in a newly expanded public sphere of debate, their participants came to imagine themselves as a collectivity. A saurayi who routinely discussed politics with fellow fadantchés told me that without freedom of expression, there could be no fada. Taking the case of Gadhafi's Libya as an illustration, he explained that "People there do not discuss politics for fear of being kidnapped." He implied that as political projects, fadas could not blossom in a country where dissent was not tolerated and anyone speaking out of turn could be carted off to jail.

Niger is an overwhelmingly Muslim country, though this hardly means everyone there agrees on how to define Islam. The liberalization of national politics in the 1990s enabled Nigériens to debate what it meant to be Muslim, among other things. Intensified global flows of image, capital, and information, new forms of associational life, and the use of media technologies facilitated the spread of new ideas about Islam. One movement in particular, the Jama'at Izalat al-Bid'a wa Iqamat al-Sunna (Society for the Removal of Innovation and Reinstatement of the Sunna, or Izala for short), spread quickly. Its members promoted religious education for all, insisting knowledge would liberate ordinary Muslims from "superstition" and idolatry (Masquelier 2009b). While they angered Muslim clerics by denouncing them as parasites living off a credulous population, the vision of an egalitarian society they promoted was embraced by the disenchanted. Frustrated young men with few prospects welcomed Izala's denunciation of Sufi corruption, social hierarchy, and conspicuous consumption. If the liberalization of media, markets, and politics enabled young Nigérien men to join religious associations, it also encouraged the dissemination of youth-oriented forms of musical culture (such as hip-hop), which found in the fada a most fertile ground. The religious landscape of Niger has since further diversified (Sounaye 2009). Aside from the multiplication of Islamic associations and modes of proselytism, Christian churches, in particular evangelical and Pentecostal churches, have proliferated as well. In its various configurations, Islam continues to provide a framework for scrutinizing practices that are vital to processes of generational affirmation and self-making. Thus exploring the place of hip-hop at the fada necessarily entails tracing samari's engagement with Islam (see chapter 4).

Portraying the fadas as the positive face of democracy tells only part of the story, however. With the democratic experiment came donor-mandated cuts to welfare and education that led to social fragmentation—and rising unemployment. While the ensuing precarity and insecurity threatened sa-mari's futures, they also provided opportunities to rethink oversight, regu-lation, violence, and security, and with them, the place of samari in urban space. Allow me to backtrack momentarily. Following the 1974 coup that ousted the first postcolonial government of Niger and established Colonel Kountché as the country's new president, a complex surveillance apparatus was set in place to bolster the regime. The secret police, known as *la Coor-dination*, suppressed political opposition while supposedly keeping corrup-tion in check.[8] Each year at the onset of the farming season, police raids targeted idle male youths in Niamey, shipping them back to their home villages so they could take part in farming activities. The promotion of agri-culture was the official pretext offered to justify the drastic measures. These "purges" had more to do with the regime's preoccupation with security, however (Issaka 2010). Unemployed young men who loitered represented a threat to the social order. At night military patrols policed neighbor-hoods, breaking up gatherings in the streets of the capital. This informal curfew effectively discouraged any expression of street sociality.

After Kountché's death in 1987, his successor, Ali Saïbou, was pressured by international lenders to shrink social services and trim the security bud-get as part of the first wave of structural adjustment programs. Large-scale layoffs and reduced recruitment in the civil service signaled the retreat of the state as enforcer of law and order. In a context of austerity com-pounded by rising unemployment and, in 1994, the devaluation of the CFA franc by half, new forms of urban violence reportedly emerged, trig-gered by the quest for survival.[9] In urban areas, insecurity became a serious concern. Residents reportedly refrained from sending children on errands for fear that they would be robbed by petty thieves (Göpfert 2012). These perceived threats, in turn, prompted the creation of an array of policing organizations operating largely beyond the grasp of the state: private se-curity companies contracted primarily by nongovernmental organizations (NGOs) and businesses as well as neighborhood militias known as *'yan banga*.[10]

'Yan banga were originally deployed in the 1950s in northern Nigerian cities to compensate for the lack of effectiveness of the police and deal with rising crime (C. Casey 2008). Local Nigérien leaders, hoping to simultane-ously restore security and give unemployed young men something to do, soon adopted a similar strategy. The *'yan banga*, who patrolled neighbor-hoods and kept thieves away in exchange for food and cash, were originally under the supervision of *chefs de quartier*. Soon they operated on their own. "They went where no policemen dared go," is how a friend put it. Tchanga,

who served as *préfet* of Niamey in the 1990s, reportedly encouraged *'yan banga* to take the law into their own hands and even kill the thieves they caught (Issaka 2010). As a component of what William Reno (2002) called "the politics of insurgency," the young vigilantes drew their legitimacy from their role as rescuers and the fact that violent justice was increasingly normalized.[11]

The *'yan banga*'s reign of terror is said to have started waning with the Nigérien military's return to power in 1996, following the coup that installed General Ibrahim Barré Maïnassara as head of state. By then the young vigilantes had lost the support of much of the citizenry (Lund 2001). People spoke of how they routinely colluded with the villains they were supposed to capture and referred to them as hoodlums. The press eagerly joined in the vilifying, portraying them as rascals that belonged in jail. Years later they are still remembered in some neighborhoods as lawless hooligans, though elsewhere some of them allegedly continue to patrol the streets at night. Searching for new ways to protect their homes and businesses, people turned to the young men who had taken to sitting together in the street until the wee hours after President Saïbou lifted the de facto curfew (Göpfert 2012). They plied the most dependable ones with tea, cigarettes, and beans and tasked them with guarding their *quartiers* at night. Samari's informal gatherings, which had come to be known as fadas, were progressively incorporated in the informal security apparatus. "People sleep better with the fadas keeping watch," I was often told. Since their inception in Niamey during the early days of the democratic experiment, fadas have proliferated in urban neighborhoods across the country, proof that ingenuity often emerges out of exigency and that spaces of belonging can be stitched together out of the very vulnerability of urban existence.

Researching Fadas

I first became aware of the existence of fadas in 2000 as I was researching the impact of the Islamic revival on women's lives in Dogondoutchi. On my way to visiting people, I would come across groups of young men sitting together in the street. They would hail me, and after exchanging greetings, I would sometimes join them for a while. Our conversations were often punctuated by servings of heavily sweetened green tea. I got to know some fadas quite well, and before long I was immersed in the daily concerns and aspirations of a number of local samari. Initially the fadas were merely a convenient place to meet young men when I was exploring the place of Islam in youthful subjectivities. The book I planned to write at the time was to feature no more than one chapter on the fada as a manifestation of emergent male sociality. Eventually I realized I could not do justice to the creativity and complexity of fadantché life in a single chapter and that to capture the "structures of feeling" (Williams 1977) in urban Niger, I should make the fada the focus of the monograph. So I switched course and embarked fully on a study of the lifeworlds of young men on the streets of Dogondoutchi. As an ethnographic vantage point, the fada provided a privileged entry into a set of overlapping concerns about youth, gender, consumer culture, and social reproduction in this region of Africa.

I was always welcome at fadas as long as I was willing to answer questions about life in the United States or my own life as an academic. I suspect many fadantchés viewed me as a welcome distraction from the daily tedium. My presence also offered validation of their pastimes and projects. It was proof of the fada's "charisma." Not everyone paid me attention, however. When I joined a cluster of samari engaged in conversation, the Scrabble or backgammon players, focused on their game, often ignored me. Once introduced to a fada, I was generally expected to visit regularly, if only briefly, as a matter of courtesy. This could be a challenge when two fadas scheduled an event on the same night. Only once did I feel a distinct unease while sitting with four fadantchés. They were polite but reserved, deflecting some of my questions (though they happily discussed how they tripped up and beat passersby). As I was walking away after bidding them goodnight, a neighborhood elder told me they were thieves and "thugs" who terrorized the neighborhood and I should stay away from them.

In the face of growing risks of expatriate kidnapping by Al Qaeda in the Islamic Maghreb in rural Niger, I relocated my research project to Niamey in 2008. Doing research in Niamey was advantageous on several levels: it gave me a sharper sense of the ongoing trends (stylistic and otherwise) at fadas across the country, and I could use Dogondoutchi as a basis for comparison. Having a wider territory to canvas, I was better able to assess the diversity of fadantchés' practices both within and across neighborhoods. Through the work I conducted in 2013 when I served as a consultant for the World Bank, I gained a better grasp of how the dense traffic between rural and urban areas has contributed to the diversity of the fadascape and the texture of fada life with its tastes and trends. In 2015 I spent my time photographing the inscriptions fadantchés etch on the walls against which they sit and taking stock of the transformations some of these walls (photographed on earlier trips) underwent over time, something I discuss in chapter 2.

Fadas, to quote Mbembe and Sarah Nuttall (2008), are "subjects *en fuite"* (25). They routinely outpace the ability of analysts to capture them in their scholarly descriptions. Mbembe and Nuttall are referring to the elusiveness of cities, but I argue the same can be said of fadas, as both instantiations of street politics and aesthetic projects forever subject to changing fashions. Fadantchés' inventiveness in the midst of want is astonishing. Their ability to respond to trends, shift registers, and create fresh idioms and new modalities of expression challenges our attempts to fix the meaning of these urban projects. As a locus of competitive sociality, the fada must continually reinvent itself to retain its power to impress others. It provides a remarkable exemplification of how the imagination, as a collective force, emerges as "a staging ground for action" (Appadurai 1996:7). Insofar as it constitutes a subject "on the move," it can be captured only provisionally in our accounts. As I write this introduction, some fadas are becoming training grounds for the choreographed dance performances samari now engage in during neighborhood competitions—an emerging trend that will likely be followed by others. No doubt, the fadantchés reading this book will find some of what I am describing somewhat outdated already. I hope nevertheless they will recognize themselves in the pages that follow and that they like what they read.

Although the ethnographic, archival, and photographic research on samari took place during five trips to Niger between 2004 and 2015, some of the material I draw on in the following has been collected over several decades. It spans hundreds of interviews, images, and archival documents and hundreds of hours spent hanging out at fadas. The limitations of what one can do in a book means I can only touch briefly on certain issues and must ignore others altogether. As is customary, I have changed the names of my interlocutors to preserve their anonymity but retained the names of public persons, such as politicians and well-known musicians. The names of the fadas and the nicknames of fadantchés I cite are real. Despite the fervent protests of many of my interlocutors, I have omitted the locations of these fadas for the sake of privacy.

Dogondoutchi, where I conducted the first half of the research, is a provincial town of roughly 80,000 inhabitants (when we include the seventeen surrounding villages in the urban district). It is the administrative seat of the *département* that bears its name and the capital of Arewa, a small territory of semiarid savannas lying at the western edge of Niger's Hausa-speaking region. Most of the town's residents identify as Mawri, with the rest composed of Fulani, Tuareg, Hausa, and Zarma mostly. The government's pattern of appointing civil servants away from their native regions and other forms of migration have diversified the population's ethnic makeup. In the past Hausaphone Mawri wore an "ethnic" mark, a double scar that cut the cheeks on each side. Today babies are no longer scarified. Although so-called Mawri are lumped into the larger Hausa ethnolinguistic group, they are the result of an "ethnic *brassage*" (Alidou 2005) and often claim ties to both Hausa and Zarma populations. For the younger generation, the idea of "Mawriness," or "Hausaness," while important, is secondary to the development of identities integrating them into larger communities defined by a shared Islamic consciousness, a sense of national belonging, an educational experience, or hip-hop culture.

Described in the 1960s as a large village endowed with the administrative services of an urban center (Guillon and Hernandez 1968), Dogondoutchi bears simultaneously the markings of tradition and modernity: it has only two paved streets, its older residential neighborhoods feature mud-brick dwellings, and it seems removed from the hustle and bustle of city life. Yet one could argue that it is almost as cosmopolitan as the capital itself. Young people can download the latest hip-hop songs from Dakar on their cell phones, local markets feature a wide variety of fashions, including the newest Ivoirian styles, and the recently opened Western Union office means people no longer have to travel to the capital to pick up remittances sent from abroad.

Niamey, where I conducted the second half of the research, is a multiethnic, sprawling metropolis and Niger's center of gravity. It has a population of over 1.3 million people, half of whom are native Hausa speakers or identify as Hausa.[12] With its large avenues, its roundabouts, its multistoried office buildings, and its rows of opulent villas whose surrounding walls are swarmed by bougainvilleas, it exhibits all the trappings of modernity. But the city is also home to modest, densely populated neighborhoods where large, mud-walled compounds may well house several families. Less than half of these compounds have electricity, and even fewer have running water (Hamidou and Ali 2005). While commercial areas and affluent residential neighborhoods feature a number of well-appointed stores, most shops everywhere are housed in cramped shacks made of corrugated roofing sheet or straw, and the sidewalks teem with ambulant vendors and *tabliers* (traders who display their goods on a small table). Niamey thus confounds any attempts to separate the so-called modern from the so-called traditional. The two are intricately interwoven, reminding us that modernity should be seen less as a historical condition than as a political project, whose aim has always been to center the West and marginalize the rest (Comaroff and Comaroff 1993).

Originally a cluster of small fishing villages lying on the edge of the Niger

River, Niamey has grown into a large cosmopolitan center with expansive new districts—some featuring elegant three-story mansions, others displaying rambling alleys lined with humble mud-walled structures. Every year it attracts thousands of rural migrants hoping to escape poverty and environmental degradation or attracted by the anonymity and possibilities urban living affords. In this respect, Niamey is as much a "nodal point" in multiple circuits of exchange as it is an "anchor point" for more settled livelihood strategies (Pieterse 2010:208). Many of the young men I spoke with in Niamey were born elsewhere. Some of them came from towns such as Gaya (in the south) or Agadez (in the north), and they now consider their birthplace part of the "bush." The Hausa term *gari* (town) marks the qualitative distinctions between urbanity and rurality, but the logic behind what gets defined as urban as opposed to rural is contextual. While Dogondoutchi is referred to as *gari* by its inhabitants in contradistinction to the surrounding area, it becomes part of *daji*, the bush, from the perspective of Niamey residents for whom anything beyond the boundaries of the capital qualifies as rural. If Niamey is for many *the* city in Niger, many fadantchés nevertheless view it as peripheral to the centers of global capital and commodity production. Striving to be seen as global citizens, they have renamed their *quartiers* to make them "cool": Boukoki thus becomes Book City, Gamkallé is now Gam City, and Lacouroussou is referred to as Lac City.

Whereas the fadas I came across in Dogondoutchi were often composed of young men who had grown up in town, those I visited in Niamey were heterogeneous—a reflection of the city's changing demographics and the long history of rural to urban migration.[13] In Niamey I worked primarily in the *quartiers* of Lamordé (one of the original villages later absorbed into the emerging city), Banifandou, Gamkallé, Boukoki, Lazaret, and Aviation. Save for rare exceptions, I have not differentiated the Dogondoutchi-based fadas from the Niamey-based ones. All are products of Niger's cultural and ethnic blending. In some ways the average Nigérien exemplifies the slipperiness of ethnic identities. Urban youth, who are increasingly born to interethnic families, attach less significance to ethnicity than to other markers of identity, including fada membership. To be sure, some fadas have a distinct ethnic makeup that fadantchés may highlight by giving it a recognizably ethnic name. Many don't, however. The ethnic heterogeneity is, in fact, a source of pride among fadantchés, as it suggests that their bonds are based on something more tangible than accidents of birth. "What we share is poverty," more than one fadantché told me, putting the stress on want and vulnerability while simultaneously downplaying any notion that fadas are based on exclusion.

Structure of the Book

The book chapters that follow are structured not chronologically but thematically. Each chapter includes some ethnographic material as well as a set of theoretical questions driving the discussion. Using the fada as both the material setting and the conceptual frame within which to consider the lived experience of young men in urban Niger, I explore the multiple facets of fada life to address a seeming paradox at the heart of male sociality. On the one hand, the fada is the concrete manifestation of young men's inability to find jobs and fill their time with meaningful occupations. It is a place for sitting, created for the specific purpose of waiting now that waiting has become an endemic condition. On the other hand, the fada is a place of busyness where the exigencies of entrepreneurial pragmatism and the disciplines of care are both sources of virtue and symptoms of time well spent. To reconcile these two inconsistent narratives—one about stasis, the other about motion—I examine a set of activities (tea making, dress practices, wall writing, and so on) through the lens of time. At the fada multiple temporalities converge, intersect, coexist: the seemingly endless wait for jobs, wedding preparations for a fadantché, the rhythm of Muslim daily prayers, weight-lifting routines, listening to the news on the radio, a cell phone conversation with one's girlfriends, and so on. Time is not just lived, it is also constructed, Nancy Munn (1992) argues, through a process she calls "temporalization" (104). Though not all the chapters are ostensibly about time, they are all part of my attempt to trace the multiple forms that futurity takes for samari and to wrestle with the multiple temporalizations unfolding at the fada and emerging most visibly through an implicit tension between stasis and movement, waiting and working, idleness and productivity.

Chapter 1 explores the texture of teatime at the fada and, specifically, how time is socialized through ritual performance. I discuss the making and sharing of tea, a practice young men have come to value greatly as they struggle to fill their days with purpose. Tea here refers not only to the leaves (and the drink made from them) but also to the whole apparatus (teapot, brazier, tray, glasses, and so on) required for its preparation and consumption as well as the experience derived from it. In the absence of other temporal markers punctuating daily life, teatime becomes a key happening, enabling samari to carve out meaningful temporalities and reconfigure their relation to the future. Chapter 2 examines the fada as an aesthetic project through which locality is materially and socially produced. I consider the wall writings samari design as a cultural production that makes visible their presence in public space and transforms the street into a key arena of masculine sociality—a space for dwelling. A major argument of the chapter is that fadas both claim public space and constitute places of intimacy. Understanding the fadas' relation to space also means considering their temporalities. The walls and the inscriptions they carry bear the imprint of time, and in so doing, I contend, they can be read as evidence of the dynamic, performative quality of places young men create. When fadantchés reach adulthood, they often turn over their fadas to younger siblings. My focus on visual culture is therefore an attempt to think about space in generational terms. In chapter 3 I turn my attention to the largely invisible women of the fada. Although the fada is viewed as a masculine space, I argue that women, especially 'yammata, are critical to the definition of masculinity and to the fada itself, as an institution whose continued existence hinges on the performance of female labor and social engagement. My discussion of women's contributions to the fada centers on the realms of domesticity, fantasy, and nighttime. It is often said that the fada is where samari were bit by the hip-hop bug and where they dreamed of becoming rappers as they listened to the radio. In chapter 4 I consider the role of hip-hop in the constitution of samari's Muslim identities and moral sensibilities. Though young men often recognize that hip-hop is "un-Islamic," many of them nevertheless see it as an ethical project aimed at fighting social injustice and improving lives. They describe rap as a form of awareness, a tool for teaching rights and denouncing wrongs. Rappers' claim to speak the truth gives them legitimacy because of the moral value people attach to gaskiya (truth). Through a focus on gaskiya as moral practice, I discuss how samari negotiate the contradictory ethical requirements of being Muslim and being rappers (or rap enthusiasts). Chapter 5 explores the workings of what I call "street ethics" as a dimension of the everyday at the fada. The concept of street ethics puts the accent on the moral ambiguity of projects, such as bodybuilding, that test the limits of the good. Weight work, diet, and other practices (which I refer to as "small disciplines") young men have adopted instantiate their quest for respect and their struggle to carve spaces of belonging. Street ethics also refers to the work that samari do. Through a discussion of night watch at the fada I show how sitting is transformed into a type of work and an expression of ethical commitment. In chapter 6 I consider how samari's dress practices are bound up in the definition of youth as both a stage of life and a lifestyle manifested by particular experiences of inclusion and exclusion. I examine how young men use dress to perform a range of improvisational identities so as to map out alternative life trajectories, at times to access adulthood, at other times to claim youth. Drawing on the concept of zigzagging, originally developed to refer to the unpredictability of entrepreneurial projects in the Global South (Jeffrey and Dyson 2013), chapter 7 examines how young men navigate a volatile political landscape that requires improvisation while hampering any long-term planning. Focusing on the case of a young man who aspired to a career in politics, I discuss how his trajectory exemplifies what I call "zigzag politics." Zigzagging is ultimately about being constantly on the lookout for new opportunities, mindful that these opportunities may evaporate as quickly as they arose. Solid opportunities arise mostly within the networks of patronage samari insert themselves in, reminding us that relations of dependence and obligation are critical to achieving social maturity and becoming a man in Niger. The conclusion draws together the book's larger argument about the fada as site of experimentation where young men overcome boredom and redefine the terms of belonging.

ONE

Waiting for Tea

Tea is like a member of the fada.

—Engineering student, 2004

It is ten in the morning on a dusty November day. I thread through narrow and winding lanes to reach a home tucked away behind an enormous neem tree. I have scheduled a chat with Boube, a twenty-five-year-old university graduate who is jobless, and his friends, all members of Bienvenue. We agreed to meet that morning at Boube's home. Upon entering the *zaure*, the entrance porch that buffers women's quarters from the street and is used by men to entertain friends, I discern four sleeping bodies. One of them appears to be Boube. I wait for the youths to rouse. When Boube finally awakens and sees me, he groggily asks whether I'd like some tea. Soon everyone is up, hot coals are brought from a woman's cooking fire, and tea preparation begins. Lawali, who was last to wake, sends a child to buy two cigarettes from a nearby street vendor. "Let's get some food," Hamissou, Boube's brother, declares. He empties his pockets but comes up with only 75 francs.[1] Together with the 50 francs Boube receives from his mother, it is enough to buy bread with a dollop of margarine for the four of them. "When you wake up and you must ask your parents for money to scuff some grub, you're reminded of your poverty," Boube laments.

Boube, Lawali, and Amadou (the fourth saurayi) have been friends since high school. After Radio Dallol was created in Dogondoutchi in 2000, they started listening to shows aimed at youthful audiences. Soon Bienvenue, their fada, was born. When organizing a cleanup in their neighborhood, they sent invitations to other fadas via the radio. They were full of hope and ambitions. Upon completing high school, some attended university while others took odd jobs. When I met the fada, Boube, who had earned a degree in history, had been trying to secure employment for two years, while his younger brother Hamissou, a high school dropout, was contemplating moving to Cotonou to look for jobs.

As the four young men wait for the tea to brew, the conversation turns to the problem of migration. One of Boube's friends recently found out his visa request was denied by the French embassy for the third time:

"You should have seen him, he was livid," Boube says as he lights one of the cigarettes the child returned with. "What's wrong with them? He just wants to sell his artisanry. Now that the tourists are gone here, selling abroad's the smart thing to do." He takes a small puff and passes the cigarette to Hamissou.

"Me," Lawali, now wide awake, chimes in, "I'm proud to be Nigérien. Better stay home than travel somewhere you're not wanted."

"Me too! Even if there was only one franc left in the National Treasury, I'd stay in Niger," Hamissou says, after inhaling and passing the cigarette to Lawali.

"Now why would anyone go to France? I heard they made smoking in public places illegal," Amadou blurts out.

"You know what that is?" says Lawali, who studied law. "It's an attack on civil liberties."

"But what's the point of being colonized?" Boube interjects. "We should be able to go there whenever we want."

"Come on, there's no reason to leave. Niger needs its children," says Amadou. "As far as I'm concerned, the fences [French president] Sarkozy set up, it's a good thing"—he pauses and turns to me—"limits the brain drain."

Migration was a frequent topic of discussion at Bienvenue. Boube's older brother lived in Senegal. In the past year alone, several members had considered going abroad to enhance their career prospects. Though emigration from Niger is negligible compared with that of neighboring countries such as Mali or Nigeria, many young men migrate seasonally to neighboring countries and many others dream of moving permanently to Europe or North America. Some years earlier Lawali was all set to attend university in Russia until he found out at the last minute his scholarship had been awarded to a more "meritorious" student. The experience had left him embittered. As their banter that morning suggested, the quartet held ambivalent views about migration. Nevertheless they admitted they would leave

Niger in a snap, if given the chance. "Holland, that's where I'd like to go. I heard women there are tall, big, and beautiful," Hamissou told me.

For conversation to flow smoothly, samari will tell you, it must take place around a pot of simmering tea. Indeed the routine of preparing and serving tea is widely considered the raison d'être of the fada. "You cannot have a fada without tea," is how an eighteen-year-old student put it, echoing a widely shared sentiment among fadantchés. Several times a day, young men engage in lengthy tea-making rituals involving brewing tea in minuscule metal kettles set on funnel-shaped braziers. Contradicting elders who see tea drinking as a frivolous activity serving no purpose, samari insist it is a fruitful way of spending time together. Anxious as they are to get on with their lives, they experience enforced inactivity as a torment. In this context, the lengthy preparation and consumption of tea not only participates in efforts to imbue life with future-oriented expectations but also constitutes a form of time management. As we shall see, through their absorption in the anticipatory experience—what I call the *jouissance*—of teatime, youth who are otherwise temporally suspended transform waiting into a goal-oriented, meaningful practice that helps them cope with the burden of waiting.

Tea, fadantchés claim, is the fuel of youth (*le carburant des jeunes*). Not only does it impart energy and fight boredom, but it also helps sustain the forms of sociality upon which un(der)employed young men depend in their struggle to make life purposeful. In this chapter I explore the distinct temporalities arising out of what Craig Jeffrey (2010), in his discussion of educated jobless youth in India, calls the "culture of masculine waiting" (4)—an experience that, while characterized by tedium and restlessness, is hardly purposeless. Rather than focus on what is lost under conditions of crisis and privation, I consider instead what is produced, and in particular how value, exchange, and affect emerge in the context of daily routines at the fada. In the absence of other temporal markers punctuating daily life, the practice of preparing and consuming tea is a critical event, enabling fadantchés to carve out purposeful temporalities and reconfigure their relation to the future.

The Art of Waiting

The economic downturn of the past decades has had a profound impact on young people's ability to attain social adulthood throughout the world, but particularly in the Global South. Like Amadou, Boube, and Lawali, who bemoaned their dependence on their parents for their livelihood, youth confronted with job scarcity are denied opportunities for advancement. Many are forced to delay marriage and family formation. Thwarted in their quest for growth and unable to found households, they are, to borrow an expression used by Karen Hansen's (2005) Zambian informants, "stuck in the compound."

Educated samari feel particularly victimized by joblessness given the prevalence of male breadwinner norms and the extent to which adult masculinity is defined in terms of financial stability. Additionally, their schooling was often prioritized over that of their sisters. Therefore much hinges on their ability to achieve societal betterment. Samari's failure to assume the role of provider and fulfill social expectations of masculine success is a stark reminder of their exclusion from Euro-American modernity—a predicament James Ferguson (1999) has characterized as "abjection" (236) to translate the debasement and humiliation experienced by mine workers impacted by the disastrous implementation of structural adjustment programs and the dramatic rise of poverty on the Zambian Copperbelt. Niger's low rank on the UN scale of human development further exacerbates un(der)employed samari's sense of degradation. When they didn't voice their suspicion that the UN rankings were based on falsified data, young men often confessed to me the deep shame they felt for being almost always *derniers* (last).

In their attempts to confront their abjection, young men throughout the world seek refuge in configurations of male sociality that offer solace from the world "out there" from which they feel excluded. In Ouagadougou and Bamako the *grins*, informal tea circles created by unemployed youth, have become the nexus of political engagement through which members negotiate access to various resources as they fashion rigid forms of street masculinity (Bondaz 2013; Kieffer 2006). In Meerut College, north India, unemployed young men have founded a club called Generation Nowhere. They meet once a month to commiserate about the worthlessness of their degrees (Jeffrey 2008). In Arusha, barbershops act as hubs for the dissemination of information as well as centers of male bonding in which young Tanzanian men weave connections to imagined elsewheres while defiantly proclaiming their exclusion from the world (Weiss 2009).

Although their expectations for the future are tinged with anxiety, educated young men (and to some extent their less literate counterparts) everywhere continue to hope that things will work out. Rather than taking poorly paid jobs for which they have neither inclination nor training, many delay their engagement in the working world in anticipation of possible opportunities. In barbershops and at tea stalls, in casual discussion groups or through their participation in formal associations (such as political parties), they engage in tactics of "deliberate waiting" (Jeffrey 2010:33). This trend is so pervasive in some places that Gérard Heuzé (1996), referring to India's idle youth, quips that waiting "may become a profession" (105).

Tactical as it may be, the waiting leads to ennui, apathy, and temporal anxiety. Yet it is not totally unproductive. Those who feel left out often occupy places that turn out to be critical spaces of cultural production and political practice (Das and Poole 2004; Tsing 1993). How the experience of rupture and alienation leads to the emergence of improvised techniques for making meaning and organizing social life is precisely what I examine here through a focus on the fada as a space of recreation. Passing time at the fada has led to the cultivation of an elaborate economy of leisure centered on the practice of making and drinking tea. Tea preparation (and consumption) obeys rules designed to ensure a heightened degree of masculine conviviality among participants, whether they be two or twelve. The tea maker is generally called *teaman* or *shaiman* (*shai* means "tea" in Hausa). At one fada, he was referred as a *fakir*, after the Muslim religious ascetic who lives off alms, a term at once self-deprecating and enabling that captures something of the distinctive masculinities young men forge at the fada through the display of a "form of empowerment which expresses the fact of 'powerlessness'" (Mazumdar in Jeffrey 2010:93).

Waithood versus Waiting

How youth negotiate the terms of their social participation in the face of great uncertainty has implications for the way we conceptualize youth as an indefinite, rather than transitional, stage of life as well as for the way we understand agency as more than simply a function of autonomous selfhood. To capture the predicament of young people in contemporary Muslim societies for whom the transition to full adulthood is fraught with difficulties, Diane Singerman (2007) coined the term "waithood." Waithood now describes the period of prolonged adolescence experienced by un(der)employed youth everywhere. When the rate at which young job seekers enter the market outpaces the capacity of local economies to provide employment, youth find themselves in waithood, a period of stagnation characterized by helplessness, dependency, and boredom. Unable to find steady jobs, marry, and start families (or, in some cases, to educate themselves), they are said to spend years in social limbo.

The concept of waithood superficially captures the predicament of young Nigérien men trapped in informal jobs or facing long unemployment spells, but it is not adequately nuanced to address the specific temporalities emerging out of their attempts to confront the mixture of ennui, detachment, and trepidation that is inevitably part of the waiting. Waiting, I argue, cannot be reduced to a passive experience of suffering but should be understood instead as a "tactical mode of life" (Makhulu, Buggenhagen, and Jackson 2010:12) out of which samari generate meaningful temporalities. In his discussion of barbershops in urban Tanzania, Weiss (2009) observes that

> subjugation is frequently approached simply as an absence of assertive capacity. Talk about subjugation often threatens to shatter the agency of those who endure it. If there are "weapons of the weak," weakness per se is not often counted among them. Discussions of social misery all too easily reduce the experience and expression of oppression to mere evidence of dependency, if not deprivation: but the concrete forms in which such suffering is felt and lived are rarely explored in themselves as meaningful socio-cultural phenomena. (216)

In this chapter I address emerging perceptions of time, sociality, and productivity through a critical examination of young Nigérien men's tea rituals at the fadas. Tea rituals are a coping mechanism through which samari invest themselves in the here and now, transforming "experience without qualities" (Goodstein 2005) into modes of self-affirmation and introspection. Despite young men's insistence that tea making is a legitimate occupation, for elders it typifies the younger generation's apathy and is symptomatic of a worrisome shift in the temporalities of youth. Aside from revealing how widespread anxieties about social reproduction have translated into tense debates about youth, their agency, and their temporality, my discussion of informal tea ceremonies sheds light on how young men go about their lives in contexts of privation and precariousness.

Meeting at the Fada

Like other youthful expressions of associative life elsewhere in the world, fadas have reconfigured the logics of sociality and the spaces of citizenship in Niger. After independence in 1960, the Nigérien government under the presidency of Diori Hamani mobilized the country's youth through the creation of a rural animation network. In 1976 Seyni Kountché, who succeeded Hamani, launched the Samarya, based on traditional models of associative life, to mobilize rural energies and create popular support for the regime.[2] For thirty years, the Samarya constituted a springboard for the recruitment and control of youth by the political leadership. In the wake of the liberalization of national politics in the early 1990s, the Samarya disappeared: "It was killed by democracy," is how one of my interlocutors put it. In its stead the fadas spontaneously emerged. Here is how a high school teacher described the shift from state-controlled mechanisms of civic training to street-centered configurations of informal citizenship:

> The Samarya, it's over. Before Kountché, it was a cultural tradition. But the state *a mis la main dessus* [grabbed it], forcing girls to dance for political meetings and when heads of state visited. Now with the education youth have received, no young agronomist or even high school student wants to dance with the drums in front of visitors. And then there's the influence of US rap, you see. . . . The Samarya, really, there's nothing left of it. Everywhere now, even in the countryside, you see young men with their big radios. They are going to listen to rap and to artists like Mali Yaro and Boureima Disco.[3]

Recall that the fada is widely associated with the advent of democracy in Niger. The first fadas are said to have appeared in the streets of Niamey in 1990 when students, teachers, civil servants, and trade unions held strikes to pressure the government to institute a multiparty democracy. Against the backdrop of growing popular discontent, they provided a forum where striking students could pass time, exchange news, and debate the future of the country while drinking tea. Like the Yemeni *qāt* chews described by Lisa Wedeen (2008) as "sites of active political argument" (145), they were privileged forums for the performance of citizenship. Soon, the fadas spread to other towns.

As the high school teacher's testimony above suggests, the portable radio has been a vital component of fada life, while the fada, in turn, has become a privileged vehicle for the dissemination of hip-hop in Niger (see chapter 4). In Dogondoutchi, Zinder, and elsewhere private radio stations established in the wake of media deregulation played a critical role in the emergence of fadas.[4] Young men would often point out to me that the fada was the place where they listened to their favorite musical programs with friends, and in fact many fadas formed out of the shared musical interests of groups of adolescent boys. Fadas are more than sites of musical experimentation and vectors of hip-hop culture, however. By harnessing the potential of radio, they emerged as a critical forum for the articulation of both political consciousness and collective intimacy. To make sense of the fada as a space of debate one must consider, if only briefly, the role of fadantchés as consumers of radio programs and as members of an engaged public.

Following the liberalization of politics and media in the early 1990s, a dozen private radio stations were set up across Niger, broadcasting news, discussions, and musical entertainment in various languages and providing an alternative to the state-sponsored programs of La Voix du Sahel and international radio stations such as Radio France Internationale and Deutsche Welle. Boom boxes soon became an essential ingredient of fada sociality, second only to tea (and it remained so until cell phones appeared to provide individualized forms of entertainment). To subsidize their programs, radio broadcasters encouraged youths to buy *cartes d'auditeurs*, cards that entitled the buyer to select a song and send radio greetings to a limited number of friends. Once greeting requests were sent to the radio announcer, young men would huddle together next to their radio and listen to their names being broadcast. Radio has the distinctive capacity to simultaneously bind listeners and radio hosts in a shared intimacy and constitute audiences as collective subjects (Fisher 2013). In the late 1990s and early 2000s radio sounds animated the private space of the fadas throughout urban Niger. By broadcasting the names of youth identified on greeting cards, DJs created a close, almost "private" relationship with some of their listeners while also encouraging fadantchés' recognition of themselves as a collectivity that mattered. The intimacy created through the greetings to individual listeners and the capacity for "collective abstraction" (the emergence of a self-aware audience) that these personalized greetings entailed provided the expressive architecture of fadas. Put differently, private radio stations, by cultivating a youthful public, became an important catalyst in the launch of fadas as both spaces of intimate sociality and self-conscious collectivities produced through mediatized address.

Broadcasters invited youths to debate issues ranging from national politics to personal matters. On Dogondoutchi's Radio Dallol one radio show known as *Le Jardin des Roses* (The Rose Garden) was designed specifically to enable youths to talk about their romantic woes and invite responses from the audience, thus contributing to the development of an "intimate public sphere" in which "emotional contact, of a sort" (Berlant 2000:vii) could be made. Other programs aired fada proceedings and interviews with fada leaders, affording the public unprecedented access to the intimate life of fadas. By promoting the formation of an "intimate public" whose participants shared "emotional knowledge" (vii) derived from a common historical experience, private radio stations helped institutionalize the fada as a collectivity and a nexus of enduring ties. In turn, the mediatization of fada activities fueled fadantchés' participation in this amplified sociality, affirming their connection with "a vaguely defined set of others" (Berlant 2008:7). Put simply, the radio provided the possibility of mutual recognition.

In the past two decades, the number of fadas has mushroomed, leading to new forms of solidarity and social activism. Some of them act as de facto NGOs and take on specific projects (providing assistance to Malian refugees fleeing their country's civil war in 2012 for instance), thereby contributing blueprints for imaging a decentralized, grassroots civil society in Niger. Responding to mounting poverty and inadequate infrastructure with innovative approaches, they have offered platforms for training and development or provided startup funds to young men lacking the social or material capital needed to jumpstart their careers. Many fadas function as *tontines*, with members making monetary contributions to a fund that is given as a lump sum to contributors on a rotating basis. This role is reflected in fadas' names. One fada in Dogondoutchi was named BIA, the acronym for Banque Internationale Africaine. Another was called Taimako (Assistance). These funds may finance a fadantché's wedding or provide assistance to financially strapped members while also helping buy necessities like tea, sugar, cigarettes, and food. "This is what the fada is really for, to provide assistance to the person in need," a young man explained. "When a member is sick, or someone in their family died—any type of problem—we help you." Members of a fada I knew in Dogondoutchi used the funds they received to travel to Niamey in search of jobs during the dry season. Another fada planned to establish a business center where youth could type and print their resumes, fax documents, and use the Internet. They had already purchased or received two desktops, a fax machine, and a couple of desks, and were looking for an adequate venue to house their center. Other fadas offered their services to municipalities (cleaning schools, planting trees, and so on) and earned cash through musical performances or the sale of harvested food (such as the fruit of the ron palm).

Not all fadas have a civic mission; some serve as nodes in drug distribution networks or meeting grounds for petty thieves. A young man I knew received his daily dose of amphetamines at the fada: "We pull our money together, someone buys the pills, then we share them amongst ourselves: we take *rima*, a yellow pill, *cinq* [five], one that makes you fall to the ground and then smoke comes out of your mouth, and also *allura* [needle, shot]. That one makes your entire body shake." During elections, a number of fadas become campaign headquarters for political parties. Others are more interested in generating social capital through artistic or musical channels. Over the years, many fadas have become part of the security infrastructure; since young men sit in the street until late, they can be on the watch for possible criminal activity at night. As a space of sociality, the fada thus encompasses a diverse range of projects and pursuits. Their diversity notwithstanding, the significance of these projects and pursuits cannot be fully grasped outside the context of austerity and anomie within which the fada, as a crucible of reflexivity and a space of experimentation, emerged.

The fadas' main agenda is to provide a space where jobless and impecunious members can voice personal anxieties, frustrations, and longings and receive support from other young (and often equally cash-strapped) men. "The fada allows us to cultivate ourselves," a fadantché said. "We discuss problems: unemployment, poverty, politics, our problems with our parents." When I join the members of Bad Boys one Saturday morning, they have just returned from a naming ceremony held for the newborn son of a fadantché's older brother. Someone is collecting the members' weekly contributions to the fada's treasury while the *shaiman* is washing the glasses and teapot in preparation for the first round of tea. A young man who moved to town six months before says he can't pay his share this week. He has shifted from one temporary job to another: working as a mason, offloading trucks at the nearby market, and selling boxes of facial tissue at large intersections. Money, he says, flies out of his pocket as soon as it's in.

"Here life is expensive," a saurayi who worked part-time as a watchman sympathetically notes. "The money I earn, once I pay my rent, a bag of rice, and water and electricity, pfff, I'm left with nothing."

"In the end, we work to survive and we survive to work," says a bespectacled young man who has been looking for work. "There's no evolution. It's a vicious circle."

"In this city, even to shit, you have to pay," interjects another unemployed saurayi.

"Yeah, that's true, but it's better to be poor in Niger than in France. At least, here, there's always someone to feed you," says the bespectacled young man.

The others grudgingly agree. The conversation soon veers toward the World Cup. Ghana, which qualified for the finals for the first time, just beat the United States. With Côte d'Ivoire eliminated, the Bad Boys are rooting for Ghana. But they are worried about its chances of beating Brazil, a superpower in the world of soccer.

Critical as the fada may be to idle young men whose day-to-day existence is ruled by waiting, it is worth noting that a number of fadantchés are gainfully employed while others are full-time students. In Niamey some fadas are composed almost entirely of university students who meet in the evening and on the weekend—with senior students serving as de facto tutors to their junior peers. In other fadas members are primarily working men. The fact that men remain in their fadas while moving in and out of employment suggests not only that fadas exhibit substantial diversity but that they evolve over time—with younger members occasionally replacing elder brothers who, because they left town or married, may be unable to meet regularly with age mates.

In Hausa, Niger's lingua franca, the term *fada* conventionally designates the court of the *sarki* (chief or emir) or the council of the *mai gari* (village chief). It is also the place of public audience and deliberation where rulers receive visitors, meetings are held about community affairs, and news is shared and spread. In short, it is where "people meet to talk." In contrast to the private courtyard where women engage in domestic tasks and conversation, it is a masculine space par excellence. In the 1990s the fada's connotation as a customary form of community assembly was recuperated by young men to designate their own social gatherings. Eager to escape the family compound and its matricentric activities, unemployed young men got together in a particular locale during their waking hours. Those who had jobs (or were still in school) met their fellow fadantchés in late afternoon to enjoy a game of *belote* (card game) and a few rounds of tea. Among adolescents these informal gatherings evolved into formalized organizations, taking their cues from the original chief's fada and other structures of governance. They were headed by a president assisted by a vice president, a secretary, and a treasurer elected by the membership. A DJ and an organizer might supervise the planning of festivities. Today some fadas feature a *conseiller* (counselor), a *contrôleur* (controller), and a *jugeman* (judge) variously tasked with promoting amity and enforcing discipline. Other fadas appoint a *taxeur* (or *taxman*) who levies taxes on fadantchés caught engaging in inappropriate behavior (see chapter 5). Some have a schedule of the themes they discuss (Monday is national politics, Tuesday is international politics, and so on).

More often than not, fadas bring together young men who have known each other since childhood. Aziz, a university student and member of Face Cachée (Hidden Face), explained how his fada evolved organically: "When we were younger we went to school together. Some of us didn't want to go home after school. So we chatted, drank tea, and ate together. Then we went home." With time, the informality of early gatherings gave way to a formal configuration with an elected leadership. The concept of fada thus covers a diverse set of social configurations ranging from informal discussion groups to highly structured associations requiring members to adhere to rules and regulations, wear uniforms, and engage in ritualized expressions of sociality. Gainfully employed older men with households to support still meet friends after work, but their gatherings tend to be informal, devoid of the performative quality their fada membership once may have had. Having successfully attained social adulthood, they no longer need to call themselves into existence by identifying as members of, say, Young Money or Killer Boys. Yet, the affective ties they share with peers remain strong.

Before they became the Cowboys, a group of longtime friends met daily on a street corner next to a tailor's shop: "We lived on the same street. We hung out together." As the friends got older, they felt the need to formalize their affiliation. Saidi, a university student, explained: "'Cowboy' means *enfant de vache*. We picked the name because we liked the lives of cowboys. One day we were together, wondering what name to give our fada, when one of us hit on the name 'cowboy.' We all stood silent, but we knew right away, this was our name!" Aside from publicizing the young men's infatuation with Hollywood westerns and US culture more generally, this fada's name betrays the enduring appeal of the American cowboy as a figure of heroic masculinity.[5] Although not enjoying the same currency as Bruce Lee and other martial arts heroes, the cowboy is nevertheless an icon of toughness and bravery for young Nigériens grappling with their inability to inhabit normative masculinities. The Cowboys founded their fada in 1996. A decade or so later, most members had moved away. Those who hadn't saw each other sporadically. Yet the corner was still known as Fada Cowboy.

By meeting daily at the same spot, fadantchés mark these locales with the visible signs of their presence, transforming previously undifferentiated street spots into meaningful spaces—"dwellings," as Heidegger (1977) called them to bring attention to the fact that it is through their awareness of place (and the "lived" relationships they maintain with it) that people relate to space. Though these territorial appropriations are largely symbolic, they become literal when members etch the fadas' names on the walls against which they sit—sometimes adding an arrow that marks the spot. In this regard these inscriptions are comparable to the graffiti through which European and North American inner-city youth excluded from the world of work and wages make ephemeral conquests in their urban neighborhoods. By "branding" public spaces, graffiti writers are reclaiming jurisdiction over spaces controlled by government and corporate authorities. The value of their artistry is grounded in the act of trespassing: by leaving a tag that functions as an "I was there," the graffiti writer deliberately tests the limits of authority (Sontag 1987). Fada graphics too are a means of laying claim to a place, but the aim is not to provoke so much as to provide a mooring for social gatherings, preferably with the blessings of neighborhood elders (see chapter 2).

One of the fada's essential features is its capacity for inclusion. The extroverted nature of these social gatherings is occasionally reflected in their names: Galaxie City, Sai Kun Zo (Till You Get Here), Ko Da Wace Ka Zo (Come Whoever You Are), and Planète (Planet). Along these lines, RFI, an acronym for Rassemblement des Frères Intimes, the gathering of intimate brothers, also stands for Radio France Internationale, a French public radio station that broadcasts across the world in several languages, including Hausa and Kiswahili. Members of RFI, most of whom had attended university, described their daily gatherings as *une radio mondiale*, underscoring not only their unique relationship to the French radio station (which they routinely listened to) but also the fada's consciousness of its links with the wider world. "At the fada," an RFI member told me, "we talk about everything and we are open to everyone. It's the RFI club." This deliberate reference to a global order that knows no boundaries bespeaks young Nigériens' efforts to insert themselves in a worldwide network of communicative practices from which they feel excluded despite their growing reliance on cell phones and Internet servers. At the local level, it is also about creating what Michael Warner (2002) calls a "co-membership with indefinite persons" (76), that is, a form of engagement with an audience of imagined others—including members of other fadas. RFI members liked to think of themselves as enlightened and classy. They were the epitome of the *'dan bariki*, the *évolué* or city slicker who demarcates himself from "rustic" neighbors through his refined manners, his sophisticated grasp of the world, and his adoption of urban "chic." They displayed their competitive spirit by holding annual feasts during which they impressed guests by offering them large amounts of food in classic potlatch fashion.

Note that RFI's slogan underscores at once openness ("we are open to everyone") and closeness (members are "intimate brothers"). The fada brings together young men who share a sense of helplessness at being trapped between youth and social adulthood. At the same time, it affords a refuge from the constrictions of the world of work and responsibility. Indeed the preservation of intimacy occasionally becomes central to the fada's identity. Take the case of Face Cachée. The name, Aziz told me, implies that "[outsiders] don't see us, don't know who we are," illustrating fadantchés' need to secure a space where they can be themselves without fearing opprobrium. When young men, feeling rejected by disapproving elders, leave the parental household or stop talking to their parents, fellow fadantchés take on the role of surrogate kin, offering moral support as well as material sustenance. According to Aziz, "In the fada, we help each other. We educate the younger ones. The fada is like a family." More than one youth I met referred to their fadas as a second family, acting as a bulwark against the daily humiliations they experienced in their quest for a viable future. They stressed the affective ties uniting fadantchés and the importance of shared rituals (playing cards, making tea, sharing jokes, etc.) for making life bearable.

As sites of masculine conviviality, fadas offer an antidote against loneliness, boredom, and despair, enmeshing young men in an "economy of affect" (Richard and Rudnyckyj 2009) that counteracts the damaging impact of the economic downturn. "With the problems we have, if we stay alone we'll go crazy. We must confide in friends," is how one young man, whose girlfriend had left him after he lost his job, put it. His faith in the fada's ability to assist him at a moment of great vulnerability hinged on the trust he placed in his fellow fadantchés. As he saw it, the fada was his last and best resort. One could say that joining a fada means entrusting oneself to

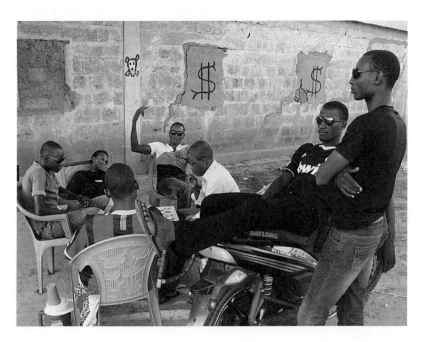

the care of others (and vowing to care for them in return) based on the certainty that one is interacting with individuals committed to the same definition of reality one adheres to. In the absence of concrete solutions to the problem of joblessness, samari find that having discussions with other young men, similarly confronted with an overabundance of time, alleviates worries about the future: "When you have nothing to do, you are left with your thoughts. Too many thoughts." Conversation, they claim, "is a useful thing,"[6] for it helps unburden the overabundance of thoughts and combat feelings of helplessness.

In theory anyone can join a fada. Before joining certain fadas, however, applicants are interviewed and must prove their good faith and secure the existing membership's approval. Fadantchés' attachment to their fadas and to each other runs deep.[7] "At the fada," a member of Top Star Boys said, "we share everything. When we go visit girls, we go together. We share ideas, we share resources, we share problems." When joining a fada, the new member agrees to follow the rules of fada etiquette designed to preserve harmony and integrity. He is further expected to help friends in need. "The fada," twenty-two-year-old Bashir explained, "it's about sharing problems." Through their active cultivation of loyalty, and despite the jealousy and competitiveness that routinely infect relationships, young men create networks of solidarity that endure, even after members marry or move to distant cities: "You migrate; when you return home, at the fada nothing's changed. Your friends are still here." In the face of great uncertainty, fadas constitute an affective nexus out of which fadantchés forge some sense of belonging. As we shall see, tea rituals are critical to this process.

Boredom and Temporality

Regardless of where they hail from, youth are typically perceived as the paradigmatic figure of national futures. In Niger young people are often described as holding the key to the nation's future. In past decades, this image has been undermined by rising unemployment. Unable to outgrow their juvenile status and assume the mantle of responsible adulthood, young men in particular are perceived as problematic beings by the older generation. Without jobs, they are ineligible to enter normative structures of conjugality and participate in social reproduction. In the current socioeconomic conjuncture, youth, once viewed as a finite stage of initiation and experimentation, is now significantly extendable. Rather than being seen as a source of productivity and potential, it has become an object of anxiety.

In a more immediate sense, young men traditionally symbolized secure futures for aging parents in need of economic assistance. It was with such a future in mind that parents sent their children, especially sons, to school. At independence young men who had received an education went on to become Niger's first professional cohort. As salaried civil servants they were able to provide financial support to elderly parents. So did the following generation of educated Nigériens. For pious Muslims, sending sons to school provided additional assurance that they would eventually subsidize their elders' pilgrimage to Mecca. Now that schooling no longer guarantees stable employment, however, parents cannot count on the young generation to support them. Instead of reaping the benefits of their investment in education, they must continue to provide for sons who, despite having reached chronological adulthood, cannot afford to feed themselves. In fact, a growing number of parents now financially support unemployed sons who have married and fathered children. As a reversal of the normative model of obligations that binds adult children to their elderly parents, such an arrangement constitutes what Claudia Roth (2008) calls an "inverted intergenerational contract." Elders have complained to me that they work while male youth do nothing but drink tea all day. For the older generation, the figure of idle young men sipping tea conjures visions of a severely compromised future.

Aside from personifying endangered futures, penniless tea-sipping male youth evoke a distinct temporality, disconnected from the tempo of industrious life. Recall that they are disparagingly referred to by Hausa-speaking elders as *masu zaman banza*, "those who sit idly." More than simply communicating idleness, *banza* signifies worthlessness. Describing someone as *banza* not only means that he is an unproductive, lazy person but also implies he is self-indulgent and dissolute. Unless he is straightened out, he may end up leading a life of delinquency.

Elders equate the idleness of youth with a futile, often decadent, and occasionally criminal form of existence that leads to moral indiscipline, sexual license, and economic failure. To be sure, I met sympathetic parents who understood their sons' need for companionship and spoke of fada activities as harmless distractions. "Our parents do not criticize the fada, the fact that we get together. They know you need friends. What they criticize is the fact that we're not working. They don't like us sitting, doing nothing," is how a saurayi put it. When the younger generation's failure to achieve social mobility is couched in moral terms, the fada emerges as a signifier of decadence—a place that nurtures young men's inclinations to lounge around rather than work. "Youth must learn there is a time for leisure, and there is a time for work. But most don't know the difference," a school administrator explained. Disillusioned parents told me it was at the fada that young men picked up bad habits such as smoking and drinking—not to mention taking drugs. It was allegedly there as well that they learned to disrespect elders and steal from them. Muslim preachers, too, accuse fadas of corrupting young men who develop addictions (to card games and tele-novelas), prompting them to ignore the call to prayer. Meanwhile newspaper editorials attribute low exam scores and, in particular, failure to pass the *baccalauréat* to the fadas' harmful influence on male youth. Paradoxically, according to a teacher, thousands of young men are given diplomas each year *just* to sustain the fada system. Such commentary provides a measure of the climate of cynicism (and hopelessness) surrounding the new cohorts of jobless graduates. Although fadantchés largely deny any involvement in crime, they are commonly identified by community leaders as *voyous* (hooligans) and accused of running gangs and engaging in criminal activities (Seidou 2008). Some have acquired a thuggish reputation for frequenting bars, picking fights with members of other fadas, and selling drugs. With the rise of fadas involved in community-oriented engagements, however, the perception that fadas are dens of delinquency is changing.

Even as they continue to submit applications for administrative or teaching positions, young men harbor few illusions about their ability to obtain secure jobs. Paradoxically, they remain hopeful that something will change and life will improve. Trapped in a state of ambivalent expectation, they feel disoriented, unable to channel their energies toward particular tasks. Instead of finding fulfillment in the spread of time, as people normally do when the activities they engage in create a sense of progression in their lives, they are jammed in a place where nothing happens. Out of their disengagement with the flow of things arises a distinct feeling of alienation and anomie. The result is what Walter Benjamin (2003) calls "the atrophy of experience" (316). In a word: boredom.

Despite substantial evidence that boredom is a key component of the experiential texture of modern life everywhere, anthropologists, save for notable exceptions (Frederiksen 2016; Mains 2012; Musharbash 2007; O'Neill 2017), have been remarkably silent on the subject. On the other hand, philosophers, psychologists, and cultural critics have produced an extensive literature on boredom, although they cannot seem to agree on precisely what it is. For Charles Baudelaire, boredom is a demon, whose emergence is tied to processes of modernity. To be modern, according to the poet, is to be bored, caught in a dull state of permanent anticipation that heightens one's awareness of the "futility of being in this world" (Anderson 2004:746). Reinhard Kuhn (1976) defines boredom as a state of ennui that filters experience through a screen: What is filtered out and lost is precisely that which gives life meaning. Such a definition approximates young Nigérien men's experience of life as dull and depleted as well as their feeling of being denied the gratification that is presumably accessible elsewhere (Jervis et al. 2003). So does Heidegger's (1995) characterization of boredom as a state of suspense that—by taking one away from one's normal focus—opens one to the world. Young men told me that thanks to their idleness they were better positioned than people caught up in the pace of their laboring lives to appreciate how the world had changed: after all, what is a fada if not a place of productive observation, a ground-level *mirador* from which to watch the world go by? Some samari named their fada Kallon Kowa (Watching Everyone), suggesting they saw their meeting place as a privileged site for observing what went on in the neighborhood.

Whether conceived as loss or longing, confusion or sharpened awareness of what one is missing, boredom is directly connected to the perception of time. It therefore provides a convenient window into the experience of young men who are deprived simultaneously of meaningful work and of the small pleasures that ideally follow moments of toil. For young Nigérien men waiting for jobs that do not materialize, boredom is arguably a central dimension of everyday life. From the moment they awaken until they go to sleep, they are forced to live a diminished existence in which there can be no time *off* since time (in the form of meaningful engagement in the world of work and wages) is never *on* in the first place. Devoid of the various happenings that punctuate social life, their time stretches out amorphously, endlessly. It is felt as a vacuum into which each slice of time fades without leaving an imprint in the form of a memory (Raposa 1999). Like the bored Aboriginal Australians studied by Yasmine Musharbash (2007) at the Yuendumu settlement to whom nothing ever happens, jobless samari experience the flow of time as "an endless repetition of the same" (313).

Consider the samari who, unable to escape life's tedium, baptized their fada MDR, an acronym that stands for Manger Dormir Recommencer (Eating Sleeping Starting Over) (Hassane 2003). Unable to escape life's tedium, they embraced it by boldly proclaiming their boredom and disengagement from the world. For these fadantchés, the acronym implies, life was experienced as a daily repetition of dull routines structured around the mundane tasks of eating and sleeping, not as a progression toward a future that was qualitatively different from the present.[8] Whereas time ideally oscillates in such a way that daily life is experienced in terms of both endless repetition and inexorable change, for members of MDR every day was essentially more of the same.[9] Their experience of time had dissolved to the point of irrelevance. Put simply, at MDR, there could be no future: life was one long, dead stretch.

The MDR acronym was an ironic commentary on the meaninglessness of life when there appeared to be no purpose to one's existence but to fill one's stomach and catch some sleep. It captured something of the absurdities of the current era in which rather than embodying the hopeful potentialities of their country's future, samari were made to bear the dystopic implications of neoliberal policies that relegated large segments of the population to "bare life" (Agamben 1998) by excluding them from meaningful social existence and rendering them dispensable. The MDR moniker was also a defiant admission of failure. By literally spelling out the dreary regimen their lives were reduced to, MDR fadantchés signaled that they wanted to be noticed for what they had become: young men for whom time would stand still for as long as they were denied the livelihoods and social positions their education entitled them to. Boredom, they forcefully reminded us, was a form of disempowerment.

Though, at some basic level, the concept of boredom so dear to modernist theorists translates adequately the numbness felt by MDR fadantchés, it does not quite capture the spatiotemporal experience of reduction I am trying to describe. The French concept of désœuvrement (generally translated as "idleness") comes closer to summing up the combination of dullness, dread, frustration, and restlessness that characterizes young Nigérien men's temporalities. By implying imposed inactivity, it evokes the condition of enforced presentism in which un(der)employed male youth are trapped as well as the frustrated (yet also hopeful) anticipation they experience. Désœuvrement is at once an emotional state and a tactical posture from which young men deploy a horizon of expectations as they debate the form that their future will take. When asked what he and his friends talked about at the fada, a saurayi responded, "We speak of our future. It's very important to us," illustrating how sentiments like hope and anxiety orient people to particular kinds of expectations, thereby creating the possibility of a future.

Young Nigérien men's aspirations, it is worth noting, are fairly ordinary: to have a secure job, achieve financial independence, marry, and found a household. Yet these expectations are projected against the backdrop of an idealized past fostered by narratives of normative masculinity (the pervasive man-as-provider ideal) and nostalgically sustained by elders. Put differently, young men's temporal anxieties are inextricably tied to a discourse of loss and decline that is itself shaped by intergenerational interactions

(Berliner 2005). Tea rituals, perhaps because they are *not* associated with elderhood, have become a vital medium for young men's articulation of viable futures.

Preparing Tea

Young men's infatuation with tea, it is widely acknowledged, started with the rise of unemployment. In Mali the association between tea and youth unemployment is captured in the expression *thé-chômeur* used to refer to youth's conversation groups. Before neoliberal policies began to have an impact, the practice was primarily associated with Tuareg people for whom tea is a central part of daily life,[10] though civil servants were also known to break for tea in the afternoon. As secure job opportunities evaporated, young men confronted with the challenge of what to do with their time took to drinking tea while hanging out with friends. Before long they were hooked. "Tea drinking caught us like a virus," twenty-three-year-old Issa explained; "we were contaminated by the Tuaregs." There is no space to unpack the rhetoric of contamination that shapes youthful understandings of joblessness, poverty, and leisure. Allow me to simply point out that the language of disease resonates powerfully with the recent history of political repression and social discrimination suffered by Tuareg minorities in post-colonial Niger. By alluding to the Tuareg "infestation" that turned young Nigérien men into tea aficionados, Issa implicitly compared the current situation of unemployed youth to Tuareg populations' marginalization from Nigérien society: both groups have been victimized by national policies aimed at preserving the privileges of an entrenched oligarchy.

More than simply infectious, the sugared infusion is also addictive. "Tea is our drug," I was told. "Once you start you cannot stop." A young man once referred to tea as *thé fatal* to imply that one could not resist the tantalizing drink while also stressing how one became dependent on its strengthening qualities. Just as Tuareg people have long relied on the for-tifying effects of tea (as well as its power to numb hunger pangs in times of famine), so samari now count on tea to give them the necessary boost in depressing times. "Tea is young people's gasoline," Issa observed.[11] To benefit fully from the stimulating effects of tea, one must consume it in the company of other drinkers, never alone. As a site of intimate sociality, the fada provides the ideal setting for tea drinking. Indeed teatime has be-come the quintessential ritual of fadantché life; no gathering at the fada is complete without at least three servings of frothy tea. "Tea is like a member of the fada," a young engineering student explained. "When there's no tea, we say that there's a member missing. If you see a fada not sharing tea, you know something is wrong." Such a vision of commensality suggests not only that life at the fada centers on tea drinking but also that the very act of sharing tea forges the bonds out of which the experiential fabric of fada life emerges. In the way they orient young men to proper comportment (slurping is allowed but sipping all the foam out of the glass is considered selfish) as well as more encompassing dispositions expected of fada members (such as the deployment of seniority within the egalitarian setting of the fada), the micropractices that structure tea consumption are constitutive of lived experience at the fada. Ordinary gestures, such as drinking from the same glass, symbolize the trust, fondness, and intimacy that the members of a fada share. In some cases, rather than pouring a serving of tea for each participant, the tea maker pours the entire content of the kettle in a large glass from which everyone drinks. It is by leaving some tea in the glass for the next drinker that fadantchés strengthen the web of friendship and solidarity in which they are enmeshed. If *oikos* (family) was stipulated as those who feed together in ancient Greece (Lacey 1968), it seems fair to say that the fada is stipulated as those who drink tea together—or more accurately, those who drink tea from the same glass—in contemporary Niger. Note again that the value of this form of commensality lies in its capacity to create sociality. "Tea unties tongues," a saurayi volunteered. "When you bring tea to people, they're happy, they'll want to talk to you," another fadantché explained.

The significance of tea as a medium of conviviality is captured in the distinction samari make between Lipton tea (black tea), which is made quickly, necessitates minimal tea-making skills, and is drunk individually, and Tuareg tea (green tea), which requires patience and dexterity on the part of the tea brewer, is obtained following a multistep procedure, and must be enjoyed by a party of at least two (but preferably more) people. (Members of Lipton fada, who preferred Lipton tea to green tea, were a notable exception to this trend.) According to Boube, the unemployed university graduate from Bienvenue, "Tea is something you share. *C'est la convivialité.* You cannot drink a whole teapot on your own. That's the difference with *thé* Lipton. *Thé* Lipton, you make a cup, then you drink it alone. You don't need anyone else. Whereas as soon as you start [preparing] Tuareg tea, someone comes. They may be in their car but they come to have tea with you."[12] More than one young man told me that they struck new friendships while preparing tea: "Some guys stopped by when they saw me making tea and we became friends."

Not only is preparing tea a complex process but it is also a time-consuming affair requiring a precise calibration of experience and intuition on the part of the tea maker, as Michael Ralph (2008) demonstrates in his analysis of tea ceremonies in urban Senegal. The *teaman* first lights coals and waits for them to start glowing. Then he fills the kettle with tea and water. Since three servings are obtained from each batch of tea, the tea maker measures the proper quantity of tea for optimal taste: too much tea will make the first round of tea too bitter; too little will make the third round too weak. Then he sets the teapot on the coals and waits for the water to boil, fanning the stove to keep the ambers burning. Here again, a mixture of precision and patience is key. If the tea boils too quickly, it will bubble over. If the coals don't stay hot enough, the tea will not brew. Meanwhile everyone else sits around the tea maker and chats, pleasurably anticipating the moment when tea is finally served.

When the tea starts frothing out of the pot's spout, it is time to add the sugar. More waiting is then required. As the tea boils again, bubbling around the sides of the lid, it diffuses a fragrant smell, signaling to the *teaman* that he can proceed to the next step. Now comes the most delicate procedure as the *teaman* pours the tea into the metal glass, holding the kettle low, then high, and finally low again as the glass fills. Pouring from a height aerates the tea and creates the *mousse*, a thick layer of foam that protects the brew from dust and flies. Once the tea is poured back into the kettle, it is "cooked" further. This last step is repeated several times until the concoction reaches the right color and consistency. When the tea is ready, it is poured into shot glasses and served. The beverage is drunk in slow, slurping sips. Once the glasses are empty, water and sugar are added to the teapot and a second serving of tea is prepared. And then a third. By the time all the flavor has been extracted from the clump of tea leaves at the bottom of the teapot, an hour or two has elapsed.

Making tea is a skill that most young Nigérien men acquire, though some claim they never did. Through a graceful economy of motions informed by the canons of tea-making etiquette, the *teaman* distills not only tea but a whole aesthetic experience where auditory signals interact with visual, gestural, and olfactory clues. Fadantchés follow strict protocol. The proper display of manners during tea rituals signals more than a concern for preserving sociality. It also entails a practical form of ethical self-cultivation that is crucial to the valorization of timepass in the face of elders' disapproval. The fairly high degree of proficiency—a mixture of skills and sensibility—required to orchestrate a successful performance (not a drop of tea should be wasted) means we can perhaps speak of the art of tea making at the fada. The gurgling sound of the tea splashing into the metal glass (or the soft crunching sounds of embers being stoked), interfacing with the fragrant smell of hot coals coated with drops of the sugary liquid and later the taste of sweet tea, constitutes an epicurean experience that makes participants forget their fears and pain. By immersing themselves in the here and now of teatime—a temporality ritually set apart from the rest of their otherwise dull waking hours—un(der)employed young men escape the oppressive weight of idleness to delight sensually in the texture of time.

Teatime

Ideally the temporality of everyday life combines recurrence with linearity. As Edmund Leach (1968) noted, life is experienced through a tension between series of repetitive phenomena and the sense of irreversible change. Although it is structured around endless repetition (from light to darkness and darkness to light), we experience each day as unique, different from previous ones. Repetitive actions such as eating, working, and sleeping are themselves embedded within larger cycles of repetition (weeks, seasons, years, and so on) in which each cycle is experienced as qualitatively different from previous ones. These temporalities are irregularly punctuated by special or unexpected events (a wedding, political elections, a famine, and so on). It is this tension between regularity and novelty that makes time flow and creates a sense of forward movement. Regularity provides a sense of stability in a world in constant flux, while linearity enables one to experience progression through time.

For jobless young men waiting for something to happen, temporality is essentially cyclical, largely devoid of the linearity that signals one is advancing in life. Instead of being experienced as a constant flow, time feels like "dead time," at odds with the drive toward progress and accumulation that should ideally shape life. Trapped within the dull temporality of waiting, samari feel excluded from the forward-moving time of modern society. The life they experience is, in Rita Felski's words (2000), "belated . . . , lagging behind the historical possibilities of modernity" (82). As they lament the lack of employment opportunities, they are keenly aware that time is running out.

Through their engagement in fada activities, samari ward off ennui by "killing time," as they say. Yet tea rituals do not kill time so much as they enliven it. In contrast to idle time, teatime constitutes a purposeful temporality; it produces a particular experience of how time unfolds when one is engaged in an activity (rather than being stuck in a moment devoid of relevance). This is what Henri Lefebvre (2004) calls "appropriated" time (76). "Whether normal or exceptional, this is a time that forgets time, during which time no longer counts (and is no longer counted). It arrives or emerges when an activity brings plenitude, whether this activity be banal (an occupation, a piece of work), subtle (meditation, contemplation), spontaneous (a child's game, or even one for adults), or sophisticated. This activity is in harmony with itself and with the world. . . . It *is* in time: it *is* a time, but does not reflect on it" (76–77). "Drinking tea gives you something to do," a jobless saurayi told me. His companion clarified further: "Tea drinking is an occupation. You cannot just sit there and watch people go by. People will say you are like a woman. Women, they gossip, they watch people pass by and talk about them." By contrasting women's unproductive gossiping to men's purposeful tea drinking, the young man revalorized male temporalities, embedding tea rituals in a time flow that "forgets time." This absorption in the preparation and consumption of tea brings fulfillment to samari, enmeshing them in the texture of time while also giving them a sense of purposeful agency, an experience aptly summarized in a young man's observation that "without tea, we samari are nothing!"

Each tea session is at once predictable and unique in the way that it produces anticipation, pleasure, and fulfillment. It shortens time while prolonging enjoyment. One could say that tea rituals resituate young men in time: time is no longer suffered but passed. Tea rituals are "in time" in the sense that they unfold harmoniously in time while also contributing to the future. It is during teatime that young men trade information regarding new job openings and engage in brainstorming sessions to find solutions to each other's problems. Tea, fadantchés say, "is the friend of conversation." In the way that it energizes young men, heartening them in the face of seemingly insurmountable challenges and acting as a catalyst for the articulation of ideas, tea is a central ingredient of the economy of hope within which young men orient themselves toward the future.

By disrupting the homogeneity of idle time and creating a distinct temporality at once purposeful and productive, tea rituals counter the crushing weight of boredom. Not only does teatime confront arrhythmia by providing a semblance of structure in the absence of other temporal markers, but tea's own ceremonial serving follows the pattern of life. The first round of tea is said to be bitter, like life. The sharp taste of green tea has not yet been weakened by several pots of water, and the sugar only partially cuts its bitterness. As young men drink from the first round, they are reminded of how harsh life is. (Some avoid the first round altogether, arguing the strong brew gives them headaches.) The second round is said to be sweet, like love. The tea has lost some of its strength; it is now a perfect balance of sweetness and harshness. The precise dosage of sweetness and strength supposedly promotes conviviality. This is the round that "makes you talk." The third round is said to be like the breadth of death. It has been considerably diluted, acquiring a smoothness that some tea drinkers find dull. Arguing that the insipid liquid is fit for women, not "real" men, many of them pass on this round. Those who drink it are reminded that life is finite and takes its full meaning when set against the larger reality of death.

It would be tempting to overinterpret this life-love-death schema: by adopting a "life is a cup of tea" philosophy, young men pierce the dull embrace of boredom. I don't think the reflective space opened up by the language of tea making stretches that far, however. Nor do I want to over-ritualize teatime. Tea making is about inventing tradition as much as it is about inventing routine. Granted, it is a signifying practice. Yet it also becomes a habitus—a set of motions one unreflectively performs—that alleviates restlessness, creates durational enjoyment, and promotes conviviality in the same way that lighting a cigarette, taking a few puffs, and passing it on to a friend furthers *détente* and intimacy. The fact that "routine" is derived from *route*, the French term for road or path, helps us appreciate further how a routine, rather than being merely repetitious, may translate as a course of action. In effect, routinely setting a time for tea can perhaps be best summed up as the process of laying down a path across a potentially shifty landscape to some destination one cannot quite see. "It is when we are talking together, around the teakettle, that we come up with plans—ideas for how to start a business or raising money for the fada," a fadantché said. For those who seek to escape the precariousness of the neoliberal present, routines, mundane as they may be, may well have some purchase on the future.

The *Jouissance* of Teatime

I have described so far how by enmeshing participants in the anticipation of sensual delights, teatime punctures the stultifying uniformity of boredom. Whereas boredom dulls experience, teatime replenishes it. Participating in teatime, I have suggested, is about looking forward to having tea as much as it is about the tea drinking itself. As they wait for the tea to brew, participants invest themselves in the moment while simultaneously orienting themselves toward a particular outcome in such a way that they reposition themselves in the flow and momentum of life. By way of a conclusion I want to probe deeper into the anticipatory dimension of teatime to consider briefly the role of pleasure in structuring the temporalities of this slice of fada life.

As a positive response to the sensual perception of the world, pleasure brings a certain fulfillment to the recipient. To borrow philosopher Antoine Vergote's (1996) words, it "touches what remains opaque in the lived body" (137) and heightens experience, making people feel more alive. Unlike the more encompassing, diffuse experience of happiness (or contentment), it entails a punctual, temporary kind of gratification. Young men have described the high they experience after drinking tea—comparing it to the blow of a hammer that wakes them up or calling it an energizing lift that makes them feel like they can take on the world—but they also mention the headaches, lack of energy, and sadness that set in when they don't get their caffeine fix. Similarly, Daniel Mains (2012) has written about the euphoria, associated with a "sense of unlimited possibility" (56–57) that young Ethiopian men achieve after chewing *qāt* and the severe depression that follows their failure to obtain their daily dose of the stimulant. Whether induced by sipping tea, puffing on a cigarette, or some other sensually gratifying engagement with the world, pleasure remains "close to the dynamism that generates it" (Vergote 1996:137). Consequently it is short-lived.

Sigmund Freud (1990) wrote that pleasure refers to not only the sensation of pleasure but also the pleasure principle, that is, the tendency to act in such a way as to avoid pain while obtaining pleasure. Pleasure, Freud argued, is always moderated. As such, it must be distinguished from *jouissance*, which, in Lacanian terms, connotes a mode of absolute enjoyment, undiluted by the pleasure principle's limitation on how much pleasure can be had. *Jouissance* is the enjoyment of one's ultimate object of desire. Since it is synonymous with excess, it ultimately leads not to gain but to loss: the loss of the self in the moment of ecstatic relief. At the fada young men pursue pleasures, big and small, largely unhindered by the burden of social obligations and the strictures of religious life. For instance, they often dismiss their card games as "just games" in which they engage to "kill" time and *pour le plaisir* (for pleasure). Yet they also admit that this enjoyment can lead to a loss of control: "*Quand ça chauffe* [when things get intense] in the game, no one wants to quit. We get so involved, we forget the prayer. Sometimes we lose control and we start a fight." Similar to Balinese cockfights (C. Geertz 1972) and Ilongot head-hunting (Rosaldo 1980), card games can be said to constitute an instance of "deep play," an intense, all-absorbing form of competitive engagement and a high-stakes venture dur-

ing which masculinity and social status are reaffirmed. They bring intense, excessive delight as well as a sense of liberation to the participants. The fact that they are considered a transgressive form of leisure (card games, assumed to involve money bets, are forbidden to Muslims) only adds to the mild intoxication they procure in the first place.

Now *jouissance* is a slippery term that resists translation. Granted, it can be understood straightforwardly as pleasure, enjoyment, a form of intense appreciation or even sexual bliss. It can also signify having rights and pleasures in the use of something, as in "she enjoys good health." Still, it has no exact equivalent in English. Being without hindrance, *jouissance* exceeds the semantic boundaries of "pleasure." Paradoxically, it does not lead to fulfillment, Jacques Lacan (1998) argues, because the kind of enjoyment it provides always falls short of the idealized standard. In other words, *jouissance* lingers between expectation and actualization; it is an enjoyment that is enjoyable only insofar as it is never truly realized. "That's not it!" is the cry that, in Lacan's famous example, signals the impossibility of fully experiencing *jouissance*. Slogans like "Enjoy Coca-Cola" promise "the real thing" to consumers, yet the latter are invariably disappointed, Lacan suggests, because the product they purchased does not measure up to the elusive object of their fantasies. Disappointment does not quell the perpetual search for *jouissance*, however. In fact, Slavoj Žižek (1989) argues, consumer culture is built on the inability of fantasy to fulfill people's desire for "the real thing." It operates on the basis that consumers will never stop searching for satisfaction for it is their desire that is insatiable. In this sense, *jouissance* is always postponed.

The quest for *jouissance* I just described matches the period of cheerful anticipation that accompanies tea preparation at the fada, while if we follow Lacan, the *jouissance* itself is what fadantchés experience when, after taking two or three sips of tea, they realize they have emptied the glass and must now wait for the next round. What interests me, however, is less the impossibility of *jouissance* in the Lacanian sense than its temporality. Scholars have described life as a symphony of temporalities (Ingold 2000; Munn 1992). From their perspective, there is not just one single set of rhythm, duration, and timing that structures human existence but a complex interweaving of many concurrent and often conflicting temporalities that actors seek to control. I would surmise that teatime at the fada is precisely an attempt to synchronize discordant temporalities so as to get a hold on the present. In fact, when all the intersecting temporalities that structure young men's experience converge in such a way that fadantchés become absorbed into the "now" of experience, teatime translates as full enjoyment. Following Vergote (1996), we could say that it transforms pleasure into a duration in which "time finds itself suspended in a density of eternity" (144). The eternity Vergote alludes to is provisional, of course. The point is that it is precisely when it is suspended in fulfillment (*jouissance*) that time can be experienced as an eternity. Having absorbed other temporalities, teatime has its own time. It is its own time.

In this chapter I have tried to discern something of the temporality and potentialities of waithood by exploring how un(der)employed young men in Niger punctuate time and create momentum in their lives through their engagement in tea-making sessions. Waiting, for young Nigérien men hoping for a better job or a job *tout court*, is hard work. As a tactical modus operandi, it is about situating oneself in such a way as to maximize one's encounter with opportunity. Although some fadantchés work while waiting, many do not because the state of readiness that waiting requires precludes full engagement in the professional world. In exploring the generativity of waiting, I have sought to privilege creativity at the expense of crisis. Attempts to capture the experience of Africans through the concept of crisis, some scholars argue, oversimplify the complexities of the lived world by reducing existence to mere survival. Understanding how samari live means paying attention to how they carve out spaces of material and existential possibility for themselves within contexts of anomie and scarcity.

More than simply providing arenas of romanticized escapism from the real world, as elders contend, teatime provides a vehicle for the articulation of hope. As a dimension of futurity, hope is an "active and even agentive modality" (Cole and Durham 2008:15) shaping the way in which samari project themselves in the future.[13] Although idle tea-sipping young men sitting in the streets of Niamey, Dogondoutchi, or for that matter any other Nigérien town are often described as lazy, bored, and uninspired, we must go beyond the terms of passivity and subjugation that have come to define them and consider critically how despite great challenges, they continue to create and aspire.

TWO

The Writing on the Walls: Ma(r)king the Place of Youth

It is the very definition of a place . . . that it is composed by . . . series of displacements and effects among the fragmented strata that form it and that it plays on these moving layers.

—Michel de Certeau, *The Practice of Everyday Life*

Much has been written on imagination as an expression of subaltern consciousness through which young people everywhere give shape to their hopes of a better world in the making (Comaroff and Comaroff 2005; Diouf 1996; Weiss 2009). What happens when underemployed young men anxious to get on with their lives reclaim their urban neighborhoods so as to bring their dull present in line with their imagined futures? In recent years young Nigérien urbanites have taken to etching the names of their fadas in large, colorful, and confident lettering on the rugged walls against which they sit: Soleil (Sun), Ba Matsala (No Problem), Baban Gari (Big City), Victoire (Victory), Star Clan, Kash Money, Jamming Rasta, Galaxie City, Adaltchi (Justice), Amerika, and so on. The writing is often accompanied by shorthand symbols (dollar signs are ubiquitous) and occasionally integrated within more complex pictorial designs that draw heavily on African American concepts of masculinity and urban "cool" and other cultural repertoires. The trend, which has radically reconfigured the look of urbanscapes in Niger, signals that youthful aspirations increasingly find expression in a search for visual appeal. As an instantiation of what Jean Baudrillard (1993 [1976]:76) calls a "new type of intervention in the city," this relatively recent form of cultural production provides a constantly evolving commentary on the world at large while making visible how samari collectively deploy artistry and imagination to anchor themselves within a sense of place. This chapter is precisely about the sense of place—that is, the emotional attachment to a place and the active sensing of that place—that young men create for themselves by inscribing their presence in the street, simultaneously asserting their "right to city" (Bayat 2010a:15) and forging spaces of belonging.

To mark their neighborhoods with visible signs of their presence, fadas draw on diverse registers ranging from popular culture to vernacular expressions of faith and ethics to the language of sociality and the geography of utopia. Their etchings, which I refer to as wall writings, constitute a veritable "archive" (Quayson 2014) of expressive practices at the intersection of verbal and pictorial repertoires. On a single street block, references to imaginary hinterlands (Les Americs; Pacifick City) thus coexist with references to the local topography: Forage (Drilling Well), Nouveau Marché (New Market), Shakwana Mutuwa (Deadly Turn, the name given to a bend in the road where accidents are frequent). On the next block, mottos of solidarity (L'Union Fait la Force [Unity Makes Strength]) jostle with moral sayings (So Mai Sonka [Love the One Who Loves You]) and messages of self-affirmation (Matassa Alkawali [Youth Who Fulfill Their Promises]). Some fada inscriptions flaunt the religious identity of their membership (Imani [Faith]; Islamique; Sabon Rai don Kowa [New Life for Everyone], a Christian fada) while others advertise their popularity with women (Amitié des Belles Filles [Friendship of Beautiful Girls]). Yet others convey emotional or political concerns (Tazartché [Continuation]; À bas l'AFC [Down with AFC])[1] or more prosaic matters such as the pleasures of tea drinking (Atayo [Tea]; Casino [Brazier]). Although they are part of a wider textual ecology that includes advertisement billboards, storefront signs, as well as traffic signs and other graphics, fada inscriptions rarely compete with other signage for space and visibility. They typically flourish on the adobe and cement walls that surround family compounds and afford residents a measure of privacy. In contrast most commercial and traffic signs are affixed on posts, billboards, or storefronts. Local neighborhoods thus provide aesthetically ambitious samari with an ample supply of blind walls on which to transfer their customized vision of masculine solidarity. As a conspicuous (and occasionally dramatic) feature of the visual landscape, fada inscriptions occupy an aesthetic niche of their own whose boundaries are defined not by material infrastructure so much as by "the built form of the spoken word" (De Boeck and Plissart 2004:235).

At one level these inscriptions work as signs, drawing attention to the existence of fadas even in the absence of their members. At another they have a metapragmatic function, helping samari project themselves in an imagined space of global possibilities. Whether they structure future-oriented dreams with names such as Territoire des Milliardaires (Territory of Billionaires), conjure up distant elsewheres with names such as Kilombo[2] and Kensas City (*sic*), or advertise their members' valor and toughness with names such as Black Warriors or Samourai, fadas are vehicles of identity affirmation enabling fantasies that cannot find another language. In the words of Istada, a member of Les Américain (*sic*), "We are Les Américain. All the members are from the neighborhood. We chose the name because we like the Americans. They get the job done. We too want to take initiatives. Together we can do things, that's why we created the fada. Together we can do extraordinary things." By naming their fada Les Américain, Istada and his friends hoped to capitalize not only on the inherent strength of the United States as an economic power but also on a certain esprit de corps—a capacity to set the group's objectives ahead of individual selfish desires—which they associated with American people. It was, Istada implied, because of their willingness to engage in teamwork that Americans were efficient ("they get the job done"). When I spoke with Istada, the young men had yet to organize any social event that would foster fame and recognition for the fada. Nevertheless they saw themselves as walking in the footsteps of their role models and were hopeful that, as a team, they would one day "do extraordinary things." Like the hip-hop barbershops of urban Tanzania described by Weiss (2009), fadas "create a frame of action in which participants feel their claims have validity—in short, a world to which they belong" (52).

In this chapter I explore how fada inscriptions affirm what Asef Bayat (2010a:26) calls the art of presence, namely, the resolve to "assert collective will in spite of all odds" in urban environments that no longer meet the needs of rapidly expanding populations. Across the continent, the infrastructure of African cities has not kept up with the phenomenal urban growth of recent decades. In an age of fiscal restrictions and shrinking state services, some buildings—and at times, entire neighborhoods—remain unfinished while others slowly fall prey to decay. Yet, as AbdouMaliq Simone (2006) observes, the cities that Africans make work on a number of levels. Scholars (Chalfin 2014; De Boeck and Plissart 2004; Diouf and Fredericks 2014) have documented the tremendous ingenuity with which city dwellers in Dakar, Kinshasa, and elsewhere appropriate and recycle infrastructural fragments to reorder urban space, anchoring their livelihoods in the makeshift combinations of spaces, objects, and practices that emerge in the process. By building homes illegally, erecting shacks out of salvaged materials, or simply carving out symbolic spaces for themselves through the use of graffiti, sound architectonics, and bodily praxis, people gain temporary control over urban space and its organization. Tentative as this process of encroachment may be, it is nevertheless a sure sign that in their effort to secure precarious livelihoods, the poor and the marginalized actively participate in the production of their urban environment. As a form of cultural production that loudly proclaims—and legitimizes—the presence of male youth in public space while also typifying the random appropriation of that space by ad hoc collectivities, fadas constitute a distinct example of how the street has become a key arena of youthful masculine sociality and solidarity.

Built form, in this instance, is the product not of strategic urban planning but of tactical moves that, by clandestinely inserting themselves in the urban stratum, disturb the relative permanence of authorized infrastructure (Certeau 1984). In an essay on the intifada in the occupied West Bank during the late 1980s and early 1990s, Julie Peteet (1996) describes how the appearance of political graffiti on street walls profoundly altered public space and led to the activation of a wide, multifaceted readership. By textualizing the resistance, Palestinian graffiti transformed the street into a medium through which total strangers could establish furtive communication through a recognition of either shared sentiments or divergent interests. As part of a diverse repertoire of actions of civil disobedience, they derived their communicative power from the risks entailed in their production: these "public" scripts were a blatant demonstration of the occupying forces' lack of territorial control.

At some level, fada inscriptions function like the Palestinian graffiti that territorialize the city by radically altering the materiality of walls and other surfaces and, with it, the meaning of public space. In fact, some of them follow the graphic style and textual conventions of graffiti. In the way they seize space, they appear to belong to the tagging register rather than what we might call the artistic register. Like graffiti writers, some fadantchés advertise themselves to their peers by branding public space with their signature. Most fada inscriptions nevertheless differ from graffiti in significant respects: graffiti force themselves in visual space to signify nonconformity and defiance. Though they may at times be irreverent and even provocative, fada inscriptions are not generally transgressive. They betray young men's desire to forge solidarities and spaces of belonging, and this is what interests me about these aesthetic projects. Aside from modifying public space by creating the perception that walls can "speak," they legibly emplace the fada as a fixture of the urbanscape and establish moral points of reference in the absence of any visible infrastructure. By making use of what is available and carving out new spaces within which to make themselves seen and heard, young men collectively, if disparately, assert their right to use public space and engage in practiced modes of intimate sociality.[3] Indeed a feature of fadas I discuss at length below is their capacity to simultaneously become part of public space and constitute private spaces. In this respect, though fada inscriptions may appear to have created an insurgent landscape, I argue that they are part of an ongoing process of place-making.

Through a focus on the relations between built form and social practice, this chapter examines how youthful claims to the street take concrete shape at the fada and how, in turn, the physicality of space shapes the social life of male youth. While the extraordinary number of fadas dotting the urbanscape of Niger appears to signal the resounding victory of lived space over "abstract space" (Lefebvre 1991), one must nevertheless bear in mind how ephemeral this type of infrastructure can be. Friendships may stand the test of time, but the physical sites anchoring the fada in space rarely do. A main argument of this chapter is that attending to space must necessarily entail attending to time, for aside from the fact that the emplacement of people is by definition temporary, places themselves always exists in time. One can therefore speak of the durability or, conversely, the impermanence of places—not to mention their plasticity. By virtue of their relative legitimacy, fada graphics enjoy a longer life than the graffiti that emerge furtively within spaces of repression and suffer systematic erasure. They must nevertheless contend with certain environmental constraints, such as decay and their susceptibility to reinscription by rival fadas. Mindful that inasmuch as the walls of Nigérien towns can be said to tell a story, that story is constantly unfolding, I read these aesthetic projects as evidence of the dynamic, performative quality of places. At another level my call for a sustained engagement with the spatiotemporalities of youthful urban practices is also an attempt to think about space in generational terms. Given the relational nature of youth, one cannot discuss their struggles to carve spaces of belonging without taking into account the complicated generational relations within which they are embedded.

The Place of Young Men

"The dream of every saurayi is to be an adult, to have his place," Soumaila, a twenty-two-year-old motorcycle washer, dispiritedly noted, during a conversation we were having at his fada. By "place," Soumaila was referring to the generational position an individual occupies at a particular moment in time. What he left unsaid but what everyone in attendance understood was that in an age of diminished economic capacities and unfulfilled youthful aspirations, young people widely struggle to secure a place in a society that apparently has none to offer them.

Whether they discuss politics, unemployment, or Nigérien society more generally, samari often bring up the urgent necessity for elders to make space for the younger generation. Their claims for space exemplify how efforts to define youth as a social category necessarily call for the control of spatiality (Massey 1998). To be sure, generational struggles are often concretized through border crossings, territorial claims, and spatial transgressions. According to my respondents, it is the previous generation's unwillingness to relinquish their stranglehold on the public sector that prevents young people (especially those who have received a formal education and aspire to earn a living as civil servants) from finding secure employment and getting on with their lives. The language of spatiality that Soumaila employed to refer to adulthood is also a reminder of how tangled up the spatial and temporal dimensions of the lived world are. In fact, given how language always captures movement and duration in spatial terms (Bergson 1911:250), the so-called spaces young men expect elders to vacate may not literally map onto physical terrains; they might more adequately be understood instead as durations, that is, positions on a temporal axis. At another level, the notion of place Soumaila brought up allows us to describe belonging as an embodied experience. If, as geographers and anthropologists have by now amply demonstrated, to be in place is to become aware of one's sensuous presence in the world, the concept of place is particularly useful for exploring how self, space, and time come together in lived experience.

As a perpetually evolving configuration that is constituted by and through human interactions, the fada offers a critical window into the spatiotemporalities of youth. In examining how the fada offers samari what Steven Feld and Keith Basso (1996) call a "sense of place" (as well as a sense of being *in* place), I consider how young men's efforts to imagine the future shape the materiality of the fada and how, in turn, their sense of place at the fada affects their imagined futures. By meeting routinely at the same spot to drink tea, engage in leisurely activities, and experience the warm embrace of friendship, fadantchés create a place for themselves that "holds out, beckoning to its inhabitants and, assembling them, making them manifest" (E. S. Casey 1996:25). It is the stabilizing persistence of the fada as a container of experience that gives it such appeal in an age of widespread uncertainty about the future. This sense of stability is nevertheless undermined by the physical dispersal of fadantchés who, upon obtaining jobs, may move to different parts of the country. The stability of the fada as a physical space is further challenged by natural decay and the occasional projects of renovation local residents engage in over time. Faded or peeling paint, eroding mud walls that bear the impact of successive rainy seasons, construction debris piling up where a group of fadantchés once sat, and luxurious foliage climbing over buildings all attest to the passage of time. By reminding us of the impermanence of material forms, decay (and the traces it leaves behind) calls attention to the contingencies of fada life and the provisionality of fadantchés' activities—an issue I return to.

Young men look forward to joining their friends at the fada, whether they intend to spend most of their waking hours there or remain only long enough to catch up with everyone's news. The affective networks they build, the memories they make, and the dreams they share with friends all contribute to making the fada into a place they grow attached to. The fada is the place fadantchés associate with good times. It is also the place they escape to when they seek solace. Places, Edward Casey argues (1996:24) following Heidegger, "gather things in their midst." More specifically, they gather experiences, memories, and words as well as feelings. The enduring character of a place, the hold it has on people, derives from its capacity to gather, enabling them to return over and over again to the same place (that progressively fills with the experiences of previous visits). This capacity to gather is fittingly captured in the expression *bon coin* that has inspired the naming of several fadas in Niamey and elsewhere. A *bon coin* (lit. "good corner") is usually taken to mean a "good spot" (as in "a good fishing spot"). More often than not it implies that the so-called corner is a "good place to stay," which is why Le Bon Coin is a popular name for cafés and restaurants in the francophone world. As a place that exudes a mix of comfort and intimacy as well as a friendly, hospitable atmosphere—in short, a warm and inviting place—a *bon coin* enfolds people in its midst, making them feel that they belong. In the way it gathers experiences and histories, it beckons to passersby (or potential customers) with the particular aura it projects. In this sense, all fadas are perceived as *bons coins* by those who contribute to their making by filling them with memories.

As a gathering place, the fada is basically constituted by the individuals who sit together around a simmering pot of tea. It is, in fact, the gathering of people that makes up the social relations in the site they occupy while also effectively constituting that site. Or to paraphrase Edward Casey (1996), if samari completely disappeared and the fada remained empty, it would cease to be a place and become a void. Although some fadas meet under a neem tree or a thatched shelter (often built with materials supplied by politicians aiming to secure votes), the vast majority of them have no visible infrastructure, save for a few portable seats. It is the young men themselves who, by congregating at a given spot, make the fada what it is as both a locus of sociability and a field of lived practice. One might say that the fadantchés themselves constitute the infrastructure of the fada: it is out of their engagement with space and material forms that the fada, as a platform that generates a certain mode of being in the street, takes shape.[4]

By the same token, it is at the fada that young men forge social identities as members of a constituency whose mission becomes formally defined in the charter they establish following the founding (and naming) of that constituency (see chapter 5). Samari who do not belong to any fada may be disparaged or ridiculed. When I asked a young man why he and his eight fellow fadantchés had created a new fada rather than join an existing fada (the block he lived on already counted at least three fadas), he told me that they wanted their own place where they could enjoy good conversations: "It's not good not to belong to a fada. If you go to someone else's fada, you may not be well received. They may tell you to leave." Although my interlocutor was intimating that many young men create their own fada to avoid the dreaded possibility of being rejected by an existing group, it is nevertheless not unusual for samari to join previously constituted fadas. Perhaps a more significant point raised by this saurayi is that not belonging to a fada is "not good." Nigériens routinely stress that people benefit from each other's company and loneliness is a dangerous thing. When I explained to some fadantchés that young people in the United States did not join fadas (or congregate daily in the street), they were appalled. "American youths must lead very sad lives," one of them commented. As he and his friends saw it, the sociality the fada indexed was essential to their constitution as persons. It contributed to not only their maturation but also their emotional well-being, helping to sustain webs of solidarity that protected them from the distress, alienation, and despair they faced on a routine basis. My interlocutor's comment also provides a clue for understanding why the youth who does not join a fada may become an object of contempt and suspicion: when not motivated by the perception that tea circles are "for losers," that they promote criminal activities, or that they are un-Islamic, the refusal to belong to a fada implies a selfishness that has no place in the fadantchés' vision of the neighborhood and its sticky webs of reciprocity.

Whether they are jobless, intermittently employed, or have full-time jobs, fadantchés are expected to make a daily appearance at the fada or else send word that they won't make it because they are traveling or facing an impediment. Absences are noticed and may prompt a visit to the fadantché's home to check on his health. When a fadantché's father died, the other members of his fada took off all at once to pay their condolences to the grieving family and keep the young man company—a typical thing to do for a friend in mourning. That day, no one met at the fada and the teakettle remained empty.

As a spatial field of action, the fada is continually undone and redone by the movement of people who come and go over time. What this means is that the fada is not a passive stage on which social life unfolds but an interactive process fueled by the multiple "lived relationships" (Basso 1996:54) that members maintain with the place and with each other. At the fada place and mobility, far from being antithetical, are co-constitutive. On the weekend, for instance, everyone converges at the fada, but while some members may get there early in the day, many do not show up until later, and how long they stay depends on the lives they lead—to the extent that they have a life outside the fada. À la descente, as French-speaking, formally employed Nigériens call the end of the workday, there is, in contrast, an intense traffic of persons at fadas that count stably employed members. The fada is generally the first stop young men make after leaving the office, the market, or the classroom. Some of them sit at the fada until late into the night whereas others stay there only long enough to enjoy a round of tea. Yet others take their leave soon after exchanging perfunctory greetings, but they will likely return later in the evening. They have a girlfriend to visit or a course assignment to complete before they can enjoy their friends' company. The sweet smell of tea escaping from the fada's bubbling teapot may well convince a newcomer to stay and enjoy a glass of the heavily sugared infusion. Teatime is after all what anchors the fada as a space of conviviality and relaxation. The fact that fadantchés speak of poser le thé (lit., "put down the tea") rather than prepare it further hints at the connection between tea making and locality. Far from ever being stabilized, however, the fada is produced out of the bundle of relationships solidified—or conversely tested—through verbal exchanges and the quotidian performance of mundane acts, such as when the shaiman pours tea for a group of seated young men whose body postures and affective engagement with each other actualize the place as a gathering of experience.

At sunset, when it is time to perform the mangariba prayer (the fourth of the five daily prayers required of Muslims), some fadas are deserted: practicing Muslims exert pressure on their fellow fadantchés so that in the end, all (or most) worship together at the nearest mosque. Once prayer is over, they return to the fada to enjoy some rice and beans, go over the details of an upcoming wedding, catch an episode of the telenovela of the moment, or simply sit contentedly next to each other while fiddling with their smart phones until the call for *isha*, the last prayer required daily of Muslims. As a place, the fada is continually regenerating and reinventing itself. In sum, it is more an event than a thing. Tracing the constitutive relationship between people and their physical environment, Edward Casey (1996) argues, means attending not only to the spatial dimensions of these places but also to their temporal orientations. From this perspective, fadas are not inert, stable formations but ongoing processes of place-making.

Each time an additional person shows up, greetings are exchanged, an additional seat is brought out (or a section of the bench is offered while the others squeeze themselves in the remaining space), and conversations and card games resume. The newcomer is expected to shake everyone else's hands. Rounds of ritual handshakes thus routinely punctuate ongoing discussions. Inconsequential as they may seem, these shakes are nevertheless a critical part of how newcomers become incorporated in the fada and how the fada itself is acknowledged as a sociospatial entity whose boundaries are constantly shifting. Thus the fada instantiates the way that places are not sites with defined boundaries but must be understood instead as points of intersections for social relations. As a place of gathering, it consists of "articulate moments" (Massey 1994:154) within a social field defined by the continuous circulation of persons and things.

In sum the significance of Nigérien conversation spots is bound less in the mastery of space than in the making of place. "The fada is a meeting place," is how many youths put it, highlighting the sociocentric character of these spaces. Like the sitting area of East Africa in which conversation routinely assembles both the space and the participants in the conversation as a *baraza* (Weiss 2009; Loimeier 2005), the fada as a place and as a gathering of people is concretely instantiated by the social interactions it enables. Emerging out of diverse social relations, "meeting and weaving together at a particular locus" (Massey 1991:28), the fada is both an occupied space and a spatial practice. In what follows, I discuss what it means to occupy public space and how the fada is constituted as both a tentative means of extending the intimacy of the familial compound into the street and a tactical process of generational affirmation.

Public Intimacy

The hundreds of fadas that dot the urbanscapes of Niger may be taken as signs that young men have heeded Lefebvre's (1968a, 1968b) utopian call

for the restructuring of urban space so that it may meet the needs of urban dwellers. Lefebvre's description of the mutually constitutive relation
between people and places is by now well-known. Allow me nevertheless
to describe it briefly. The production of urban space, Lefebvre contends
(1991), does not limit itself to the planning of the material space of the
city. It also entails transforming the social relations that are bound up in
that space. By planning, commoditizing, and policing urban space, capitalism has radically transformed the everyday lives of ordinary urban residents. City planning under capitalism does not take into account the everyday lives of these residents or their visions of a good life. Instead, Lefebvre
argues, it creates zones of exclusion and practices of discrimination that
reproduce social inequality while denying many people the right to participate in the production of their own environment. Lefebvre (1996) pro-
poses that residents reclaim urban space so as to tailor it to their needs
and aspirations, a move he calls the "right to the city." The right to the
city, he writes, is "like a cry and a demand . . . a transformed and renewed
right to urban life" (158). By investing in small-scale projects—community
gardens, graffiti, and the like—that counter the claims of capital, people
reclaim their local environment, if only momentarily. Susceptible as they
may be to the pressure of capital, such instances of micro-urbanisms nevertheless redefine the social practices that shape these spaces. In sum, and to
paraphrase David Harvey (2008), the right to the city means we can change
ourselves by changing the city.[5]

As tactical forms of engagement that empower young men to transform
their immediate environment when they lack the capacity to transform the
wider landscape of social practices, the fadas can be said to exemplify "the
right to the city." Recall that some fadantchés have stable jobs and show
up at the fada only in the evening or during the weekend. Others are full-
time students. The majority are unemployed or underemployed, however.
For those who are excluded from the arenas of power and authority, the
fadas they belong to can rightly be said to constitute an "appropriation"
(Lefebvre 1996) of space; by scribbling on walls and carving out spaces in
which to sit together, they turn the street from a "non-place" (Augé 1995),
a place people are just passing through, into a place of intimacy and shared
concerns, a place of belonging.

Let me stress that "appropriation," as Lefebvre calls it, has more to do
with emplacement than with ownership. For Lefebvre (1991), the students'
occupation of the Latin Quarter in Paris during May 1968 epitomized
the appropriation or rather the reappropriation of a space that had been
usurped by the system. He thus writes that once rid of automobiles, the

Boulevard Saint-Michel became once again a promenade—a space pedestrians could inhabit. Meanwhile the black and red flags that students hung at the Sorbonne radically transformed the look and feel of the building. By dwelling in the street, young men who meet daily at their fada similarly make active, or rather participative, use of a space they previously used passively by driving or walking through it (Bayat 2010a). But let me be clear. Describing fadas as a takeover of the street as an undifferentiated public space would be misleading. The kind of street I discuss here is a more diffuse realm that is persistently, yet unevenly, morcellated by dispersed groups of young men through informal acts of seizure that are made widely legible through the deployment of a rich repertoire of names and images. By marking segments of the street as their own, groups of fadantchés fragment the street into a series of intimate spaces that act as "pivot[s] for the mobile dispersal of persons and things" (Weiss 2009:79). This is an ongoing, irregular, and constantly renegotiated process.

Like the barbershops of urban Tanzania that offer a situated grounding from which to engage with the world, fadas have the distinctive capacity to encompass the street within themselves and extend themselves into the street, and it is this capacity that enhances their significance in the eyes of young men eager to escape the matricentric space of the family compound yet unable to join the public world of mature adulthood. Consider the fada known as Glissement Yobi Yobi. The name itself refers to a *coupé-décalé* song by Ivoirian artist Dj Consty. Initially associated with the flashy performances of Ivoirian migrants in Paris, the musical genre known as *coupé-décalé* (scam and scram) has by now conquered Nigérien airwaves with its highly danceable beats and its gleeful mood. Chosen by Alkassoum, a fadantché born in Abidjan who identified strongly with Ivoirian popular culture, the fada's name also captured the rest of the membership's great fondness for *coupé-décalé* music. Keen to stake out their place in the neighborhood, the fadantchés, who met at school, asked a commercial painter to produce a mural that would evoke the exuberance of *coupé-décalé* and saturate the wall with its spirit of lightheartedness. The wide-eyed saurayi pictured in the mural embodies through his movements the insouciance and inexhaustible joie de vivre that local youth associate with Ivoirian musical culture. Significantly, the boom box that is so frequently featured on street walls that it has become iconic of the fada's pictorial economy is nowhere in sight. Yet the implicit message is that the young man is dancing to the sound of *coupé-décalé*.

When I met the members of Glissement Yobi Yobi, most of them were high school students with ages ranging between seventeen and twenty-two. The rest were school leavers who made a precarious living by repairing cell phones, driving motorbike taxis, hawking fruit, or selling car parts. One

worked as a loader in a Lebanese-owned grocery store. They met every night at the same spot. There they set up benches and chairs around a small coffee table. Those in charge of refreshments brought plastic glasses and a plastic water jug. The *contrôleur* took attendance, the *serviteurs* (servants) served water to all those who were present, the SG (*secrétaire général*) read the agenda, and the president moderated the discussion so it remained on topic while allowing participants to bounce ideas off each other. Later in the night, once the pot of beans and rice prepared by the appointed cook was ready, all sat down to eat. By meeting daily at the same spot, the members of Glissement Yobi Yobi marked the locale with the visible signs of their presence, converting the anonymous space of the street into a place they inhabited and made their own.

As a locus of friendship and intimacy, the fada blurs the line between the home and the street. It is both private and public and yet fully neither. Consider Glissement Yobi Yobi. By its very location on a residential street, the fada's wall is in full view of passersby. One might say that it discloses itself to the public eye in the sense that even in the absence of fadantchés, it hints at the activities that take place there, thereby conveying some of the dynamic interaction that exists between persons and places (Munn 2013). At a more literal level, the mural's large white letters dancing against the bright blue backdrop contrast so strikingly with the ochre walls of the neighborhood that the whole composition catches passersby's attention even from a distance. Inasmuch as visibility is a defining quality of public space, the wall writing's conspicuousness firmly situates Glissement Yobi Yobi as part of the street. Nineteen-year-old Alkassoum told me that when designing the fada's mural, he and his friends selected bright, contrasting colors that would be noticeable from afar. "We want every person who walks by to pay attention to our fada," is how he put it. Aside from hinting at the material (and emotional) investment the creation of a fada presupposes on the part of its founding members, his statement betrays the pride fadantchés take in the loud and colorful artistic compositions that function like "totemic designations" (Baudrillard 1993:76) of a group's identity while also proclaiming their appropriation of public space.

Even those for whom the meaning of head-turning wall inscriptions remains somewhat cryptic (the use of foreign words and idioms often renders the writing inaccessible even to literate Nigériens) are forced to recognize that fada wall writing constitutes an art form in its own right. I have heard some parents speak proudly of fada inscriptions as evidence of the younger generation's creativity and resourcefulness while others lauded what they took to be their sons' attempt to beautify urban space. Some fadas rely more on imagery than text to publicize their presence in the neighborhood. Like Nigérien political parties, who use the symbols, colors, and hand signals that stand for their political platforms to make themselves visible in a nation with high rates of illiteracy, these fadas acquire prominence through the colorful murals they produce. In the way it translates agency, efficacy, or value, an image is radically different from a verbal explanation, Roy Wagner (1986) observes. It does not convey meaning the way texts do. In fact, the sensual, affective registers through which we apprehend meaning often exceed language (Moore 2011). Fadantchés appear to be well aware of the power of images, and they use it to attract attention and awe. By naming their fada Zaki (Lion) or Coeur de Lion (Lionheart), young men wish to capture some of the qualities associated with lions. (Lions are widely admired in Niger for their courage and combative qualities; their image is used to symbolize strong political leadership.) However, the skillful drawing of a lion on the fada's wall endows the place with a totemic force and a visual appeal the written word itself lacks.

Paradoxically the fada is also a space of practiced interiority. Through scriptural and social performances aimed at excluding outsiders and enhancing the unity of the group, its members aim to cultivate high levels of privacy and, at times, secrecy. The signage of some fadas is occasionally cryptic, illegible to nonmembers. Like many graffiti, it functions as coded communication between members of the fada's subculture through references to figures, concepts, or narratives of global popular culture that enjoy limited currency outside youth circles. The low literacy of a significant number of Nigériens of all ages further guarantees their exclusion from the scriptural economy that has surfaced with the fadas. "We named our fadas Scientifique Show because we're educated and we like science. But some of our neighbors don't even know what science is," a saurayi explained. The fact that a number of fadas represent themselves only through acronyms, leaving passersby no clues as to what the letters stand for, also contributes to the sense that fadas are exclusive organizations that cultivate their auratic power—their charisma—through the use of esoteric language. More generally this signals that the streets are increasingly opaque and readable only by insiders with the ability to decode the rapidly evolving repertoire of signs and symbols fadantchés opportunistically deploy. In Niamey such a repertoire further serves to operate distinctions between Niameyze (in Zarma, those who are born in Niamey and whose sophistication and skills enable them to navigate the urban landscape) and the rural, rustic, and somewhat gullible kawyeyze or villagers (Sounaye 2012).

Strategic inscriptions are important practices of place-making, but they are not the only modality through which young men carve space for themselves. Aside from picking fada names and motifs that appeal to a distinct constituency, samari have devised an elaborate (and perpetually expanding) lexicon that keeps out those who are not in the know. Specific registers of talk, notably the use of code words and expressions, define a space of intimacy by acting as linguistic markers designed to exclude the older generation and, at times, nonmembers while affirming the cosmopolitanism and "coolness" of fadantchés. Some terms such as *meuf* (girlfriend) are borrowed from French slang, but most come from English (*crew, killer,* and so on). Others, such as *farotage* (showing off), originate from Nouchi, an Ivoirian urban slang. Yet others, such as *fadantché,* appear to be local linguistic inventions.

Privacy is strengthened through adherence to certain rules of fada etiquette (see chapter 5). A cardinal rule of conduct all fadantchés learn is that what happens at the fada remains at the fada. The bond of trust that develops between fada members solidifies over time through the exchange of personal confidences. Fada members are fiercely protective of each other's secrets. Candidates wishing to join a fada must first and foremost earn the trust of the membership by proving their loyalty and dependability. In this context, switching fadas—and effectively transferring one's trust to a rival group—is seen as an act of betrayal. The individual who shifts allegiance to a new fada is nothing but a "turncoat" whose actions threaten the closeness his former friends have cultivated over time. More specifically, the secrets he was privy to are no longer safe. To discourage members from ever leaving—and prevent potentially embarrassing details of a person's life (family disputes, failed romances, and so on) from leaking out—some fadas include in their code of conduct the prescription that a steep fine will be levied against anyone intending to jump ship.

Privacy at the fada is further affirmed through domestic activities that enact the cohesiveness of the group while enhancing its inward orientation and intimate character. Culinary endeavors, notably cooking rice and beans—a fada staple—enable fadantchés to imagine themselves as part of a virtual domestic unit whose existence is structured around meal preparation and consumption. Far from seeing cooking as a wifely duty that feminizes them, fadantchés often brag about their culinary skills, claiming their *wake da shinkafa* (beans and rice) tastes better than women's. Occasionally, the fada becomes an extension of the familial compound when it merges with young men's *ghettos,* where they sleep and socialize. I once visited a *ghetto* that was built in the family's walled compound but with a door that opened on the street (an oddity given that compounds typically feature a single street entrance) so the occupants could come in and go out at will. Three young men, one of whom did not belong to the household, slept there.

Elsewhere two brothers built a thatched shed in the street as an extension of the familial compound so that members of Show Boys Clan, their fada, could meet in total privacy. The straw shed, which was lavishly furnished with plush armchairs and coffee tables and featured a separate sleeping area, was a perfect instance of "houseless domesticity" (Appadurai 2000:643), enabling samari to indulge in domestic plenitude as their future narrowed. "We have a phone, a TV, and a CD player but we don't have electricity yet," Abdoulaye, one of the brothers, known for buying expensive clothes and visiting dancing establishments, told me. The riotous assortment of flags, plastic flowers, and Bob Marley posters adorning the place gave it the appearance of a colorful cocoon that offered protection from the harsh world outside while testifying to the fadantchés' need to stabilize the place by amassing things, or as Kathleen Stewart (1996:144) put it, by amassing the place around them. I once witnessed a senior woman engaged in the meticulous sweeping of the fada grounds abutting her compound. In the Sahel sweeping the leaves, rubbish, and animal waste that accumulates in courtyards is part of the daily battle against dirt. The deliberate care the woman took to clear the place of litter suggests that she saw the fada as an interior space that, just like her own courtyard, required daily tidying. In fact, by pushing detritus into nondescript street space, she was literally tracing with her broom the boundaries between the fada (part of the domestic space that must be swept) and the street ("outside" space in which to discard rubbish).

At the fada, as these practices of homemaking variously demonstrate, the domestic spills over into the street. The fada is a space that is both "in" and "off" the street. It blurs the distinction between "life inside" with its familial pressures and "life outside." As a small bubble of intimacy that is also part of the street, the fada can be said to constitute an external private space; as a space of civic discussion that gathers the world into its fold, it serves simultaneously as an "internal public space" (Cooper 1997). In short, it is a hybrid space.

I noted earlier how some fadas make a mark on the urban landscape through their investment in material infrastructure. Young men keen to anchor themselves in the neighborhood may build a thatched shed or pay a mason to pour a concrete slab at the foot of "their" wall. The platform is delineated by painted markers at the corners. Others simply line the ground with a row of cement bricks to delimit the surface they occupy. Passersby avoid walking through these spaces just as they avoid walking through prayer spaces marked by mats. More often than not, it is the brittle mud wall against which many of them sit that receives a coat of cement before being used as a canvas for their totemic inscriptions. The use of a cement base to support the process of "stamping" the street with their fada's name recalls the widespread use of plaster on adobe walls to water-proof and decorate façades in the classic Hausa tradition. By buffing the wall before etching the vivid symbols of their group affiliation, fadantchés frame their aesthetic interventions as a decorative practice that beautifies the neighborhood. "We want people to say ours is the most beautiful sign" is how a member of Jardin d'Eden put it. At another level, it is their friend-ships and social obligations that fadantchés literally cement upon the ur-ban landscape by pouring a permanent foundation for their fada.

Fadas' investment in permanent structures is rare, nevertheless. Save for their wall inscriptions, signs of fadantchés' presence in the street tend to be provisional, flexible. For instance, fadantchés may leave a bench painted with the fada's colors (or better, two of them displayed in a cross pattern)

on the spot where they usually sit to fill the space and mark it as theirs in their absence. Most fadas don't even feature this kind of mobile infrastructure, however. As instantiations of an "infrastructure of paucity" (De Boeck and Plissart 2004:235) defined more by the absence than the presence of material structure, they exist through the sensorial, corporeal, and affective engagement of young men with the street and one another. It is thus by filling up the space with their bodies, their conversations, their music, and the sweet fragrance of tea escaping from bubbling kettles that many fadantchés produce the lived spaces—the dwellings—they call fadas.

When considering how the "quiet encroachment of the ordinary" (Bayat 2010a:14)—the furtive, dispersed, yet prolonged way in which samari take over the street—materializes, we must recognize that far from being fixed entities surrounded by mobile chaos, fadas appear out of a tangled web of encounters. They are not defined by boundaries, nor can they be said to contain activities. Instead they arise through processes of mobilization, vacillation, and negotiation. As contingent gatherings of things, practices, and memories, they can be said to be assemblages "whose properties emerge from the interactions between parts" (DeLanda 2006:5). It is the fada's internal heterogeneity and its relationality to the outside that enable it to function as *un espace de l'entre-deux* (Boyer 2014), a space of the between that is neither fully private nor public.

Scriptural Economy

Fada wall writings come in a diverse array of representational styles, ranging from barely visible inscriptions to elaborately designed images; some of them feature awkward self-portraits and childish scribbles (with the last letters of the fada's name bunched together for lack of space), while others are more sophisticated compositions, demonstrating graphic skills, compositional deftness, and spatial savvy. Yet others take the form of aggressive tagging bursting into public space "like a scream, an interjection, an anti-discourse" (Baudrillard 1993:78). By dramatically marking blind walls with the signs of their presence, young men transform anonymous spaces into personalized places that bear their emblems and their colors as well as their visions of what the future might hold. Through their use of an extremely varied range of mottos, acronyms (fada names are often abbreviated to their initials such as ABC for All Boys Clan), musical references, and cultural emblems, they have contributed to the emergence of an entirely new scriptural economy that enlivens urban neighborhoods while

enabling the upcoming generation to voice their struggle for recognition. Young boys often scribble words on walls in imitation of their older brothers and in anticipation of the moment when they will join a fada.

Fadantchés' wall displays aim not to provoke so much as to interpellate passersby; capitalizing on their visual, auratic power, they attract attention and stand out while nevertheless operating within the logic of an existing discursive ecology rooted in street life. Unlike street artists whose unsanctioned, clandestine artwork needs no authorization precisely because it seeks to challenge the codified order of urban capitalism, the large majority of young men are keen to obtain approval before investing in paint and cement. Today most elders give their consent; knowing that adolescent boys meet at the same spot every day translates into peace of mind for parents—even if not all fadas serve as a refuge from violence and crime. As a fadantché explained: "Our parents don't know what we do at the fada. But they don't mind fadas because they know where we are. They know where to find us. We're always in the same place." It is often when they realize what creative impulses drive these social projects that parents become advocates of the fada system. Unlike graffiti that are widely considered a form of defacement, fada inscriptions aspire to function as legitimate urban transcripts or what we might call, following Certeau (1984), "proper names" (103): they are socially acceptable and rule governed.[6]

More than one fadantché nevertheless admitted to waiting until their parents became used to having the fadas gather outside their compounds before floating the idea of using the street-facing walls as canvases on which to etch their groups' names. Others remembered colonizing the walls progressively and surreptitiously. Interpreting their parents' absence of condemnation as a sign of tacit approval, they gradually added new features and new colors to the walls until their projects were completed. I once met a group of fadantchés who had been forced to erase the name they had just painted. When I first saw the barely visible inscription "CELTIC SHOW" on the wall, I assumed I was staring at the traces of a "defunct" fada that had been recently repossessed by a new group. Only later did I learn that the erasure of the fada's name, far from being the result of natural decay, had been intentional. The fada's founders, three youths who attended the same high school, had painted "CELTIC SHOW" in bright white paint only to find out that the household head (one of the youths' father) disapproved of their artistic project. They were compelled to scratch off the name (and the drawings accompanying it) as best they could. To the property owner, the fada's inscription was "out of place" (Douglas 1966). It was a threat not only to the wall on which it had been etched but also to the wider social order that assigned value, legitimacy, and integrity to walls and other elements of the city's infrastructure in the first place.

Fada wall writing is both a literal and a figurative form of name making. Fadantchés express great pride in the material inscriptions that act as stand-ins for the fada even in the absence of its members, just as graffiti symbolize a gang's presence in a neighborhood (Phillips 1999). A young Niamey resident told me that wall writing "served as a kind of publicity for the fada." His friend, a motorcycle taxi driver known at his fada as Tupac, further explained: "People see how we represent the fada. They may like the name but what's important is that they also admire our style. This makes them want to become part of the fada." Implied in Tupac's statement was the way that name writing serves as a message of positive affirmation, a sort of totemic designation promoting the values shared by the fada membership and proclaiming the strength of that membership. While fadantchés typically etch the name of their fada in a single spot, it is not unusual to see the name of the same fada inscribed in two distinct spots facing each other: members who sit against one wall in the morning move to the opposite wall in search of shade in the afternoon. Yet others may write the name of their fadas in half a dozen locations, thereby surrounding themselves with visual manifestations of their own existence. By drawing arrows to direct passersby to the actual spot (the *siège*, or seat, as they call it) where the fada meets, they "weave themselves into their own neighborhoods" (Phillips 1999:124) in a manner reminiscent of urban gangs' use of graffiti to delimit the boundaries of their respective territories. Fadas' modes of inscription differ nonetheless from gang graffiti in that fada territories overlap—occasionally creating a vibrant textual mosaic on a single wall surface—whereas gang territories, which exist on a much vaster scale, do not. This means that a fada's struggle for recognition does not translate into territorial battles even if it occasionally leads to violent confrontations with members of a rival group (see chapter 5).

Fada inscriptions must occasionally contend with the environment they seek to transform. Wall surfaces, especially when the wall is made of mud, can be rough and irregular. Doors and windows at times create interruptions. While long, uninterrupted planes are generally favored by fadantchés, a good location is often the number one priority, overriding the writing surface. Certain inscriptions are thus shaped by and ultimately resonate with the wall's formal properties, such as the color of a shutter, the height of the structure, or the geometric design of a gate. In some cases, they appropriate the wall by adapting to its pattern of solids and voids. This appropriation may result in an awkward visual composition with sets

of words crammed between two windows; elsewhere a roof extension or a post will be used to frame a fada's inscription. In this respect, fada inscriptions work like graffiti that insert themselves in—and are shaped by—an existing landscape. They bring to mind Roland Barthes's (1991) observation that what constitutes graffiti is "neither the inscription nor its message on the wall, the background, the surface (the desktop); it is because the background exists fully as an object that has already lived, that such writing always comes as an enigmatic surplus" (179).

To insert their signature in a visual field saturated with signs of existing fadas, newcomers may opt to recruit the services of a professional painter who will create a distinctive, eye-catching design—replete with references to the good life, tough masculinity, pop culture, or whatever theme the fadantchés choose. Fierce creatures (lions, snakes, and dragons in particular) commonly serve as avatars of fadantchés aiming to visibly manifest their toughness, virility, and bellicosity. Abstract symbols too enjoy wide currency. In Niamey dozens of fadas have chosen the star or the dollar sign as their emblem; the heart, seat of emotions and symbol of romantic love, is an equally popular fada icon. The colors a fada selects are an additional means through which it can assert its unique identity in a landscape overrun by graphic expressions of masculine solidarity, power, and fierceness. Fadantchés often told me that black was the number one choice of color, with red coming close behind. A quick drive through any *quartiers*

colonized by fadas will nevertheless establish the preponderance of white paint on the walls, whether as the sole color or as part of a color scheme (with black used to create an achromatic background for the white text, for instance). Sky (or turquoise) blue and white or yellow and black combinations are also popular options. When a group of fadantchés opts for uniforms, the color of their uniforms matches that of their wall painting.

Some fadas go as far as tagging their benches and their teapot using the same color scheme.

By juxtaposing vivid, intense colors such as white and blue (or yellow and green) to spell out the fada's name, fadantchés create a maximum visual contrast that electrifies the wall and acts as a magnet, attracting people's attention and (fadantchés claim) inviting them to stop by. The goal ultimately is to make themselves visible. Not all fadas succeed in effectively deploying color, design, and semantics to achieve the desired end. Yet, when tasked with making aesthetic decisions, many fadantchés seem implicitly guided by what Jacques Rancière (1999) calls the "partition of the sensible" (22), namely, the conditions of possibility for perception. Since what is apprehended with the senses is conditioned, the sensible delimits what is included from what is excluded in a community. According to Rancière's principle, fadas are thus divided into two categories, those one sees because they have a "logo" and those one does not see because they lack the logo that makes them stand out. A saurayi explained: "You take a name when people don't know you. Once you are known, you don't need the name. To become known, it helps if people recognize your name, you see. When they see it on the wall, they identify it right away."

Sophisticated and stylish montages created by professional painters speak of particular aesthetic choices that are themselves conditioned by class, education, and degree of urbanity. Urbanites distinguish themselves from their provincial peers by demonstrating their cosmopolitanism. Fadantchés from Niamey laughed deprecatingly when I mentioned the names of some fadas from Dogondoutchi. "These names are for country folks! They are not so civilized," one said, implying there was a chasm separating the city from the country in their imaginary. Fadantchés attending French-type schools demonstrate that they have "taste" (Bourdieu 1984). Consider how Salifou, an eighteen-year-old high school student who never left home without his trademark sunglasses, described the stylistic choices he and his friends had made: "After we founded the fada, three months ago, we cemented the wall. The platform in front of the wall was also cemented. We paid a mason to do this and now we're looking for someone to do the art. We used *vert sapin* [forest green] for the frame of the fada mural but for the background, the color we picked is *blanc sale* [creamy white]. And red." Salifou was a founding member of La Belle Vie des Jeunes Garçons (The Good Life of Young Boys). He envisioned the fada as a seat of self-cultivation that would contribute to the actualization of the members' life projects: "*La Belle Vie*, you know, it's the good life, the good life we hope to have." More than simply foregrounding an imagined *good* life, *la belle vie* (lit. "the beautiful life") also brought forth visions of an aesthetically gratifying life, that is, a life guided by refined judgments. By betraying an appreciation for nuanced color schemes, Salifou's use of sophisticated terminology ("forest green," "creamy white") conveyed his refined taste and affirmed his superiority over those unable to cultivate an "aptitude for practice without practical function" (Bourdieu 1984:54). Put differently, by proclaiming his engagement with urbane pleasures that remained out of reach for most Nigériens, his aesthetic preferences hinted at the way that fada art may occasionally serve to reinscribe social distinctions among the younger generation. Salifou, whose parents attended university and were gainfully employed, hoped to become a judge. Whether or not he would succeed in this endeavor, he was fairly confident about his future. He saw himself as part of a privileged minority destined to play an influential part in the affairs of the country.

Fada inscriptions often appear to echo one another, like a "forest of symbols" (V. Turner 1967) whose respective meanings can be fully grasped only in the context of their resonance with other proximate signs. Fadant-chés tend to reproduce what they see out there when they set out to colonize a wall: hence the multitude of dollar signs, silhouettes of Rasta men in dreadlocks, and drawings of teakettles one comes across when driving through Niamey's neighborhoods. It is nevertheless the ambition of many fadas to literally make their mark by drawing attention to themselves through the semantic suggestiveness of their names and the use of bold, contrasting colors and graphically complex designs. Colorful and well-designed displays of visual information grab viewers; by taking hold of people's awareness daily, they become gradually absorbed in their experiential map. When I spoke with Salifou, the fada had yet to hire a painter that would translate his and his friends' vision of life into an image of integrity, success, and beauty. The young man nevertheless expected La Belle Vie des Jeunes Garçons to become a recognized place that, by gathering things in its fold, would anchor not only the activities that took place there but also the wider neighborhood. His investment in the aesthetic project—including the careful choice of colors designed to maximize the fada's impact on the passersby's field of vision—was aimed at turning La Belle Vie des Jeunes Garçons into some sort of landmark, a place that would gain recognition as both a neighborhood sight to behold and a site of neighborly activity.

Salifou's vision for La Belle Vie des Jeunes Garçons suggests that fadas should not be seen as cut out from their surrounding environment. In fact, some fadas reproduce some of the codified order of commercial street life.

Take, for instance, Madara da Café (Milk and Coffee), a fada that takes its name from an adjacent stand that serves tea and coffee laced with condensed milk. The choice for this fada's name emerged organically out of the fadantchés' practice of meeting daily by the coffee stand. The reference to coffee and milk adds a humorous twist to the classic narrative of the fada as a seat of conviviality structured around the practice of tea drinking. By naming their fada after a local business, fadantchés laid bare their spatial tactics. For it was by identifying with an already existing place that the fada earned its claims to space. Far from proliferating anarchically across the urban landscape, some (though by no means all) fadas turn out to be localized instantiations of a wider spatial logic. Indeed Madara da Café marked its spot by borrowing the scriptural logic of local commercial signage. Painted on a wooden plank nailed to a large neem tree, the white and blue inscription signaled where the fada—composed largely of mechanics, teachers, welders, and carpenters—met every day after work. Save for the word *fada*, it could easily be mistaken for a business sign. If occupancy can be said to generate a sense of entitlement (Kim 2015), posting a sign that formally names the place created by the very act of occupying space is nevertheless a far more assertive form of encroachment.

No matter the effort and resources fadantchés expend to brand the wall against which they sit, it is in the end by acquiring a name that the group becomes officially a fada. Selecting a name that will stand out while capturing the spirit of the fada is a challenging task, as fadantchés themselves point out. One fada went through two name changes, the first time because some of its members weren't satisfied with the original name and the second time when the fada's new leader (his predecessor had died in a traffic accident) wished to leave his imprint on the organization by choosing a new name for it. Originally known as Rassemblement des Stars Dangereux or RSD (Gathering of the Dangerous Stars), the fada took the name of Lion Star before being ultimately rebaptized Big Boss Two. As the one-year anniversary of the name change was approaching, the fadantchés were discussing how to mark the event in style (many young men celebrate their fada's birthday to enhance its visibility and charisma). One member explained: "Now people know we're Big Boss Two. When you say 'Big Boss Two,' everyone knows who you're talking about. But, still, we want to have a celebration to let people know we have changed our name. We'll invite other fadas, we'll have music and food and soft drinks."

Although some fadas are named after local landmarks (a large tree, a shop, and so on) or vernacular idioms (such as Babou Maraya Sai Rago, There Are No Orphans save for Lazy Ones), the overwhelming majority of fada names are drawn from images and ideas that come from elsewhere. A member of Texas recalled how he and his friends found the fada's name: "We searched for a name in a geography book. We wanted the name of a place in the United States. Texas, it's a town over there." Fadantchés usually take pride in narrating how they came up with the name of their fada. After listening to the narratives of a number of fadas, I realized that the story behind the name was as much a part of the identity of the place as the name itself. A place name, Michael Jackson (1998) observes, is "the trace of a story, the story about how a name came to be given" (175). Put differently, if our sense of connectedness with other people is critical to our definition of who we are, so is an appreciation for the way that stories connect us to the enduring but external life of the land.

By naming the place where they meet daily Texas, Revolution, or Ruff Ryders, fadantchés endow the place with meaning. It is by acquiring a name that a space becomes a place (Basso 1988). Names are not simply markers of places. They also gather meaning, experience, and ultimately history. It is, Jeff Malpas (2008) writes, "through naming, through the way the word calls up the thing, and the place with it, that language is also a happening of place and place a happening of language" (266). In other words, names collect semantic content about places. Insofar as it becomes "remarkable—worthy of a story" (Frake 1996:238), a name therefore enables stories to gather around the space it delimits in such a way that the mere mention of that place becomes evocative of things that happened there. Some university students who all identified as Tubu, an ethnic group concentrated in northeastern Niger, informally named their fada Ambassade du Qawar. Qawar is a mountain range in the northeast along whose western side are nestled oases known for salt and date production. As members of an ethnic minority that has suffered discrimination ("a Tubu could never be elected president of Niger," one of them told me), the students felt marginalized by their peers at the university. "We are ambassadors for the Tubu, you see. But nobody knows we're here." The pompous name, alluding to a marginalized region of Niger, was a self-deprecating reminder of their invisibility but also evoked their elite status as *intellectuels* (lettered individuals). The fada was also a comforting space of Tubuness away from home. A fada that is named becomes a place that gathers and is itself gathered (Malpas 2008). Ambassade du Qawar gathered in its fold the lives of its members. Aside from conveying a sense of its links with the wider world, its name brought together local histories, persons, and relations. Each memory in turn contributed to the thickening of young men's relationship to the fada. As the fada becomes saturated with its occupants' identities and histories, it leads to what Munn (2013) describes as the centering of "persons in places" and "places in the action-field of persons" (374).

In contrast to Tanzanian youth, who express their alienation from the places they long to inhabit through their pictorial representations of remote elsewheres (Weiss 2009), young urban Nigérien men engage in street projects that often appear confident, anticipative, and aspiring. By conjuring up names of distant places such as Texas, Kansas City, or Mexico, they effectively create a sense—however fragile and provisional—of being at home in the world. The "elsewheres" they make reference to in their wall writings are predominantly framed as demonstrations of hope and potentiality. "I really like America. Right now I am learning English. I want to get a job that will allow me to travel to the US," a member of Les Americs told me. Save for some notable exceptions, narratives of fadas, their creation, and their naming are generally couched in the language of aspiration. In the way it develops into an aggregate of fadantchés' stories, memories, desires, and prospects, the space of the fada, animated by visuals that reference the treasured legacy of older brothers, an enjoyable pastime, or the much anticipated future, becomes the "objective correlative of [their] inner lives" (Jackson 1998:175).

The Spatiotemporalities of Fadas

Insofar as the walls of the fada can be said to tell stories, these stories, far from being stable, continuously unfold. For one thing, the lifespan of fada inscriptions is relatively short. When a cohort of fadantchés reaches social maturity, some of them move away for professional reasons while others may invoke conflicting commitments to justify their absence from the fada—though they might still meet whenever time allows. Their younger brothers might take over the fada, or the place might become once more undifferentiated street space, the fading inscription on the wall standing as the only clue that, in a not so distant past, young men sat there daily to chat and drink tea. Alternatively, a new group of fadantchés may grab the site and quickly cover the peeling paint with a fresh layer of colors in a deliberate effort to wipe out any trace of their predecessors' connections to the site. They may etch the name of their new fada by borrowing a paintbrush, or they may decide to wait until they have amassed enough funds to hire a professional painter before renovating the wall. If their ambition is to compete with rival fadas by creating the most eye-catching design, the site may well look unfinished for months while they ponder how to proceed. Meanwhile exposure to rain and sunlight causes even the most vivid and colorful murals to fade in a matter of years. The process of decay is hastened when the support is a simple mud wall that will erode slightly with each rainy season. The wall of a particular stretch of street may thus display half a dozen fada murals in various stages of deterioration that (insofar as they can be deciphered) speak of the values, aesthetics, and imaginaries of multiple generational cohorts.

The temporal lives of fadas can be traced through the residue of street art that sticks to the walls, layering present experiences over faded pasts. Nigérien teenagers grow up in an environment that is literally saturated with traces of former generations seeping through the washed-out layers of paints. There are street walls on which the inscriptions compose yet also compete with one another to create a vibrant mosaic of utterances and images. At times, the lettering and drawings intersect with each other in such a way that the overall effect is disorderly, cacophonous. Because new fadas colonize abandoned spaces and write over existing inscriptions, the remains of cumulative coats of paintwork over certain walls create a multilayered record. Fading hues meld into one another to produce new color schemes that are progressively absorbed into the façade. The blended effect created by successive coats of color applied over time can be quite striking—so much so that, to the untrained eye, it may appear intentional.

Color is not the only thing that fades, however. Layers of scribbles neutralize one another as they grow fainter, turning walls into palimpsests, visual compositions that reveal some of their past—as when a parchment was reused once the first layer of inscriptions faded. Julia Kristeva (1984) speaks of the "productive violence" (16) that takes place at the site where new layers of inscription are superimposed on older ones, at once erasing existing works and adding to the overall record. In the way it is both destructive of earlier depositions and accommodating of new ones, the palimpsest is the art historian's nightmare. If, in some places, the remaining deposits break through the surface of the wall, providing evidence of past activity, the process of erasure is nevertheless thoroughly intertwined with the layering process, defying any attempt to separate the successive episodes of deposition from one another. What this means is that some wall inscriptions have become illegible over time.

Note that this palimpsestic look is not simply the result of inter-fada competition or generational changes (with new inscriptions intentionally covering old ones). After a few years, some fadas attempt to freshen up their wall with a new coat of paint. Ironically, these preservation attempts often end up further contributing to the palimpsestic quality of wall writing. A professional painter complained to me that rather than turning to the person who originally designed their murals, fadantchés often opt to refresh the design themselves when the paint starts fading or peeling. As they awkwardly trace over the original motifs with borrowed brushes, they often "mess up" what used to be graphically complex compositions. "This is why you see some fada signs that no longer look like the original design," the painter concluded mournfully. As the newer layer of paint fades over time, it acquires a certain transparency, letting the original design that lies underneath seep through. This creates something of a pentimento effect that hints at the changes the surface of the wall experiences over time.

As palimpsestic canvases that retain traces of former dwellers, the streets of Niamey in particular remind us that space cannot be seen as "a static slice orthogonal to time" (Massey 2003:108). Brash or subtle, legible or illegible, the marks that fadas leave on the environment evidence the dynamic qualities of places and the "spatializing" (Certeau 1984:97) dimension of social practices. They point to the ways that places are always in the process of being shaped out of people's engagement with the world (Bender 2002). While I have argued that in the absence of concrete infrastructure, fadas must be seen as practiced spaces, I have also tried to stress the importance of attending to the materiality of places and to their material alterations over time. We often take for granted the stability of matter,

Tim Ingold (2007) writes. Our engagement with matter, he notes, starts once the stucco has hardened on the façade or the ink has dried on the page. We see the building but not the materials it is made of, the words but not the ink. We should recognize that places are simultaneously materialized and dematerialized as the stuff they are made of disintegrates over time. Thus plaster on the wall crumbles and ink on the page fades. Whether or not they can be read as evidence of neglect, the fading paint, crumbling surfaces, eroded mud walls, and overgrown vegetation are part of the history of fadas. They remind us that these street projects unfold in time and that it is precisely in the tension between stability and transience that life as a fadantché finds its full meaning. Put differently, the fadas exemplify how space has "its times" (Massey 2003:108) and cannot be held still. The traces fadas leave behind point not only to the impermanence of material forms but also to their contingent relations with their surroundings.

Fadas and Generations

Fadas, I have argued in this chapter, are always becoming. They cannot be understood as inert scenes, readymade containers for human activity, but must be seen instead as events produced through people's reiterated engagement with space. Moreover the spatializing practices that give form and substance to fadas and the localizing inscriptions that situate them in space also unfold in a temporal register. In short fadas are marked by openness and impermanence. As I hope to have demonstrated, they are driven by creativity, hope, and ambition. As concrete instantiations of young men's affirmation of the "art of presence" (Bayat 2010a:26), they signal the ingenuity with which some urban residents turn their environment into a canvas for their aspirations. For if fadas often provide a scaffolding for samari's vision of the good life, they are also, importantly, aesthetic interventions into urban space.

In this chapter I have examined some of the ways in which fadas—as both material signs and social practices—exist in time and what happens as they grow, mutate, and decay. Insofar as fadas never stand still, they must be apprehended as spatiotemporalities with distinct rhythms, some of which are cyclical, having to do with regular activities such as tea drinking or weight lifting, and some of which are linear, having to do with the maturation of yet another generation of fadantchés. It seems therefore fitting to end my discussion of the mutually constitutive relationship between people and place with a man's description of his former fada and of its members' engagement with their environment:

When we were young, we created a fada called Adalci. It's a Hausa name that means "justice." A bunch of us spoke Hausa, which is why we picked a Hausa name. We all agreed on the name. This was in 2001. We met after school, we organized dances, we drank tea and listened to music. We spent a lot of money on clothes. We were competing [with one another] through dress.

Now we have left such things. We don't need a name anymore to feel important. The name of the fada, all those things, it's for the immature youths who act without thinking. We've left all this behind. We have jobs and families. We still meet, but we don't call ourselves a fada. We drink tea, we talk, that's it. No music, no fancy dresses. Grown man must behave. I have a wife and three children. I must get up in the morning to go to work. When we were young, we wrote the name of our fada on the wall. ADALCI. We did it ourselves. Now the inscription on the wall is almost completely erased. Our little brothers have picked up the fada. For us, none of those things matter. We are grown men and we aren't concerned about such things. The fada, you see, is principally a means of evolving. So it plays an important role. You can't stay a youth all your life. When you are in contact with other people, you learn.

One would be hard pressed to find a more explicit description of what happens over time to the relationship between a fada and its members. As a place that maintains the "living present" (Munn 2013:371) of earlier times through both the traces of a former occupation (that is, through the wall's mnemonic potential) and the memories these occupants have accumulated, Adalci recapitulates the original members' coming of age. Today members of an emerging cohort have taken over the fada and added their imprint on the space so they can (figuratively and literally) stake out their place in the world. This is what Munn calls "the becoming-past-of-places" (359), that is, the ways that places are meaningfully constituted over time through the interplay between discursive and more concrete place-making practices. Adalci's capacity to accommodate the vision of a new generation of fadantchés coupled with its ability to presence the past reminds us that what gives a place its specificity is not some sense of ongoing history (though it can be that too) but the fact that it is constituted out of a "particular constellation of social relations" (Massey 1994:7) that comes together at a distinct locus.

The brief sketch of Adalci's evolution further suggests that the kinds of street politics I have discussed in this chapter are rather ordinary, in the dual sense that they occur daily and they surface under the radar, away from the nexuses of administrative and political power. It is through daily use, or what Certeau (1984) called *pratiques quotidiennes*, that fadantchés come to inhabit the street and develop a sense of rootedness to a place. Their wall writings nevertheless situate them within what might be characterized as a kind of subculture, on the fringe of urban life. Thus the invasion of public space by fadas—a process at once surreptitious and bold-faced—is a perfect instance of "colonization from below" (Appadurai 2000). By erecting a new architecture of belonging through a whole array of discursive, aesthetic, and other practices, samari provisionally stake their claims to the city.

At another level this so-called invasion is part of a wider process of social reproduction. Young men occupy the street because they have nowhere to go, but they do so by replicating existing forms of male sociality (the chief's fada) and guided by the expectation that they will eventually move on to bigger and better things. In this regard, I have argued here, the wall writings that saturate the urbanscape with civic and aspirational messages are explicitly aimed at figuring life in the twofold meaning of helping young men make sense of their current place in the world and giving shape to their yet undetermined futures. In the way they encode a wide variety of relationships at the shifting intersections of here, there, and elsewhere while scripting how elders might be re-placed, these writings function as strategic tools of intergenerational struggle. They also remind us that fadas should be seen as contingent projects, anchored in the urban landscape by scriptural and social practices that briefly endow them with an illusion of permanence.

THREE

Snapshots: Bringing (Invisible) Women into View

A fada without women is not a fada!

—Motorcycle repairman, Niamey, 2013

"Hey, princess, how are you?" Salifou called out to a young woman who was exiting her compound, across the street from where he was sitting. Although he seemed to be watching a kettle of tea simmering over a bed of hot coals, the young man, a member of La Belle Vie des Jeunes Garçons, did not miss any of his neighbors' comings and goings and paid particular attention to the young women who appeared within his field of vision. His two companions, previously hunched over a backgammon board, lifted their heads to look at the girl. She smiled confidently and uttered something back. She appeared unaffected by the familiarity of Salifou's greeting despite the inappropriate implications of intimacy it conveyed. She and Salifou had known each other since they were children so she didn't mind his cheeky ways. Moreover, she thought of herself as a modern girl, who did not shy away from young men's company despite the tight surveillance her parents kept over her movements. Yet she was also mindful of the importance of cultivating a reputation as a respectable girl and that to meet social expectations of propriety—and enhance her marriageability—she must project an image of demureness and modesty. Though she occasionally came over to chat with the young men, briefly inquiring about their families or their studies, she did not partake in their activities. When a uniform-clad adolescent girl walked by minutes later on her way to school, the three young men gazed at her for a while. She appeared not to notice.

In Niger the act of sitting with one's friends around a pot of tea is unambiguously gendered. While young men may gather in a public space, young women do not typically loiter in the street: they have places to go and things to do. Not only do their domestic obligations often prevent them from partaking of the kind of leisurely activities fadantchés engage in, but it would also be improper for them to sit among young men in full view of the neighborhood. While male passersby acknowledge the presence of sitting fadantchés, responding to their salutations and, at times, even stopping to engage in a bit of conversation, young women who walk by the fada typically mumble a quick greeting before walking away. Or they simply ignore the young men whose gaze lingers appraisingly on their faces, "the slow rotating movement of the buttocks" (De Boeck and Plissart 2004:54), or the graceful motion of an ankle protruding from under a flowing hijab.

Based on the near total absence of women at the fada, one could easily conclude that they are excluded from such settings. After all, the fada is understood to be a space designed for samari by samari themselves. Modeled after the council of elders, an all-male structure that assists traditional authorities from the emir to the village chief, it is centered on male activities, male concerns, and male aspirations. Not only is the fada a primary outlet for the performance of boastful masculinity, but it is also part of the street. In a social environment where gender segregation operates to restrict women's access to public spaces, the fada is a quintessentially masculine space created to satisfy young men's needs for sociality and their desire for self-affirmation.

The apparent absence of women from the fada should not lead us to exclude women (young and older) from our analyses, however. Inasmuch as the construction of masculine spaces is predicated on the exclusion of women from these spaces, women matter—if only in a negative way. In his ethnography of homelessness in Bucharest, Romania, Bruce O'Neill (2017) uses the concept of the photographic negative to capture the essence of moments when nothing happens. Drawing on Benjamin's observation that when taking a snapshot, photographers produce a negative of the scene they are trying to capture, O'Neill interprets the boring times and places his interlocutors are trapped into as "ethnographic negatives" (115–17), inversions of the dense and vibrant social world that is ethnographically observable. When the ethnographic record is conceived as a negative, O'Neill contends, what was obvious recedes to the shadows while what was obscured (or simply less visible) can be brought into view. I find the concept of the ethnographic negative fruitful for exploring the gendered dynamics of the fada. Viewing the fada as the negative of the snapshot, one that records an inverted gendered world, enables me to situate the samari, their activities, and their aspirations as the dark backdrop against which the women's presence and their contributions are brought to light.

By momentarily treating the fada as a photographic negative, I seek to complicate the picture of homosociality that emerges from popular and scholarly representations of the fada. Women, I argue, are critical to the definition of masculinity that unfolds at the fada. Indeed they are critical to the fada itself, as an institution whose continued existence hinges on the performance of gendered labor and social engagements that are often unacknowledged. In this chapter I draw on O'Neill's concept of the negative to highlight women's importance to the fada along three different registers, namely, domesticity, fantasy, and nighttime. First, I describe the labor women invest daily at the fada. Women, especially older women, contribute substantially to the fada, but their contributions go unnoticed because, since they fall under the rubric of domestic work, they are not seen as part of street life. Second, I consider the centrality of 'yammata in male spaces of fantasy. Whether the discussion centers on sex, romantic preoccupations, or *projets de mariage* (marriage preparations), young women are often the focus of men's conversations. Third, through a focus on nightlife, I discuss how the cloak of darkness that shrouds 'yammata's movements enables them to join the fada without incurring opprobrium. Being attuned to the nighttime economy of fadas, I suggest, is essential for grasping the place that women occupy in these male spaces.

The Gender of the Fada

The fada is often described as a homosocial island where young men find respite from the incessant demands of girlfriends (and wives)—a training ground of some sort where, away from familial pressure, restless, insecure samari mold themselves into strong, confident men (see chapter 5). To be sure, there exists no formal obstacle to women's participation. In fact, many fadantchés told me that they did not bar 'yammata from joining: "They can come if they want." Some of them admitted they would welcome the presence of girls but knew such a move would bring disapproval on the part of elders. "We do not bring 'yammata to our fada because we'd be criticized by the neighborhood. But we appreciate women and what they do," is how a young man put it. His comments hinted at the fact that 'yammata were occasionally enlisted to prepare a meal or arbitrate a friendly dispute between two members in need of an impartial judge. Yet all the same, the forms of sociability 'yammata engage in do not typically include sitting and drinking tea "with the boys." Like the women whose presence in the boxing club on Chicago's South Side was tolerated only so long as it remained infrequent (Wacquant 2004), 'yammata are not expected to hang out at the fada. Nor are they supposed to parade themselves in the company of young men, for their moral character (and, ultimately, their marriageability) rests precisely on the ability to project an appearance of modesty, chastity, and virtue. "Some girls come to the fada. But the *mace ta kirki* [good girl] should not wander everywhere. She cannot drink a Coke in front of people. Easy girls do that. They are *bordel* [prostitutes]," a saurayi explained, intimating that respectable girls—whom young men married because their parents approved of them—stayed home rather than openly socialize with young men. School-educated 'yammata, who are more comfortable in gender-mixed settings than their nonliterate peers, may drop in on a fada—where they will usually be offered a seat—but their presence ultimately disrupts the group's social dynamics and its carefully cultivated intimacy. As an essentially masculine space, the fada is (ostensibly) predicated on the gendered division of labor and pastimes. After all, women too have their own structures of solidarity. In Niamey many of them belong to a *foyandi*, a Zarma term referring to an informal association that serves as a *tontine* and a space of sociality and solidarity.

Take tea drinking, for instance. As a practice aimed at enhancing friendship and intimacy, it is marked as masculine. Samari often joke that tea is "too strong" for women, or they point out that the third round of tea, watered down by the recycling of the tea leaves, is fit only for women. In her work on gender and gift exchange Marilyn Strathern (1988) has persuasively argued that people, like things, are composed of the relations that they in turn engender. From this perspective, tea can be said to be both representation and performance. Aside from being a stimulant, as a potential symbol of strength (and bitterness), it is also a creator of experience—and of masculinity: by passing on the third round of tea, samari perform masculinity through their rejection of weakness while reinscribing the fada as a male space from which frailty and faintness are excluded. Among married fadantchés, manhood is further asserted through banal utterances such as "I have to go home," by which they imply they have a wife waiting for them at home. Being married translates as being fed—having a wife prepare your meals. A saurayi told me the best thing about marriage, aside from ending l'adultère, by which he meant sex between unmarried partners, was that a man no longer ate street food. The cash a married man gave his wife turned into home-cooked meals. Whereas samari boast of their feminine conquests (with some occasionally bragging they have a girlfriend in every neighborhood), married men enact their masculinity through pithy

references to (and occasionally lengthier discussions of) their domestic lives. Such references signal maturity by hinting at men's roles as providers for dependents—a critical dimension of manhood. Significantly, insofar as marriage turns men into providers, it is often at the fada that they rehearse their marital role, as we shall see. To borrow an expression from Michael Herzfeld (1988), we could say that if wives are essential to the creation of the *mutumin kirki* (good, honorable man), the fada is where men learn to be "*good* at being a man" (16).

A few fadas count young women among their members, but they are rare. Among the dozens of fadas I visited in Dogondoutchi, only three had a gender-mixed membership. These three fadas were founded with the explicit purpose of promoting the normalization of social interactions between young men and women. They were composed of young people who had grown up on the same school benches and were comfortable in one another's company. The *'yammata*, in particular, considered themselves modern in the sense that they did not feel hampered by the gender segregation that prevents many women in Niger from dwelling in public spaces. At État Major (Military Headquarters), the fada's cofounder and treasurer was a young woman who kept a tight grip on the budget, pursued relentlessly members who did not pay their weekly dues, and was unafraid of publicly dissenting with her peers. She saw the fada as a space of creativity and experimentation where she could gain the leadership experience that would serve her when she became a lawyer. She had designed the fada's uniforms and was fully involved in the planning of events, such as inter-fada gatherings, sponsored and financed by État Major. At the same time, she was fully aware of the need to protect her own reputation as a "serious" girl. État Major's meetings took place every Friday in her family's compound, under her mother's and grandmother's watchful eyes, and no project was initiated before receiving parental approval. As she put it, "Our fada is a place for work. Members do their schoolwork together."

In Niamey's poorer neighborhoods, young women's presence at the fada is actively discouraged on the grounds that Islam prohibits gender-mixed gatherings. Young women who occasionally engage classmates or boyfriends in conversations do not linger; they are mindful of the social disapproval their presence at these male gatherings may generate. A couple of unmarried girls spoke of the discomfort they felt walking in the street in front of an assembled fada. If some 'yammata acknowledge the presence of the seated young men, responding to their greetings but ignoring their teases, many do not out of kumya (shyness, shame, and respectability). One young woman confided that the thought of being interpellated by young men looking for an excuse to practice their skills as tchatcheurs (men skilled in the verbal art of seduction) filled her with dread. To minimize the risk of its happening, she dressed modestly, making sure her hijab hid the curves of her upper body, and whenever possible she avoided the streets crowded with fadas. As she saw it, the hijab was a shield, signaling that its wearer was unavailable. By deflecting the male gaze, it enabled her to enjoy "civil inattention" (Goffman 1963:84) whenever she walked down a street in full view of a fada.

'Yammata's avoidance of the fada reminds us of the extent to which Nigérien men and women live spatially divided lives. When 'yammata are not attending school, their labor is usually harnessed for the performance of domestic tasks. Consequently, they spend much of their time in the familial compound, and the street outside is simply a link between two places. For young men, on the other hand, the street has become a second home, a place where they can congregate to face jointly the tedium of having nothing to do. Given how gendered the use of the street is, samari and 'yammata are not subjected to the same moral evaluations as they navigate public space. Whereas young men are excoriated for sitting in the same spot all day long—a symptom of their social immobility—young women are chastised for not staying put. For it is the latter's excessive mobility—rather than the absence of it—that sets tongues wagging and may even compel *malamai* (Muslim religious specialists) to take action, by urging parents to restrict their daughters' comings and goings.

The Invisible Work of Women

The invisibility of women at the fada can be read as part of a wider pattern of female exclusion from male spaces in an overwhelmingly Muslim society. To be sure, *'yammata* enjoy more freedom of movement than their married counterparts, but their mobility is nevertheless constrained, especially if they belong to a devout Muslim family. What this means is that their access to certain public spaces (the market, the classroom, the mosque, and so on) is restricted and, in some cases, denied altogether. Norms regulating women's access to public space are further embedded in local conceptions of respectability and instantiated in gossip and sanctions linked to women's visibility and mobility. In Dogondoutchi information about young married women allegedly sneaking out of their homes to go to market or going places they should not circulated quickly in the neighborhood where I lived. No matter how inconspicuous they tried to be, they rarely escaped their neighbors' watchful eyes. In the gender-segregated Provençal village where she conducted fieldwork in the early 1970s, Rayna Reiter (1975) found that private and public forms of sociability provided clues to the different lives women and men lived. This could also be said to describe the case of Nigérien society where the forms that leisure takes are distinctly gendered. Like Reiter's male informants, who fraternized at the café and other public places, Nigérien men congregate in tailor's workshops, under sheds, and by food kiosks or storefronts. Meanwhile, Nigérien women visit each other's houses, just as their French counterparts in Reiter's ethnography exchanged visits and errands with female relatives, rarely socializing beyond their private realm.

Recently feminist scholars have nonetheless pointed to the limitations of assuming there is a firm division between public and private spheres. They have called for a shift from the perspective that space is fixed to a focus on fluidity and movement. The public/private binary, they assert, is an ideological one. Barbara Cooper (1997), working with Hausa women in Niger, has proposed that we think of the private spaces women use to conduct commercial transactions as public spaces. Susan Gal (2002) has similarly argued for the usefulness of considering public and private as semantic categories that are fractal. What this means is that public activities may be embedded in private spaces in such a way that what we refer to as private space is actually split into both a public and a private. Conversely, private activities may penetrate the public sphere, thereby leading to the replication of the private/public division within that sphere. The fada provides a compelling instance of how public and private are mutually embedded in fractal fashion: as a form of street life, it frames the public performance of masculinity in urban contexts. At the same time, private conversations, body postures, commensality, and the use of movable infrastructure allow for the creation of intimacy. Constructed as a particular nexus where social interactions, sensibilities, and aspirations intersect, the fada provides an alternative locus of sociability for young men anxious to carve private spaces that are somewhat distinct from the intergenerational family compound yet not totally disconnected from it either.

The fada's hybridity has important implications for the way we consider women's investments in and contributions to these projects. Notwithstanding claims by fadantchés that they cook their own meals, the beans (and other dishes) they are so fond of are routinely prepared by their sisters—or mothers. A saurayi who prided himself on his talent as a cook explained: "We take our mother's cooking pot. When it's early, girls will prepare the food for us. But if it's late—three or four o'clock in the morning—the girls are sleeping so we do it ourselves." Though rarely acknowledged, women's contributions to fada life are traceable to older, equally gendered modes of engagement. In the words of a fadantché: "There are no women in our fada. If there is a *gayya* [collective form of labor], we bring women. They prepare water and food and wipe the sweat of men's foreheads." Women's participation in communal labor becomes visible, my interlocutor implied, insofar as they feed men and care for them, thereby enabling the performance of *real* work. On several occasions I partook of a dish of macaroni or rice at the fada I was visiting. The fadantché's mother (or wife), who had prepared the meal, did not appear; a young child would bring the dish in her stead to the fada. On other occasions young men would eat dinner at home but later show up at the fada with a dish prepared by a mother or a sister. The gendered spatial divisions that operate on the surface mean that women are—largely though not entirely—excluded from public spaces. Yet, through their domestic labor, they extend their reach into the street, filling fadantchés' stomachs and nurturing male social networks. Drawing on Simone's (2004) insights, one could say that through their labor, women constitute an important element of the fada's "human infrastructure."

In her work on Gawa, Munn (1986) has shown how a person is extended and dispersed via acts of hospitality. While acts of selfishness and greediness subvert what she calls "spacetime" by negating and consuming a person's capacity to extend and diffuse her spatiotemporal influence, hospitality allows the potency of a person to be deployed via concrete material exchanges that extend that influence. When a *biki* (birth or marriage celebration) is held, the women who distribute the food they have prepared for guests will bring a dish or two to the closest fadas as a gesture of neighborliness and a demonstration of their worth. The daily care women lavish upon their homes, sweeping, cleaning, and tidying, may extend to the space of the fada. As previously noted, I once saw a woman sweep the grounds of a fada as if it were her own courtyard. Other women admitted to doing so as well. Sisters are occasionally enlisted to launder or iron a fadantché's clothes before an event hosted by the fada. Women are thus critical nodes in the infrastructure of care that sustains the fada. Yet the forms of labor they provide remain largely invisible. Women can therefore be said to inhabit the masculine space of the fada in the negative. Only when the fada is viewed as an inverted image of itself—where absence appears as presence and vice versa—does women's labor become discernable. Viewing the fada as a photographic negative and highlighting the forms of female labor that are contributed to the fada help us rethink how space is used along gendered registers and how it contributes to the gendering of people's activities.

Women as Fantasy

Another dimension of the negative space that women, specifically young women, occupy is that of fantasy. When I asked a couple of fadantchés what their favorite pastime was, one of them jestingly responded, "watching *'yammata* pass by." One may see his response as unremarkable, just another example of the kind of lighthearted humor samari engage in when in the company of peers. After all, who would counter the claim that, as an observation post, the fada constitutes the best spot for watching appraisingly young female pedestrians walk by? Yet even when samari joke about sizing up girls, there is a dimension of gravity (or anxiety) to their banter. The question of women, by all accounts, is serious business. That much emerges out of the conversations fadantchés have with each other about the mechanics of romance, the toolkit of the good lover, the promise of "true" love, and the pitfalls of "materialist" women (Masquelier 2009a). Every one of them knows that, aside from earning a stable income, wining a woman's heart is an important step on the path to manhood. As is the case elsewhere in Africa (Parikh 2015; Stambach 2000), the expansion of secondary education in contemporary Niger has reconfigured the dynamics of love and intimacy. Given the coeducational character of French-type schools, boys and girls sit side by side in classrooms. If schools are where many samari start navigating the shifting landscape of gender, sexuality, and intimacy, the fada is where they learn "how to succeed in the eyes of women" (Smith 2017:40) at a time when money is increasingly becoming the currency of love.

Among youth there is a growing perception that romance and intimacy are the cornerstone of marriage. Many young people now insist on the importance of affective bonds in cementing marital ties, thereby deliberately positioning themselves in contrast to their parents and grandparents, whose marriages were most often arranged. Marrying for love puts pressure on samari to earn women's affection while also demonstrating they can be good providers. The fada is a critical arena for learning how to seduce girls and educating oneself about sexuality. It is also where samari boast of their romantic conquests. "What do we talk about? GIRLS! We talk about girls—how beautiful a girl is. That's what we're obsessed with," a saurayi volunteered. "I am not a poet, I don't know how to use romantic words," another said. "My friends at the fada helped write the letters I sent a girl. They advised me." At Show Boys Clan, I found two members counseling a distraught saurayi who had just realized his girlfriend had another suitor. They were helping him win her back: "Your *petite*, basically, you have to *tchatcher* [sweet talk] her, like tell her you can't breathe without her." At the fada young men's preoccupations routinely center on women and how to win them over.

The ethics of love and the valorization of emotional commitment notwithstanding, religious discourse on chastity and norms regulating women's mobility limit *'yammata*'s access to the fada. Thus while *'yammata* loom large in young men's fantasies, paradoxically their presence at the fada is elusive. To address this seeming paradox, I shall map out the broad contours of what Aymon Kreil (2016:166), in his study of coffee shops in Cairo, calls the "territories of desire." By focusing on what young men imagine femininity to be, how women figure in their practices of self-making, and how the fada grounds their romantic aspirations, I will briefly trace some of the contours of this affective geography.

At the fada young men routinely exchange tips on how to pick up girls. They advise friends on what to say to sustain a girl's interest and how to balance the material and emotional dimensions of romance.[1] Granted, they often tease each other about their amorous strategies, and at times they compete for the same girls. Yet they are also supportive of one another whether they experience romantic triumphs or disappointments; the provision of care and encouragement is what fada sociality both requires and enables. At the fada, samari are initiated into not only the art of living but also the art of loving. In the words of Salifou, a member of La Belle Vie des Jeunes Garçons: "We tease our friends when they go to see a girl. *Les dragueurs*, we call them. But at the same time, we're here for each other. When someone wants to meet a girl but she doesn't pay attention to him, he comes to us with his problem and we tell him what to do, how to talk to her, how to come on to her. We give him advice. And then he gets the girl." Operating in a supporting environment means samari can borrow "props" (such as a cell phone or a motorcycle) from one another to enhance their desirability as potential suitors. Many *'yammata* expect their dates to pick them up in style, that is, riding a motorbike: "When I took my *chérie* to the restaurant, I borrowed a friend's Daylong [motorbike]. Women expect it." Young men forward links to pornographic videos to one another on their cell phones so they can educate themselves about sex. They discuss the pros and cons of marrying early, the difficulties of reconciling sexual experimentation with Islamic morality, and how to navigate the treacherous waters of courtship, among other things.

Habibou, a member of Boston Junior, sought advice from his fada on how to approach a girl he had noticed in his neighborhood. His father had been supportive of his various projects, including the fada, but on the topic of romance, he was mum. "My father never asked me if I had a girlfriend. In our culture, parents do not talk to their children about these things, they feel shame." Though he was not ready to marry (he was twenty-one and practically penniless), he was very much in love. When I met Habibou, Valentine's Day was weeks away, but he was already fretting about what to get Samira, the girl he courted. In recent years, Valentine's Day has become an important celebration for lovers in Niger. *'Yammata* expect to receive chocolate, clothes, or stuffed animals from suitors. Habibou knew Samira wanted a cell phone, but he could not afford the one she wanted. "Love is very important. We live with love, we die with love," he told me to help me understand what was at stake. After consulting the fada, Habibou sold his phone and borrowed money from his older brother so he could present Samira with the model she had set her eyes on.[2] Mobile phones, scholars have suggested, are not neutral technologies of communication. They encode people's fantasies, enabling these fantasies to materialize in the act of transmission (Archambault 2017). More than a symbol of technological revolution or a sign of prosperity, Habibou's gift to Samira was above all an investment in the romance he hoped to nurture. "Girls like to be amazed, flattered. So I send Samira little messages. When she texts me back, 'I LOVE YOU,' I am all cheered up."

Samari readily admit that some of them are better than others at chatting up girls: "You're at the fada, you see a girl walking, you decide to try your luck, and so you go after her, hoping she'll listen to you. If she shows interest in you, you return to the fada telling everyone about your conquest. If not, you return with your tail between your legs, and then maybe some other guy tries to get the girl." Those who know how to talk to girls persuasively are known as *tosteurs* or *tchatcheurs*. Whereas the *tchatcheur* (or *tchapeur*) typically uses his way with words to charm girls, the *tosteur* deploys his rapping skills. Fadantchés with special talent may be dispatched to contact young women and recruit them for the fada.[3] The intent is to seduce a young woman not for oneself but on someone else's behalf—a move that ultimately benefits the entire fada. Girls represent "social capital." When a fadantché starts courting a young woman, he must present her to the fada to officialize her relationship to the group and discourage anyone else from making a move on her. Through their love affairs or friendships with members of a particular fada, 'yammata contribute to that fada's reputation—all the more so when they are widely admired for their looks and the object of intense competition between fadas.

In some fadas this form of recruitment is reportedly frequent. Mille Boy, a member of Jeunes Tosteurs Solidaires (or JTS), boasted of his and his friends' impressive record: "We attract the most beautiful girls. We want JTS to outshine the other fadas so we become the most popular fada." Earning the respect of all the other fadas was a tall order, however, and Mille Boy admitted that JTS occasionally faced setbacks: "There are fadas that don't get along. They are competing against each other. They both want the same girl to be in their fada—you know, a beautiful girl everyone admires. They try to attract her to their fada. Of course, if you manage to lure a girl who used to be with another fada, the two fadas are going to be at war with each other. That's what happened to us."

Young men frequently cited the attention they received from 'yammata as a prime motivation for pumping iron, an activity that was extremely popular in the 2000s: "Girls, you see, they like men who are strong, men with big muscles." As a tool for defense and aggression, bodybuilding was doubly tied to samari's amorous fantasies since women were generally the reason fadas fought each other in the first place (see chapter 5). I was told that clashes between fadas were provoked by young men who "stole" (or simply took too close a look at) a young woman who "belonged" to (i.e., had already been "claimed" by a saurayi from) a rival fada. Aggressions against other fadas boosted the standing of a fada not only because it demonstrated the members' fierceness but also because it spoke of their ability to attract women. Today the reputation of certain fadas remains tied to the women who are associated with it, in some fashion or another.

To attract girls to their fadas, fadantchés may organize *soirées dansantes* (dancing parties) that charge an entrance fee for young men but are free for their female consorts. These parties are often a measure of the fadas' popularity because one can gauge the number of women they attract. "You want to show that there are many girls at your fada, that they come to dance, to admire young men and be seen," a saurayi explained. Other fadas hold *kermesses* (fund-raising events) in which young women may act as the bait to induce young men to play games and spend money. The game booths may be staffed by attractive young women. In addition to monetary prizes, the winners will be awarded the phone number of a young woman, a trend that adds a new twist to the equation of girls with capital. There are, in sum, a number of opportunities for samari to pick up girls and, by the same token, enhance the prestige of their fadas. Besides raising money for the fada, a stated aim of the *kermesse* is to boost its reputation as a glamorous organization that others will want to join. As well, *kermesses* offer opportunities for encounters between young men and women—furtive and cursory as they might be.

"A fada without women is not a fada," a young motorcycle repairman from Niamey once quipped. A quick look at the names of certain fadas offers clues for how we might grasp the implications of such a statement: Manyan Mata (Big Women), Amitiés des Belles Filles (Friendship of Beautiful Girls), Rabi (a girl's name). By naming their fadas after particular women or stressing their connections to them, young men signal that they understand themselves and their relations to one another in terms of women. A group of friends named their fada Rachel to honor a young woman by that name who lived in Senegal. Rachel, who was in high school when the fada was created, often returned to Dogondoutchi for the holidays. She was reportedly "fair complexioned, beautiful, and *très gentille*." Although her association with this circle of admirers was tenuous given how far from them she lived, the simple evocation of her name was enough to permeate the fada with her "absent presence," enabling it to stand strong in an increasingly dense fadascape. The fact that Rachel lived abroad enhanced the fadantchés' claim to cosmopolitanism, expanding their fada's reputation by extending its influence in time and space (Munn 1986; Weiner 1976).

At the heart of samari's work of imagination are their self-projections into the world of adulthood, complete with stable livelihoods, wives, and children. Recall that a saurayi's ultimate goal is to marry and found a household. Such ideals, when based on romance and companionship, still occasionally run counter to parental definitions of proper marriage. "What do we dream of? To have a beautiful wife and beautiful children," Aziz, a member of Face Cachée—and the only one of his siblings to attend school—told me. There was distress in his affirmation. The previous year, instead of tying the knot with his girlfriend, Aziz had married the young woman his parents had chosen for him. "The first time I met my wife was the day of the wedding. It was an arranged marriage. I couldn't go against my parents' wishes." Aziz's wife, who never attended school, remained in the village with her in-laws after the wedding. "I visit her twice a year. But she can't live with me [in Niamey]. I'm an intellectual, I've traveled, she's illiterate. We've nothing in common." Aziz hoped to marry for love one day. In the meantime, when he was not attending classes, he spent most of his time at Face Cachée where he found solace from his marital woes.

Young men's anticipatory visions of the future and, in particular, their wedding plans are nourished by the fada's tight webs of solidarity and its aspirational politics. Except when, as was the case for Aziz, parents arrange their son's marriage, it is at the fada that wedding plans are initiated and later concretized. Members contribute funds and provide logistical assistance for a fellow fadantché's wedding. They generally cover a substantial part of the overall cost of the event, including the rental of a tent and plastic chairs as well as the food and drinks to be served to guests during the reception. "These days, you can't get married without the fada," is how one young man put it. By giving samari access to the social, technical, emotional, and material resources they need to court young women and marry them, the fada plays a critical role in social reproduction. One could even argue that the fada is an engine of social reproduction. Rather than contributing to the postponement of marriage by glorifying idleness, as elders frequently claim, the homosociality of the fada facilitates romance and promotes matrimony by serving as a forum for the circulation of key cultural and financial capital. How young men anticipate and imagine adulthood, in turn, shapes the fada's formulations and practices of sociality.

Women of the Night

At night, the city is "a different place" (285) that enables a different reading, Julia Hornberger (2008) writes of Johannesburg. She notes that after nightfall, streetlights "spread their cones of light" (285) throwing the

spaces they illuminate into prominence and neglecting all that lies between them. It is precisely what lies between the light cones, namely, the
social and sexual contacts that darkness enables, that interests me here. The
lights (or their absence) have a palpable effect that goes beyond the visual
transformation of the urbanscape. Take Niamey, for instance. At night, the
city comes alive in a way that implies a radical transformation of space,
enabling the emergence of alternate social traffics and moral geographies.
The main thoroughfares are lined with streetlights, but most of the smaller,
unpaved streets and alleys remain dark. Walking through the obscure, narrow pathways lining mud-walled compounds in the more modest neighborhoods, one regularly bumps into couples standing still, whispering to
each other. Obscurity creates what we might call inner, protective spaces
where young people who have otherwise no place to meet can experience
intimacy "in the shadows." Nocturnal life thus affords yet another means
of viewing the fada as a negative that, through the literal inversion of light
and darkness, brings otherwise invisible women into focus.

Many parents prevent their daughters from visiting fadas, fearful of their
potentially corrupting influences. Young women tend to comply with parental commands, at least during the day, when their comings and goings are
difficult to conceal. The mobility of unmarried girls may not be bound by
the same exacting moral standards as that of married wives, but it is nevertheless constrained (though much less so for members of the educated,
cosmopolitan elite). The fadas are part of the public space many 'yammata
must avoid or, at least, appear not to be associated with. As previously
noted, most of them walk quickly past where young men are sitting and
talking, in keeping with the demure deportment they are expected to adopt
in public. Having internalized the set of gendered dispositions that guide
proper conduct, they may experience *kumya*—a feeling of shame and in-
adequacy that translates as shyness and, occasionally, anxiety or dread. For
many young women who live under the moralizing gaze of elders, the fada
is both an intimidating place and a place that can sully their reputation.

At night, on the other hand, the fada becomes a "contact zone" (Farrer
and Field 2015:11) between young men and women, a space where they
may interact with a certain degree of freedom and without fear of social
condemnation. This is the time when 'yammata discreetly evade the control of elders, often waiting until the household is asleep to exit the compound. Under the cover of darkness, they make their way to the fada where
a boyfriend is awaiting them, reminding us that nightlife is inextricably
linked with transgression, romance, and sexuality. Nighttime is also when
young women forced to engage in transactional sex to survive go looking

for clients. Whether they hover around bars, loiter on dark street corners, or stand in the floodlight, they are known as *bonsoir monsieur* because they often greet male passersby by mumbling "Bonsoir, Monsieur!"

Given the widespread condemnation directed at gender-mixed gatherings featuring dancing and music, attending a dance party is a risky proposition for *'yammata* raised in strict households. To escape opprobrium and avoid having to tell their parents where they go on certain nights, they engage in clever subterfuges. Dressing in conservative outfits covering much of their bodies, some of them walk to a girlfriend's home after informing their parents that that is where they'll spend the evening. There they change into the racy outfit they brought with them. Their pursuit of romance has been greatly enhanced by the use of cell phones in the past decade. As Julie Archambault (2017) has shown, mobile communication has profoundly reshaped the experience of intimacy by allowing for some heightened degree of discretion. Recognizing the spatial tactics and expedient practices *'yammata* engage in after dark is critical to grasping the local geography of intimacy and the fada's place in it.

Note the role the *ghetto* plays in this affective topography. Far from being reserved for the exclusive use of samari, the *ghetto* after dark occasionally serves to house the tryst of young lovers looking for privacy. To hint at the experimental nature of these furtive encounters, a group of fadantchés jokingly rebaptized the space *la salle d'opération* (the operating room). Premarital sex is considered morally wrong, and opportunities for amorous trysts are few and far between. In their sermons Muslim preachers routinely stress the importance of limiting postpubescent girls' mobility and marrying them early to preserve their virginity and, ultimately, their family's respectability (Masquelier 2005). Unmarried lovers must be discreet when they meet. After dark, fadas (and *ghettos* that serve as meeting spaces) thus become valued for the privacy they afford young couples in search of intimacy.

I once remarked to members of Jeunes Tosteurs Solidaires how, despite all the talk of girls coming to the fada, I rarely saw any *'yammata* there. Did they, I asked jokingly, always show up surreptitiously, cloaked in a hijab to ensure anonymity? The young men laughed heartily and told me about a young hijab-clad woman who had visited the fada a few years before. After spending some time with her male companion in the protective space of the adjoining *ghetto*, she ran out. In her haste, she left her hijab behind. She never returned to pick it up. The fadantchés kept the hijab. Hanging on a nail on the wall of the *ghetto*, the garment stood as a tangible reminder of the fraught, occasionally volatile nature of their relationships with women. "It's kind of our flag," Mille Boy remarked while the others chuckled.

Through their emblematic role as vessels of Muslim virtue, women in Niger bear a much heavier "semiotic burden" (C. Jones 2010:624) than men. They are expected to serve as a symbol of society's moral order through their chaste demeanor and their adoption of modest dress, including hijab or other head coverings (Masquelier 2009b). In many Nigérien households, tight-fitting, form-enhancing garments have been jettisoned in favor of proper "Islamic" attire. By casting women as virtuous and shielding them from the penetrating male gaze, the hijab enables women to move freely in public areas. Paradoxically it can also serve as a cover-up: it allows its wearer to deploy an image of modesty that matches local expectations of what proper women look like while hiding her "immorality" behind a righteous façade. Such tactics of concealment are precisely what 'yammata rely on to hide their visits to the fada from elders. Cloaked in both a hijab and the darkness of the night, they become, if not invisible, at least anonymous as they make their way across generally poorly lit neighborhoods.

The hijab Jeunes Tosteurs Solidaires kept as a souvenir of premarital intimacy had the capacity to make members laugh because it functioned as an oxymoron. On the one hand it was a symbol of feminine virtue; on the other, it was an emblem of deceit, a means of disguising sexual activity. In the way it captured the essence of the fada, as both a space of playful (and occasionally illicit) experimentation and a training ground for the cultivation of responsible adulthood, the hijab truly functioned as the fada's flag—a piece of cloth that symbolized a constituency's shared ethos. Aside from pointing to the place of the hijab in the sexual culture of the fada, Mille Boy's comment sheds light on the vision many samari entertain of young women as both objects of romantic fantasies and baffling, occasionally devious creatures who cannot be trusted. Samari frequently note that while they want to have sex with women, sex corrupts 'yammata. What they mean is that a sexually active unmarried girl cannot be trusted; by consenting to have sex with her boyfriend, she signals she can easily be persuaded to have sex with someone else. She is a kyan kwance, an easy girl, not suitable for marriage. The keepsake hijab further offered confirmation that marriage should center on the containment of women's powers of seduction within conjugal relationships. Devoted as they are to the ideals of romance, samari may nevertheless argue for the necessity of segregating genders (and secluding women). If they experiment sexually with 'yammata, they nevertheless fully expect the women they marry to reserve their charms for their husbands. An economics student who hoped to work for a bank surprised his fellow fadantchés by insisting that, once married, he would keep his wife secluded. "I am a jealous man. I'll provide. She'll stay home." Though the poetics and politics of the fada are centered on male values, male activities, and male aspirations, the expressions of the masculinity that is forged in those spaces rely on the deployment of an idealized vision of womanhood. Insofar as women are confined to the fada's shadows, it behooves us to explore these "dark spaces" for the insights they afford into the fada's gendered dynamics and the enactment of masculinity. To paraphrase Ferguson (2006), shadows are not only productive metaphors to describe what remains hidden but also producers of images and narratives that can illuminate critical dimensions of the fada's moral architecture.

The Fada's Constitutive Outside

Women, a number of ethnographic studies have by now demonstrated, are essential to the performance of masculinity (Newell 2012; Weiss 2009). In his study of masculinity in rural Andalucía, Stanley Brandes (1980) claimed that even when women were not physically present with men as they worked or went out drinking, they were critical to men's own understanding of manhood. Matthew Gutmann (1996), focusing on changing gender identities in working-class Mexico City, has similarly contended that the majority of men formulate their understanding of what it means to be men through comparisons with women. Robert Morrell (2001) shows how boys and men in South Africa are crafted as gendered beings through the coaching and critical eye of girls and women. Drawing on these insights, I have suggested that despite their apparent invisibility, women play a crucial role in both the practical and the imaginative life of the fada.

In anthropology, youth has problematically been synonymous with young men, while gender was the prerogative of women. In Africa especially, youth has often been defined as an overwhelmingly male category: males must wait sometimes years before becoming heads of households and achieving adulthood, whereas females experience youth as a brief interval between the onset of puberty and marriage (or motherhood). The gendering of "youth" has a particular salience in Niger where many adolescent girls are married before they turn fifteen. Moreover, until recently, few anthropologists studied men as *men*. Men's gender was presumed rather than interrogated, and therefore it was rarely a focus of critical inquiry. By treating male actors as the "'unmarked' category" (Gutmann 1997:388) rather than gendered persons and by selecting specific aspects of masculinity to stand for universals, ethnographies often failed to capture masculine diversity. Analyzing the fada as a masculine space means identifying how samari define themselves as engendered and engendering beings through their relations to women. Mindful that gender is sometimes used as "a shorthand for an oppositional balance of power" (Cornwall 2002:968) in which women are the losers, I have examined the fada not as a place that excludes women so much as a site of imagining, courtship, and gendered labor and sexual culture.

Men and women, young and old, do not occupy space in the same ways. Their movements are conditioned, shaped by both implicit and explicit social norms (though, as I have shown, they are also subject to negotiations). This has distinct consequences for the terms of women's participation at the fada. In this chapter I have explored some of the less visible ways in which women contribute to the making of men. This has required conceptualizing the fada as a photographic negative that inverts lightness and darkness so that women, their labor, their engagements, and their histories can be brought to light. As the case of Rachel, a fada named after a girl who lived far away, suggests, women's absence is at times more significant than their presence.

Invisible as they may be, or rather because of their invisibility, women are the fada's Other against whom fadantchés can assert their subjective understanding of who they are as men. It is precisely because they inhabit a different space that women, 'yammata in particular, can be said to serve as the fada's "constitutive outside" (Butler 1993:3). As those who don't belong yet are the object of ongoing fantasies, women bind the homosocial space of the fada and "haunt those boundaries at the persistent possibility of their disruption and rearticulation" (8). Vital as they are to the performance of masculinity, they are also potentially a threat to it. In the way they can sever a romantic relationship, move on to another fada, or alternatively consume a saurayi's resources, 'yammata have the ability to test men's capacities to perform masculinity. Insofar as samari are invested in each other's romantic success, breakups may be experienced as failure (and a loss of prestige) by the entire fada. At some level, they signal the fada's inability to stage (or foster) successful performances of masculinity.

In piecing together the multiple narratives that circulate about the fada as a forum for the valorization of male subjectivities, I argue that we must not lose sight of the largely invisible contributions made by women, young and older. Whether they contribute labor, resources, affection, or prestige, women help sustain the fada as a perpetually evolving platform on which young men play with, negotiate, and enhance their masculinity. As they come and go—often surreptitiously, in the middle of night—young women, in particular, remind us that, as a "place of the possible" (Lefebvre 1996:156), the fada exists both as a site of convergence and a space of dispersal whose topography continuously unfolds. Similar to the coffee shops of Cairo, which Kreil (2016) describes as critical sites of homosociality that orient masculine desire in specific directions, the fada is a central coordinate in the "shifting geography of intimacy" (177) that allows us to map out the concerns, fantasies, and aspirations of young Nigérien men.

FOUR

Hip-Hop, Truth, and Islam

Rap revolutionizes, it condemns; it is a struggle, a form of engagement.

—A rapper, Niamey, 2000

Challenging the assumption that Muslim youth are largely responsible for the rise of radicalism and extremism worldwide, scholars have begun to interrogate the imaginative practices through which young Muslims attempt to carve a place for themselves in society. Focusing on young Muslims' embrace of playful and potentially illicit activities, they have analyzed these practices as vehicles for global youth affiliation and tools of identity fashioning (Khosravi 2007; Larkin 1997; Swedenburg 2001). Such an analytical focus has enabled them to downplay the exceptionalism of Muslim youth while highlighting the attributes they share with their non-Muslim counterparts worldwide. Through examination of the global trends Muslim youth embrace, the various pastimes they engage in, and the dating games they pursue, scholars have also drawn attention to the improvisational ways in which young people everywhere assert their youthfulness while simultaneously forging their Muslimness (Herrera and Bayat 2010; Deeb and Harb 2013; Janson 2014). Whether or not Muslim youth are religiously inclined, their combined engagement in "faith and fun" (Bayat 2010b:45) has shaped the production of their subjectivities in complex ways.

Consider the case of Abdoulaye, the sarauyi who enjoyed wearing fancy clothes, dancing, and drinking. The twenty-three-year-old had left school at fifteen and lived with his parents and seven siblings in one of Niamey's oldest quartiers. He currently sold fruit for his uncle at the local market but hoped to secure stable employment so that he could one day marry and start a family (though he was in no real hurry). Meanwhile, as a member of

Show Boys Clan, he spent much of his time in the company of other young men, many of whom were similarly underemployed. Together they often sat on a bench in front of his parents' house, occasionally watching music videos or playing cards, but mostly chatting about politics, the latest musical star, or a friend's upcoming wedding. At other times, they retreated to the well-appointed *ghetto* Abdoulaye and his brother had built adjacent to the parental compound (see chapter 2)

One day, Abdoulaye took me inside the *ghetto* and showed me the clothes he kept carefully folded in a small trunk under his bed. There were a couple of richly embroidered *riguna* (robes worn with matching drawstring pants) and a red and white *keffiyeh*, the checkered scarf Muslim pilgrims bring back from the Hijaz and which they wear draped around the shoulders. "This is what I wear to go to the mosque for *salla* [prayer]. The scarf comes from Mecca," he explained with evident pride. Tucked in was also a woman's dress: "This is for my girlfriend, when she prays." When I later asked Abdoulaye whether *malamai* still criticized youth for wearing "American" (i.e., hip-hop style) clothes, he responded confidently, "No, people are civilized now." Then, and before I could ask what he meant, he blurted out in exasperation, "de toutes façons, on n'en a rien à foutre des marabouts!" (anyway, we don't give a damn about Muslim religious authorities).

Surprising as Abdoulaye's response may be, it is also revealing of the ambivalence young Nigériens, especially young men, occasionally experience as they struggle to reconcile their social, material, and marital expectations with the religious dispositions and moral values they learned from parents, teachers, and the wider community. Although economically marginalized, Nigérien youths have been granted unprecedented emancipation thanks to the global flow of goods, information, and images they can access since the emergence of private radio and television stations, the circulation of new print media, including youth-oriented glossy magazines, and the availability of cast-off imports and pirated goods on local markets. Their sense of Muslimness, that is, the identification—as well as solidarity and pride—they derive from being part of the *umma*, the global Muslim community, has been affected substantially by entertainment culture and foreign commodities. The distinct, yet increasingly globalized identities young Nigériens have forged for themselves as members of fadas and through their participation in consumer culture are the subject of ongoing controversy. Muslim preachers routinely berate youth for their alleged disrespect for social conventions, unfettered consumption of foreign (especially "Western") things, and sexual indiscipline. In their sermons they urge them to abandon their sinful pastimes and align their conduct with the teachings of the Qur'an by marrying, praying regularly, and becoming religiously informed.

As Abdoulaye's outburst suggests, many young men resent the social control that *malamai* exert over them through moralizing discourses aimed at guiding them on the right path. To admonitions that they should act like Muslims, they often respond that religion should not dictate (at least not entirely) what pastimes they engage in, how they interact with young women, or what radio programs they listen to. For them, being Muslim is, of course, about living a life in accordance with the teachings of the Qur'an. But importantly it is also about the development of an ethical sensibility that is variously demonstrated by means of authentic self-expressions ranging from social activism and geopolitical loyalty to filial deference to neighborliness—forms of engagement a number of them demonstrate as members of civic-minded fadas. In sum, it is about being a good citizen. Aware that their demeanor may not always match locally understood Muslim norms of proper conduct, some insist that a Muslim identity is not something one exposes visibly through the public performance of a conventional grammar of practices (such as wearing Islamic dress or attending prayer at the local mosque). Others invoke their immaturity, arguing that they will be more mindful of their religious duties when they grow up—if only so they can be proper role models for their children. Ultimately many young men define their ways of being Muslim in fluid, situational, and inconsistent terms. The Muslim ethos they claim to follow is routinely contradicted by the choices they make and the stances they take based on the coexistence of different moral—and amoral—registers. How young men in Niger deal with these contradictions and justify their pastimes and pursuits is the subject of this chapter.

In past decades, there has been considerable debate in Niger about how to define Muslimness. Many Nigériens have become aware that their own ways of being Muslim, when refracted through the critical gaze of others, may not map onto what was once unquestioningly accepted as orthodoxy. Yet far from promoting a more consistent approach to religion and morality, this "heightened self-consciousness" of Islam (Eickelman and Piscatori 1996:39) appears to have intensified the ambivalence some people experience as they try to follow religious principles while also satisfying material aspirations and meeting social expectations. Samari, in particular, confront multiple and competing requirements in their quest for prosperity, social success, and emotional fulfillment. As they attempt to carve out spaces of existential possibility for themselves in contexts of economic hardship, the coping strategies they devise are often at odds—so "hardened" *ulama* (Muslim religious scholars) claim—with Islamic tradition. Their engagement with hip-hop culture has been especially controversial.

After Nelly, 50 Cent, Snoop Dogg, and Public Enemy became familiar figures on local television, the popularity of hip-hop culture spread quickly. Many samari enthusiastically adopted their idols' baggy pants, oversized T-shirts, and high-top sneakers. They ignored the criticisms of conservative Muslim elites who insisted that these clothes were un-Islamic. Abdoulaye himself spent much of what he earned on clothes of Western inspiration he purchased at local markets. Like other un(der)employed youths for whom consumption has become the privileged modality for creating social distinctions (Liechty 2002), he drew on the world of hip-hop fashion to enhance himself, using the power of clothes to forge a desirable identity. Modeling his look after those of his favorite rappers, strolling around, and having fun were part of the performative practices that marked Abdoulaye as a youth. He was widely admired by his peers for the savvy way in which he embodied coolness through his fashionable appearance, his embrace of hip-hop, and his romantic liaisons with neighborhood girls. On Fridays, however, Abdoulaye returned home well ahead of the midday prayer to put on Islamic dress before making his way to the *grande mosquée*. There he engaged in a public enactment of religiosity, identifying with the similarly clad believers who attended the imam's sermon and momentarily coordinating his practices with theirs.

Although the vast majority of samari usually present themselves as committed Muslims determined to follow God's commands, they often relate to religion in complex and contradictory ways, routinely engaging in behaviors widely perceived as un-Islamic. Some pray, fast, and visibly demonstrate their *tsoron Allah* (fear of God; faith) by listening to cassette sermons and wearing the locally tailored long-sleeved robe (*jaba*) with matching drawstring pants that is considered proper Islamic attire. A limited few have managed to insert themselves in the growing religious economy; they make a living preaching and selling CDs of recorded sermons and Qur'anic recitations in their Islamic *discothèques* (Sounaye 2011). Many of them, however, admit that they rarely pray (or only when pressured to do so); they know that the music they listen to is considered sinful and that their saggy pants are criticized by *malamai* for dragging on the ground and gathering dirt, thereby invalidating their prayers.

More than one saurayi I met saw the performance of prayer as an obligation that should not prevent them from seizing opportunities as they arose even if these contradicted basic Islamic principles. When the choices they made were in contradiction with what they knew to be the proper path, they justified them by invoking laziness, immaturity, or by taking advantage of available venues, including turning to religion or, alternatively, undermining it. Twenty-five-year-old Souley, a university student, told me he was allowing himself to "be irresponsible, drink alcohol, and chase women" until he turned thirty. After that, he would reform his ways, because "in the end, I don't want society to judge me." He prayed irregularly though he admitted that a member of his fada, who had been trying to reform him, regularly invited him to join him at prayer time. Youth's engagement with Muslim norms of morality and religiosity suggests that practices understood as Islamic do not manifest themselves in isolation, unreflectively adopted by individuals in their efforts to fashion themselves as committed Muslims. They are tangled up in wider social fields of action, their contradictions, and the experiences of those who embrace them (Simon 2009). It is precisely through their engagement with the conflicting demands they face routinely and as they move between seemingly incommensurable practices that Muslims constitute themselves as moral persons, critically attuned to the world in which they live. Therefore, rather than looking for "moments of perfections" (Schielke 2009:36) that shape ethical dispositions among piety-minded subjects, we must focus on ways through which Muslims grapple with tensions, confront contradictions, and cultivate ambiguity as they orient themselves in moral space. Heeding the warnings of scholars who caution against presenting Islam as a fixed set of principles and practices offering a straightforward path to virtue (Ewing 1990; Marsden 2005), this chapter explores young men's attempts to live Muslim lives through the analytical prism of ambivalence. More specifically, I consider how young men's attempts to navigate between contradictory moral requirements play out in the context of their engagement with hip-hop music. Hip-hop is condemned by many Muslims who disapprove of Western cultural imports or simply declare all music *haram*—forbidden by Islam. Although young people often admit that rap music does not really belong in Islam, they nevertheless see it as a moral project destined to uncover the truth (*gaskiya*) about social injustices and improve lives. Yet they are also conflicted about hip-hop and the representations of wealth, education, and gender it generates. Through a critical discussion of the contemporary discourse on hip-hop, I examine how samari cultivate a reflexive understanding of the world and of their place in it and constitute themselves as ethical subjects, and I highlight the role of aspirations, tensions, and ambiguities in the making of these moral subjectivities.

The Truth of Hip-Hop

Like a number of musical styles derived from US hip-hop, such as *hiplife* in Ghana or *bongo flava* in Tanzania, rap "made in Niger" first emerged in the 1990s. As a performative style associated with elite French-speaking youth, rap quickly gained popularity through radio and television shows, the rise of the "thug look," and the circulation of cassette tapes, CDs, and magazines. It was at the fada that samari listened to hip-hop music. Indeed, many fadas' raison d'être was to provide a space where young men could tune in to their favorite radio programs or play taped music. Once they owned a teapot, the acquisition of a boom box—the larger, the better—was therefore critical to a group's formalization as a fada. One of the earliest songs in the Nigérien hip-hop repertoire is titled "Fada Attayo" (Tea Fada). Penned by Lakal Kaney, a now defunct rap group, it is a celebration of youth culture and sociality at the fada. It opens with the following words:

> Fada Attayo
> Fada Attayo
> Fada Attayo
> Hey my friend
> If you want to see the fadas
> All you have to do is go
> Down to the streets of Niamey
> Capital of Niger
> You will see fadas
> Where tea is king[1]

It was also at the fada that many samari learned to rap and dreamed of becoming famous hip-hop performers. A number of fadas coalesced around the members' shared passion for hip-hop, while some served as career incubators for rappers who went on to earn wide recognition. The fada has thus played a critical role in the dissemination of hip-hop culture. According to some people, it is where Nigérien rap was born. Put differently, the history of Nigérien hip-hop is inextricably tied to the spread of democratization and economic liberalization, the rise of unemployment, and the emergence of fadas. Mature men recall late nights spent at the fada dropping rhymes and recording performances in between alternate servings of tea and beans to fortify themselves. In such contexts, fadas served as more than sites of rap fandom. They became a critical source of insights into the predicaments of youth, nurturing artistic imaginations, as "Fada Attayo" and other songs centered on samari's street culture attest. Early on, they also doubled as recording studios and springboards for fledgling careers.

Recall that the birth of Nigérien rap and the emergence of fadas more or less coincided with the wave of religiosity that swept the country following the 1991 National Conference and the subsequent liberalization of politics and media mandated by the new constitution. As new radio and television programs broadcast the music of US and French rappers, many samari became infatuated with hip-hop aesthetics and politics. They taught themselves how to rap by imitating the lyrics, rhyming, and mannerisms of their favorite hip-hop artists. Each year, a few lucky ones, whose performance earned them a prize during music festivals sponsored by aid organizations or cell phone companies, would tour the country (courtesy of their benefactor) in search of fame and fortune. In every town, they rapped about unemployment, the benefits of child vaccination, and the dangers of AIDS, in front of rapt audiences. Meanwhile mosque attendance went up as growing numbers of Nigériens, inspired by preachers of all stripes to follow properly Qur'anic teachings, began praying more regularly; many of them demonstrated their renewed commitment to Islam through the adoption of a variety of practices ranging from sartorial modesty to seclusion of married women to the promotion of large families. Convinced that the serious challenges (unemployment, poverty, drought, and so on) facing Nigérien society were rooted in people's impiety and immorality, they condemned the westernization of local values, the pursuit of materialist ambitions, and the absence of moral discipline in their communities. Against the backdrop of contentious debates about the place of Islam in public and private life, some of them envisioned an Islamic civil society that would provide a moral alternative to established secular models of nationhood, society, and family.

After Izala gained prominence in the 1990s, the issue of music as a possible source of unvirtuous conduct became hotly debated. Whereas Izala reformists claimed that all music, including the chanting of *zikiri* (recitation of God's divine names) in Sufi rituals, was haram, their opponents insisted that only music leading to sinful acts (sex, alcohol consumption, and violence) should be prohibited. Muslim scholars have noted that there is no verse in the Qur'an prohibiting music. Nevertheless many Nigériens believe that musical expression in all its forms is forbidden to Muslims. Anxious to align themselves with emerging models of religiosity, they speak of the past as a time of sinful indulgence during which "ignorant" Muslims engaged in un-Islamic activities such as dancing and drumming. These errors have since been corrected: Today, they say, many Nigériens are familiar with the comprehensive moral discipline that is required of all Muslims. At the urging of Muslim preachers who define music as an instrument of Satanic temptation, they listen to Islamic sermons and firmly disapprove of celebrations involving drumming and praise singing or featuring popular music. In order to comply with the prohibition on music, a young man I knew stopped and fast-forwarded the film he watched when music came on. He resumed his film watching when he got to a place where there was no music.

Far from being strictly religious, the issue of whether music is permissible is also generational, with popular music being understood by many elders as offensive, revolutionary, and largely un-Islamic. Hip-hop, especially, has aroused the ire of the older generation for allegedly promoting foreign values, encouraging impiety, and challenging the status quo. Countering claims that rap is Satanic music and leads its listeners astray, hip-hop performers, such as the prominent Nigérien crew Kaidan Gaskia (*sic*) (Acting Truthfully), invoke their commitment to truth. They stress the urgency of speaking sincerely and honestly about society's problems and rap's suitability as a weapon (*une arme de combat*) against poverty and marginalization. Their legions of fans, assembled at the fada, absorb the language of truth and later redeploy it in the defense of their own projects. The fada, many samari would undoubtedly agree, is a platform where one learns to put in practice some of the lessons of hip-hop. It is also where quick-tongued youngsters polish their skills as social critics and provide rappers with verbal ammunition: "Who is going to give us jobs?"[2] the members of Lakal Kaney, ventriloquizing jobless fadantchés, sing repeatedly in "Fada Attayo."

The Hausa concept of *gaskiya* has a broad array of significations. It occurs frequently in conversations. Often translated as truth, it may in certain contexts convey more nuanced notions, such as honesty, faith, and sincerity. In other contexts, it translates more accurately as reliability or fairness. Hence, the statement *ba ka da gaskiya* (lit., "you have no truth") may refer to an interlocutor's bad faith or dishonest methods but can just as well be taken to mean "I cannot count on you" or "I cannot trust you." As an ethical concept, *gaskiya* has a particular weight for Hausa speakers. The first vernacular newspaper to appear in northern Nigeria was named *Gaskiya Ta Fi Kwabo* (The Truth Is Worth More Than a Penny). The time was 1939. Fearing the impact of German propaganda on their African subjects, the British encouraged the launch of a Hausa periodical that would serve as a medium of enlightenment for local populations in northern provinces (Yahaya 1988).

Broadly speaking, *gaskiya* is essential to the makeup of a good person (*mutumin kirki*): a man cannot do what he considers right or good without demonstrating *gaskiya*. Indeed, it is not farfetched to say that from a moral perspective, *gaskiya* is a prerequisite to any worldly undertaking. Predictably, *gaskiya* is central to the ways people understand religion: without denying that being Muslim may mean different things to different Muslims, Nigériens all agree that there is one Islam. Islam is the Truth, something no human activity can ever interfere with. Indeed, the certainty of Islam's true and indivisible nature is what enables them to state categorically that there is one "correct" way of being Muslim. By implication, one cannot be a good Muslim without being a true Muslim in the sense of both practicing "true" Islam and being true to one's convictions. Although the nuances of *gaskiya* exceed its religious signification, as far as Muslims are concerned, Islam is the self-evidently true religion in the sense that it derives from the literal word of God and also coincides with the irresistible logic of things. Only by embracing Islam can one hope to follow accurately and truthfully God's will, and by implication, become a good person.

Traditionally a cardinal virtue indispensable to the constitution of decent, upright individuals—"before Islam," elders will tell you, personal integrity was tested through a series of ordeals to which morally upright members of the community submitted to show they had nothing to hide—*gaskiya* is now also a key component of the distinctive ideology that informs youthful critiques of what is wrong with society. In the face of injustice and suffering, those who can speak out have the moral duty to do so. Hip-hoppers define themselves as *la voix des sans voix* (the voice of the voiceless): they lift the veil of lies manufactured by those in power and describe the world as it is—even if that entails risks. By using *gaskiya* as their rallying cry, members of Kaidan Gaskia indirectly point to the way that Muslim values can be said to overlap with the aspirations of hip-hop. Like other groups that present themselves as champions of *gaskiya*, they claim to "act truthfully." They have opted for a course of action in which their music (especially their lyrics) can be read as an expression of their moral engagement to defend the rights of youth and other marginalized members of society.

According to Phéno B, also known as the *taximan rappeur*, the project of creating Kaidan Gaskia was about "respecting the truth." It was while driving his taxi through the streets of Niamey that he discovered and fell in love with the rap music he heard on the radio. Today in addition to being a member of Kaidan Gaskia 2,[3] Phéno B is a music producer. He named his recording studio, Studio Kountché, after the former president of Niger who is fondly—and at times nostalgically—remembered by many Nigériens as a man of integrity and often invoked along with Martin Luther King, Nelson Mandela, and Thomas Sankara as a hero of the cause of Africans and people of African descent.[4]

By the same token, rappers, if they are true to their ideals, do not merely reproduce scripted utterances; instead, their words speak of their social commitments. To my question about whether performers must exercise caution when criticizing the government, Issa responded gravely that being a rapper meant that you were committed and artists must never be afraid. In "Faux Gouverneurs" (Fake Governors), Issa and his brother, who performed under the name Plantation Boys, sang that "It is time to say corruption *go* / Those who corrupt and are corrupt [must be] immediately arrested." A critique of the Nigérien government, the song drew on the evocative power of the fake to denounce brazen abuses of power and the spread of deceit and forgery. "Hip-hoppers must tell the truth," Issa told me. The issue is less one of truth versus lie than one of owning one's utterances and committing to the course of action initiated in public performances. Whether in one's engagement with hip-hop or in trade, in daily life as well as on special occasions, being truthful is a fundamental virtue that earns one respect in worldly life and reward in the afterlife.

Whether rappers aim their lyrical fire at bad governance, unemployment, or gender discrimination, their mission is to "speak the truth" and shed light on the lives of the poor, the weak, and all those who are victimized under current social conditions. "Youth are miserable. They suffer because they have no work, no opportunity, no future," a rapper told me. "Our goal is to denounce our leaders' incompetence and their lack of engagement toward youth." More than one rapper invoked poverty and oppression as sources of inspiration and spoke of their urge to sensitize youth. "Hip-hop is a way of presenting reality, you know, the problems confronting youth in a country plagued by poverty, disease, and corruption," an aspiring hip-hopper from Niamey stated. By way of an illustration he alluded to the successful Nigérien hip-hop group Wassika ("message" in Hausa), whose stage name made clear that their aim was to send out a message.[5]

Hip-hop artists feel vested with the mission to sing truthfully by reporting an unmediated reality, just as they often say Muslims have a duty to follow faithfully (and in some cases, actively promote) the message of the Prophet. "The system oppresses us. We must speak out. The future of the country is in our hands," a young musician by the stage name of Raz Gaz told me. Raz Gaz lacked the means to produce his music for distribution.

When I met him, he had recorded only two singles. In his last song, "Enfants de la rue" (Street Children), the lyrics relied on clichéd images of "vulnerable" children, the delivery was dry, and the mixing was rough, unfinished. But his determination to defend the cause of the weak was moving. Like other hip-hop performers in Niger and elsewhere on the continent, Raz Gaz positioned himself as an "authoritative speaking subject" (Shipley 2010:92) who sang knowingly about injustice and suffering. Through his trenchant criticisms of a society that neglected its youth, he generated the moral capital needed to justify his career orientation. His parents, both Fulani of noble ancestry, had originally disapproved of his immersion in hiphop: in their eyes, he was nothing but a *griot* (praise singer) and therefore a source of shame and embarrassment. By presenting himself as an educated, socially aware performer who rapped with authority about the "evils" of early marriage or the fate of street children, he eventually earned their respect. Although proud of his son, Raz Gaz's father felt nevertheless uneasy about the young man's ambitions to make a living as a rapper. He knew Raz Gaz was widely admired but could not overlook the fact that as traditionally low-status members of society, musicians were frequently objects of contempt. The case of Raz Gaz, who sang about injustice as a means of becoming rich and famous (even as he looked down on uneducated rappers who lacked French fluency) while his father worried about the loss of status that a career in hip-hop implied, hints at the ways that Nigériens' embrace of rap is fraught with ambivalence.

Reconciling Faith and Fun

Did Abdoulaye, who liked dressing well, dancing, and drinking, show me his Islamic wardrobe because he wished to be perceived as a pious Muslim? Or was he hinting at the good Muslim he aspired to be once he found employment, married, and became a *cikakke mutum* (adult)? I will probably never know. What is clear is that he revealed a side of his identity that differed strikingly from the fun-loving *faroteur* (show-off) I was familiar with. Far from constituting clear guidelines for conduct, religion was but one of several registers Abdoulaye relied on to live a Muslim life while asserting his individuality. When he put on his recently purchased jeans and fancy belt buckle (which hung on a hook when not in use) and went out drinking with his fellow fadantchés, he kept the clothes that visibly manifested his Muslimness literally "boxed up." At the risk of reading too much into it, I argue that storing one set of clothes in a trunk while hanging the other set on a hook allowed him to compartmentalize his contradictory identities—and shift between them—without being seemingly troubled by them.

Roger Bastide (1955) explained this ability to live with contradictions through the *principe de coupure*, a mechanism that allows for the coexistence in a single individual of behaviors or logics that are otherwise incompatible. In his study of Afro-Brazilian rituals, Bastide noted how people compartmentalized principles and practices in such a way that they could live simultaneously as Catholics and as Candomblé adepts. The Candomblé practitioner "does not lie. He is at the same time Catholic and fetishist. The two things are not opposed but separate" (10, my translation). Abdoulaye's dress practices exemplify the "principle of compartmentalization" described by Bastide. By keeping his Islamic wardrobe in a separate location from his jeans and T-shirts of foreign origin, so that the two sets of clothes were never visible at the same time, Abdoulaye was able to inhabit two contradictory worlds of value—one Muslim, the other secular—in such a way that the distinction between *haram* and *halal* became somehow irrelevant.

Yet Abdoulaye's violent reaction to my query about *malamai*'s disapproval of *samari*'s fashions also suggests that the shift "from partying to prayers" (Bayat 2010b:46) and vice versa was not unproblematic. Indeed, the young man was experiencing serious inner turmoil at the time. His parents had been pressuring him to get a full-time job and marry. But Abdoulaye had other plans and resented these pressing demands that he abandon his youthful ways. Marriage meant he would have to provide for his wife in addition to himself, and he was in no hurry to abandon his indulgent lifestyle. At the same time, he felt obliged to respect his parents' wishes:

> Before, I got along with my parents. My mother loved me and did not like to see me cry. My father gave me a good education. I cannot do what is forbidden by the Qur'an such as adultery, drinking, [taking] drugs, smoking, stealing. All these things, I know I would never do because I have received a good education. When I decided to let my hair grow, I asked my father. He said, "No problem if you take care of your hair and wash it." Now my father wants me to achieve [financial] independence. He is retired. [My parents] must take care of my younger siblings. The Qur'an says, "Do all that your father or your mother asks you to do, except those things that are not part of religion." My parents are very religious. In my family everyone prays; if you do not pray, you cannot stay in my parents' home. You would set a bad example for my younger brothers. My parents do not let you do what is contrary to what the Qur'an says. Of course, they are right.

Although Islam played a central role in the constitution of Abdoulaye's ethical selfhood, the process of realizing himself as a proper Muslim was fraught with conflict and moral ambiguities. The young man struggled to reconcile his obedience to his parents (which he saw as one of his primary obligations) with his existential yearnings. Yet he nevertheless managed to live a meaningful life as both the dutiful son of pious Muslims and a popular youth known for his fashion savvy and his clever dance moves.

Whether actively religious or not, samari self-consciously think of themselves as part of the *umma*. In the wake of 9/11 fada conversations routinely centered on US foreign policy and what samari saw as the White House's distinct bias against Muslim populations: a number of fadantchés believed the 9/11 attacks were the results of a Jewish conspiracy aimed at putting the blame on Muslims. Since Islam prohibits such violence, the perpetrators of the attacks could not possibly be Muslims. Others described US military actions abroad as concerted attempts to fight the spread of Islam. The allegations that American soldiers burned Qur'ans and that a request to build a mosque on ground zero in New York had been rejected were raised by some as evidence of US opposition to Islam. If young men feel a sense of obligation to act as proper representatives of Islam and condemn Islamophobia (most flagrantly exemplified, in their eyes, in the US invasions of Afghanistan and Iraq), they do not necessarily equate their Muslim identity with adherence to the parameters of piety enunciated by Muslim authorities, at least not in the immediate future. A saurayi who took his girlfriend dancing on Saturday nights told me of his plans to seclude his future wives. Although he aspired to be a good Muslim "like his father," he wasn't ready to give up his status as *jeune*[6] and all the fun and experimentation associated with it: "The Qur'an forbids dancing, but until I marry, I am not really responsible for anyone or anything. At times I feel guilty [going dancing], but I know it's once I'm married that my prayers and my sins really start counting."

At times young men engage in behaviors (or express opinions) that contradict the moral stance they have taken days (or even moments) earlier. I have heard young men sipping beers and smoking at outdoor bars speak contemptuously of so-called *munafikai* (hypocrites) who grow beards and pontificate about religious duties but fail to give alms to the poor. A university student who once lectured me extensively about the moral benefits derived from praying on time admitted to regularly skipping prayer when he felt lazy or was engrossed in his studies. He prayed when in the company of friends at the fada whose own pious behavior reminded him of his religious duty.

Flexibility then is part of the habitus of youth. In the aftermath of 9/11 the same samari who vocally criticized the United States and, in some cases, celebrated the end of the "evil empire" owing to the well-known fact that Americans were "against Muslims" often expressed a strong desire to emigrate to America. As they saw it, the world was increasingly devoid of prospects, and they must be open-minded enough to grab whatever opportunity arose. Flexibility, then, was key to securing the often contradictory and increasingly tenuous promises of the current neoliberal moment when one lived in one of the world's poorest nations. In this respect, viewing youth as a "social shifter" (Durham 2004), a category whose meaning exists independently of the particular context in which it is used at the same time that it is understood anew in relation to each specific situation in which it is summoned, is illuminating. It helps us appreciates not just the transitional nature of youth in structural terms but also the ways in which youth is constantly renegotiated in sociopolitical practice. While they complain of being *petits*, and thereby subordinated to elders, samari exert comparative authority over those who are younger—whom they task with buying tea or cigarettes for them, relaying messages to friends, and so on. They look forward to the day when they, too, will be *les grands* (elders) and enjoy unquestioning submission from the younger generation.

My discussion of hip-hop as a forum for denouncing social inequities provides an entry into the broader consideration of the role of the ethical in the lives of Muslim samari. A number of anthropologists have recently examined social practices and everyday comportment as forms of "ordinary ethics" (Lambek 2010) in an effort to enrich their ethnographic analyses. Ethics, Michael Lambek (2010) notes, is "neither prescriptive nor universalist" (6) in the sense of promoting the same rights for everyone on earth or striving for a sense of the common good. More closely associated with performance than decency and with the good than the right, ethics is a cover term that stresses how complex, and often inconsistent, human action can be. Through a focus on ethics as a modality of social action, I consider how young Muslim men in Niger define hip-hop as an expression of their moral selfhood even as they strive to reconcile its contradictory messages on class, wealth, and gender.

Roots and the Quest for Fame

Truth for Nigérien hip-hoppers is about not just bluntness but also transparency. Like the Sumbanese Protestants described by Webb Keane (2007: 186), for whom sincere speech arises from within to expose the speaker's inner state of being, rappers ideally use words to self-consciously reveal something about themselves. "We really have something to say," a young musician declared, adding that "rap, it's the reality we describe. We make claims, we criticize. We speak with our guts."[7] Anger, frustration, and indignation, young men claim, are what fuels their inspiration. Although those who describe themselves as the "voice of revolution" insist that the words come from within,[8] their critics—including some rap artists themselves— frequently note that hip-hop in Niger is more about fashion than about social engagement. Young men turn to rap music hoping to strike it rich and become someone[9] but know little about the social roots of hip-hop. They are largely inspired by the US videos (replete with images of luxury automobiles, large mansions, and sexily clad women) they see on television. Rather than writing about what moves them, they select themes coinciding with the agenda promoted by local NGOs. Thus, when an NGO decided to award a prize for the best rap song on AIDS, scores of rappers allegedly came out with new songs on AIDS. Some of the lyrics of these songs, critics observed dryly, turned out to be almost verbatim copies of the public service messages featured in the brochures distributed by the NGO.

Seasoned performers associated with the birth of Nigérien hip-hop bemoan the recent infatuation with rap music, claiming that it has contributed to the dilution of the movement's core message. They speak dishearteningly of young rappers' lack of commitment and the derivative character of their music. Some even claim that much of the rap music currently produced in Niger is not genuine. More generous observers, on the other hand, stress that local rappers are increasingly distancing themselves from their US counterparts and digging in their own cultural repertoires to produce a distinctively indigenized music in which local instruments often play an important role. They describe self-financed hip-hop groups as intense laboratories of creative entrepreneurship fueled by passion and driven by commitment. The groups Wassika and Lakal Kaney achieved notoriety early on by rapping in Hausa and Zarma and mixing hip-hop beats with West African sounds and rhythms to achieve a creolized performance that attested to the "Africanization of hip-hop culture" (Mitchell 2001:8). Other groups followed suit by incorporating vernaculars (Hausa, Zarma, Tamasheq, or Fulfulde) in their lyrics, at times relying on "folk" tunes that spoke of the artists' ethnolocal allegiances. In recent years Nigérien rappers have indigenized their look. Many dress in tailored baggies and shirts made of African fabric, a sure indication that the modalities of hip-hop practices cannot be reduced to a simple appropriation of American styles. In Tahoua a tailor gained fame by fashioning *des costumes de rappeurs* out of locally printed cloth. Rappers had their names embroidered on their shirts: "It makes the outfit more Nigérien," explained a musician. Whether or not one recognizes the originality of Nigérien hip-hop, what is certain is that through their tough masculinist stance, their considerable verbal dexterity, and their claims to fight for social justice, rap artists have provided a distinctive performative style that has facilitated the reconfiguration of young Nigérien men's moral agency and afforded them a window into their own predicament.

Today hip-hop is one of the dominant popular music forms in Niger. Yet even the most optimistic musicians acknowledge that the market is tough, and only a limited few will succeed in exporting their music abroad and making money from it.[10] Unknown artists struggle to reach mainstream audiences and convert musical value into economic value (Shipley 2013). Musicians I spoke with pointed to the climate of antagonism that characterized relations between rappers. Groups splinter frequently after releasing an album, and the songs they release are rarely featured more than a few weeks on the radio, limiting their chances of garnering fame and recognition. Meanwhile competition is fierce. In an age of persistent scarcity, there is limited space for cooperation and resource sharing. In their desperate quest for success hip-hop artists end up adopting strategies (individualism, backstabbing, and so on) that routinely undercut the spirit of solidarity promoted in their lyrics. They often accuse one another of taking short cuts or of mimicking more talented artists.

Amid widespread concern about Nigérien hip-hop's loss of authenticity, rappers routinely invoke the lack of financial means. They claim that in the absence of adequate recording studios and government backing, they make do with what they have. Yet as the wide array of joyful beats, folksy tunes, and clever multilingual raps makes clear, Nigérien hip-hop cannot be reduced to simple bricolage. Artists intentionally select local styles, sounds, and themes that demonstrate their loyalty to country or to some other cause. In a video, members of Kaidan Gaskia 2 are seen dancing in front of a map of Niger in a manifest validation of their territorial identities. Unlike other groups, who are criticized for having left the country to seek their fortune elsewhere, Kaidan Gaskia 2 is resolutely anchored in Niger—in fact, their patriotism has earned them unparalleled visibility as cultural heroes. Although they strive to disseminate their music beyond Niger's borders, the homeland is where they draw their inspiration and where they operate. Not all hip-hop artists share the same aspirations. Tahirou, a fledgling rapper who spoke of hip-hop as a tool of cultural preservation, knew he could not live off his music much less provide for a wife. He wondered how long he could sustain his musical passion. At the same time, he dreamed of moving to the United States and striking it rich.

As Tahirou's circumstances illustrate, young Nigérien men's embrace of hip-hop is not without contradictions. Rappers' claims to sing on behalf of women's rights are often belied by their aggressive, masculinist stance, itself inspired by the violent misogyny of much of American rap. Although young women attend hip-hop concerts, female rappers are few and far between—a reminder of the double standard of gender that restricts Nigérien women's professional aspirations. Moreover, despite its focus on social justice, Nigérien rap is perceived by some as elitist: until they started rapping in local vernaculars, performers—themselves the product of the French-based education system—excluded from their audiences school leavers and unschooled youth who did not speak French. It is by having attended school that they acquired French fluency as well as the worldly knowledge and civic training that enabled them to speak with authority about social issues such as child labor or early marriage. It is also by claiming that they speak of what they know that they have been able to dismiss the claims of Muslim elders who accuse them of immorality and subversiveness. Paradoxically, their oft-repeated claim to speak on behalf of their generation has allowed them to paper over those social divisions and paint a vision of Nigérien youth as uniformly poor, economically marginalized, and unable to sustain aspirations of social mobility.

Ethical Stances

Through their stances against social ills and their condemnation of government abuse, Nigérien rappers have had a substantial impact on public discourse. Whereas politicians rarely take notice—and when they do it is generally to threaten to jail those who dare criticize the regime—Muslim preachers routinely express their disapproval of the music and conduct of rapping youth. For rap artists and their aficionados, the denunciation of hip-hop culture by *malamai* reveals the extent to which *ulama* are out of touch with the younger generation. "We are about change, this is why *les grands* don't understand," a rapper claimed. But things are changing, I was also told. Some *malamai* are beginning to understand the value of rap lyrics—even if they still have qualms about the content of music videos. "At first rap was seen as a music of ruffians, a music of hoodlums because it criticized *les grands*," Raz Gaz told me. "Now people have understood. They realized we have something to say."

Raz Gaz's pronouncements notwithstanding, young men often feel compelled to justify their participation in hip-hop in the face of elders' scorn and skepticism. They strive to make people understand that their music, far from being sinful, is motivated by ethical considerations. The aim of rap, they point out, is to promote development and better people's lives. "We are interested in the problems of the country. This is why we picked this name for our group," explained Souleiman aka Majesty Sool, a member of Méthode de la Morale also known as MDM Crew. Mindful of the need to fashion himself as an artist driven by ethical considerations, Souleiman, who rapped with his brother Zabeirou aka Zab, purposefully chose a name that left no doubt as to the moral basis of their musical activities.

Even as they authoritatively describe rap music as an instrument of social justice compatible with the goals of Islam, rappers occasionally concede that it is not "Islamic." Inspired by consumerist fantasies and dreams of self-realization, yet anxious to avoid the label of bad Muslims, they search for ways to accommodate their musical endeavors within religion's strict moral register. It is these attempts to situate themselves within Islam's moral universe that I consider briefly for they illuminate the role of the ethical in the lives of young rap performers and their adepts. The moral terrain in which hip-hop ethics is rooted in Niger is characterized by a deep ambivalence that provides the basis for what I have called elsewhere "situational ethics" (Masquelier 2007). The ethical subjectivity of many young hip-hop artists and would-be artists is grounded in a constant alertness to the coexistence of conflicting aspirations and motives and the need to overcome the distinction between religion and nonreligion.

More than one youth told me that "true" *malamai* did not approve of their music. This condemnation of hip-hop, they believed, found justification in the fact that "music was not in the Qur'an." For Nigérien youth, the Qur'an is not simply a sacred text providing moral guidance but also a complete source of scientific wisdom. "In the Qur'an, there's everything," I was told. From "the facts of evolution to complex mathematical formulae," every sliver of empirically verifiable knowledge was allegedly contained in the Qur'an. Samari gave me detailed reports of televised shows documenting how truths uncovered by modern research had been predicted long ago by the Qur'an. Music, however, was not mentioned in the Qur'an, and could not find legitimization as an Islamic practice.

At other times, the same young men insisted rapping did not go against religion. "Hip-hop music is not haram because it seeks to improve people's lives" is how some put it. Those who sought advice from liberal-minded *malamai* were given reassurance that their moral aims were not in contradiction with Islam's commandments. A high school student was informed by his father, a Qur'anic teacher, that his activities were "not a sin, not even a problem" according to the Qur'an as long as he "sang reality." Twenty-three-year-old Hussein, who asked his grandfather, a Muslim scholar and member of the Nigérien national Islamic organization, Association Islamique du Niger, whether rap was permissible in Islam, was told, "it isn't music that is bad. The Prophet, when he left for Medina, had a companion who was a musician. He never said that music was haram." For Issa, who had learned the rudiments of rap at the fada and performed with his brother under the name Plantation Boys in front of local audiences, the world of hip-hop did not conflict with the teachings of Islam. "My father, the only thing he insists on is that religious duties not be ignored because of music," Issa told me. To stress how supportive his elders were, he mimicked an imaginary conversation between himself and his father:

—[*pretending to be his father*] "At prayer time, you leave, you do your prayer. Afterward you can do other things. I encourage you because your music, it's work. It's better than remaining with your arms crossed and every time, [*taking on an exaggerated pleading tone*] 'Dad, give me 100 francs so I can scuff some grub.'"

There are opportunities, you see. For instance, at the MJC [Maison des Jeunes et de la Culture, a concert venue], I introduce myself, I sing, and I receive 10,000 francs.

—[*impersonating himself*] "Dad, look, today I have money. Here is 500 francs to buy kola nuts."

—[*pretending to be his father*] "It's very good, my son. Where did you earn this money? Very good, my son, keep going. Be prudent, may God bless you!"

By quoting from the hadith or defining rapping as a language of truth, samari enshrine hip-hop in a moral register of its own that stands at times in direct opposition to the seemingly clear coordinates enunciated in religious teachings and at other times parallels religious normativity. Issa's suggestion that his musical engagements, as a form of labor, generated income that benefited his family brought hip-hop in direct conversation with religion. There is no intimation here that hip-hop might be part of a wider culture of conspicuous consumption that drains the pockets of many local rap artists, even relatively successful ones. In Issa's view, hip-hop was a constitutive part of the Islamic ethos that, much like the Weberian Protestant ethic, valorized hard work, discipline, and frugality. Furthermore, by showing me that he could bring gifts to his father, Issa hinted at hip-hop's capacity to help young men become good sons who cared for elders. Male youth who use their earnings as hip-hop performers to reciprocate the nurture received since childhood fulfill social expectations. Rather than provoking intergenerational strife, Issa suggested, hip-hop brought families together. In sum, it was part of the moral good.

Most youth have a fairly literalist understanding of religion. They describe Islam as a clear set of norms that classify all actions as either part of Islam, that is, permitted, or not part of Islam, that is, forbidden. Although they are well versed in the modalities of moral speech, as noted earlier, many do not subscribe consistently to the commandments and prohibitions enunciated through religious teaching. Their commitment to Islam's overarching norms and ethics is largely situational. During Ramadan, Ibrahim, the young man who sold credit to cell phone owners but dreamed of setting up shop as a purveyor of fancy handsets (see the introduction), consistently prayed and fasted and avoided alcohol. The remainder of the year, however, he generally skipped prayers and enjoyed an occasional beer with friends.[11] Like the other members of his fada, he was an avid rap aficionado. People looking to buy credit from him could usually find him sitting at the fada, with earbuds in his ears, listening to music from his phone. One evening, in an effort to make me see that hip-hop did not stand outside Islam's moral universe, he picked up the half-filled bottle of beer he was drinking: "See this bottle? It's ok to sell it if you fill it with water. It's when you sell it filled with alcohol that you're going against Islam."

The fact that Ibrahim was drinking beer even as he spoke authoritatively of the Muslim prohibition against alcohol consumption did not bother him. Determined to demonstrate the coherence of the moral universe within which he was operating, he did not see how his own actions, from my perspective, conflicted with the definition of normative ethics he had just supplied. To be sure, people all learn to live with contradictions. Ibrahim's case illustrates how individuals may provide jarring accounts of themselves without attempting to integrate them, their inconsistencies obfuscated by an "illusion of wholeness" (Ewing 1990) that makes life livable. In his account of Zande witchcraft, E. E. Evans-Pritchard (1937) warned that what may appear inconsistent when "ranged like lifeless museum objects" in ethnographies may not be so from the informants' perspective. My aim here is not to identify the presence of conflicting ethical voices in Ibrahim's narrative but to hint at the way people are "evaluative" (Laidlaw 2014:3). The moral reasoning Ibrahim engaged in enabled him to negotiate the familiar contradictions of daily life and map out a walkable path.

To return to the point Ibrahim was making, music, as far as he was concerned, was not un-Islamic per se. Like commerce, it was regulated by a set of norms that defined the boundaries between what was acceptable and what was not. Hence, it was the content of the artist's message, not his appearance or the style of his performance, that determined whether his music was haram, just as it was the content of what a grocer bottled up for sale, not the bottle itself, that determined whether his trade was morally legitimate.[12] Insofar as ethics is not about the rules guiding the choices people make so much as about virtues that entail distinctive forms of desire and motivation, it is not hard to see how for Ibrahim, hip-hop, despite being touted as un-Islamic by conservative Muslims, was a form of ethical engagement. Hip-hop enabled him to become the kind of person he wanted to be.

Fun versus Ethical

Anxious to legitimize hip-hop as an ethical practice that has a place in Muslim communities, young rappers contrast it to the supposedly vain and frivolous performances of *coupé-décalé*. *Coupé-décalé* originated in the early 2000s in trendy Parisian nightclubs where young Ivoirian men drew attention to themselves through bold music-dance performances that spoke of their shrewdness and joie de vivre (Kohlhagen 2006). Within months residents of war-torn Abidjan had adopted it. By flaunting the wealth amassed abroad, *coupeurs-décaleurs* (performers of *coupé-décalé*) promoted a climate of lightheartedness that supplanted the gloominess of the Ivoirian capital at the height of the civil war. *Coupé-décalé* soon spread to other countries; it is now one of the leading forms of popular music in some parts of the continent, competing with hip-hop and other musical styles for the allegiance of young Africans.

According to Issa, who rapped as a member of Plantation Boys, "*Coupé-décalé* is all about ostentation. It's not real. It's about people throwing clouds of money on their friends when they dance." Other rap enthusiasts denounce *coupé-décalé* as a trivial pastime motivated by a desire for self-enhancement—not the wish to alleviate poverty or social exclusion. Rap, they argue, is informed by social critique; *coupé-décalé* is a simple fad. For the rapper Raz Gaz, "*Coupé-décalé* is not decent music. Those people sing just to invite you to dance and drink. So everyone dances, and then what? 'Come and dance! Come and drink! Look at my jacket!' What about your jacket? It's cabaret music to make money."[13] By noting that *coupé-décalé* artists displayed their skills (and stylish clothes) to entertain not educate,

Raz Gaz portrayed *coupé-décalé* as a shallow practice scripted by an ideology of materialism rather than a real desire to improve the lives of the powerless.

"Rap has a real message, *coupé-décalé* has no message. It just tells people to have fun," he further explained. "We try to move society." In contrast to *coupé-décalé*, whose raison d'être was unbridled enjoyment for its own sake, rap music, in Raz Gaz's view, was decent, honorable, and principled. In sum, hip-hop was ethical, *coupé-décalé* was not. In one of their songs, the rappers of Black Daps warn: "If you continue to hang out in the *ghetto* [in bad company], you will be exposed to drugs and theft." They urge their audiences to "cultivate [their] intelligence and knowledge" and "trust in God." One of the goals of hip-hop is to help youth break away from their lives of crime so that they can lead a productive existence under God's watchful eye. Its songs ideally provide the language through which audiences distinguish what is good and moral from what is not.

Though rappers often portray themselves as victims of circumstances who cannot hope to improve their situation without vigorous external assistance, paradoxically, they also see their youth as a responsibility. They are "self-consciously young" (Bayoumi 2010:18) and invoke, through their adoption of hip-hop values, the right to speak on behalf of other less privileged youth. "We are the mouthpiece of an entire generation" is how twenty-five-year-old Raz Gaz put it. Commonly invoked as it is in the rhetoric of protest, the claim to speak for a generation is nevertheless more than a simple cliché. It must also be seen as part of a wider effort to develop generational awareness—a sense of the common concerns, responsibilities, and aspirations youths share as a group by virtue of their generational position.

It is tempting to dismiss Ibrahim's and Raz Gaz's moral positionality as mere talk—the product of opportunistic conversations with an anthropologist willing to be convinced. I argue instead that justification does not stand apart from moral action, for in the process of describing a situation, such as the one Ibrahim described, using a beer bottle as a prop, one is already making decisions that require a moral position. Striving to make good decisions is part of our ethical development, Kwame Anthony Appiah (2008) insists. By justifying the choices they make, Nigérien rap artists cultivate a critical (and essentially ethical) understanding of the world. To some extent, this reflexivity hinges on embracing the ambivalence they feel toward hip-hop. For in trying to persuade others of the veracity and morality of their practices, they are also persuading themselves. Their own explicit discourse ultimately provides a model for the kind of person they should become, helping nurture an emerging habitus (Keane 2010:80).

Ethical Subjects

Conventional notions of a Muslim worldview limit our understanding of Muslim lives and Muslim subjectivities, particularly those of youth, because they assume that doing the right thing necessarily translates into some version of following rules—something youth typically resist in their generational quest for self-affirmation. Drawing on Veena Das's (2010) observations that morality, far from being prescriptive, is born of aspirations, conflict, creativity, and ambivalence, I have explored in this chapter the complex ways in which young Nigérien men inhabit Muslimness, focusing on the fashioning of their moral subjectivities in the context of their engagement with hip-hop.

Samari recognize the supreme authority of religion, yet their definitions of morality and moral action are not always rooted in weighty theological precepts. Refusing to be boxed in by religious coordinates, they shift between different, intersecting, and at times clashing ethical registers in their attempts to cast their worldly aspirations within a moral field of action. Their self-realization as ethical subjects takes place in contexts of conflict, ambiguities, and double standards as they make excuses for their apparent lack of piety and offer justifications for pastime and political choices, self-consciously articulating their moral stances in the process. In the way it enables its members to draw from various ethical models (including hip-hop), the fada offers a privileged window into how samari "live Islam" (Marsden 2005) and how, in the process, they confront complexities, encounter satisfactions, and fulfill aspirations but just as often suffer disappointments, experience frustrations, and feel pulled in different directions.

Although Islam is omnipresent in samari's lives, for many of them this presence remains largely implicit, confined to certain moments and contexts. Islam is rarely mentioned in hip-hop songs, and when it is, the references are largely formulaic. Uncharacteristically, Kaidan Gaskia 2's latest album features a song about God. In "Allahou Akbar," Phéno and the other members of the group urge their audience to "be aware of God all the time and not just when [they] need Him." They warn that "When you are happy, you don't think of God. It's only when you face danger that you remember God and want to pray to Him." These lyrics capture how for many samari, Islam imposes its presence, yet just as often recedes into the background, available and yet also not accessible to the consciousness of its subjects. Despite the pressure placed upon young men to conform to an authoritative Muslim tradition, rap aficionados actively cultivate modes of understanding and interacting with the world that are rooted in their *own* ways of being truthful and morally receptive to the suffering of others. How these young men negotiate the terms of their moral selfhoods in the context of their musical engagements reveals something of the way they see themselves as Muslims and as youth.

FIVE

Keeping Watch: Bodywork, Street Ethics, and Masculinity

La fada, c'est la sécurité.

—Moustapha, Dogondoutchi, 2007

"We named our fada F.B.I. We really liked the idea of crime fighting. There was glamour to the name since the F.B.I. is a powerful agency in America" is how Sani explained what had prompted him and his friends to name their fada after the US law enforcement agency. The members of F.B.I., most of whom remained dependent on parents for their livelihoods, met every evening on a sandy backstreet across from a hardware store in one of Niamey's oldest neighborhoods. They brought a barbell made from an old car axle, which they took turns lifting, to buff themselves up. When I asked Sani, alias Kamikaz (after a prominent Nigérien rapper), whether neighbors minded the presence of youths sitting on their doorsteps until late at night, he responded smugly: "On the contrary people are glad we're here. We, at F.B.I., ensure security. The neighborhood gives us nothing [in exchange], but at least everyone's safe. Here on that road, there are at least five fadas along the way. There is no way a thief could come to steal from people. We're here. We make the neighborhood safe." "Making the neighborhood safe" has become the mantra of fadantchés anxious to demonstrate to skeptical elders that the fadas are working for the common good. Whether or not they borrow from the language of statehood to craft an image of authoritative justice for themselves, as the members of F.B.I. did, fadas are generally welcomed by shopkeepers, who reward them for their services by plying them with tea, sugar, beans, and other necessities. Some streets are so densely packed with fadas that nothing (and more importantly no one) escapes their vigilance. In the absence of formal policing by agents of the state, fadantchés take great pride in their role as gatekeepers of the neighborhood. But as we shall see, it was not always the case.

Recall that popular concerns with security can be traced to the transition to democracy in the early 1990s. The end of Colonel Kountché's military dictatorship in 1987 and the subsequent advent of democracy in Niger signaled the retreat of the police state. The dismantling of the security apparatus put in place by the late dictator triggered a widespread sense of insecurity in urban areas. As the nation confronted a mounting economic downturn provoked by falling uranium prices and the implementation of the first wave of structural adjustment reforms, there was a sharp rise in petty crime in urban areas. Initial public optimism that democracy would translate into widespread economic progress gave way to deepening concerns about delinquency in the face of the state's struggle with lawlessness.

Responding to the perception of growing insecurity, private security companies emerged to provide protection for NGOs and private businesses. They dispatched security agents equipped with truncheons, knives, and walkie-talkies to those willing to pay for that protection. Concerns with crime further led to the rise of vigilante groups known as 'yan banga.[1] The 'yan banga were composed of disenfranchised youth unable to secure jobs. In fact, the very marginality of these youth is what enabled this form of civic vigilantism to be at once tactically innovative and subject to cooptation by local powers (Pratten 2006). Sponsored by local leaders and businessmen, the 'yan banga saw themselves as "superheroes" (Smith 2004), vested with the mission to rid urban neighborhoods of crime. Their quest for violent justice took place in a twilight space that accommodated practices of deception and the withdrawal of lawful norms (Sen and Pratten 2008). Armed with truncheons and cutlasses, they reportedly beat individuals they caught wandering after dark (in places they shouldn't be) before handing them to the police. Occasionally, they even mugged them. Initially their brand of swift justice received widespread support from a populace genuinely concerned with crime and the state's ineptitude. When reports of abuses surfaced, however, approval gave way to ambivalence. As the line between law enforcers and perpetrators grew increasingly blurred, the young vigilantes lost public support. A Niamey resident explained: "The problem is that they took the law into their own hands. At times, they beat up thieves real good before they could be handed to the police. At other times, they let them escape in exchange for payment." Pressured by citizens to intervene, local administrations eventually disbanded the 'yan banga (Göpfert 2012).

Fadas too stepped in to fill the void left by the police state. After the de facto curfew imposed by the Kountché regime was lifted, jobless samari who started sitting together in the street during much of the night could monitor the comings and goings of passersby and thwart unwanted intruders. The fadas thus became the eyes and ears of urban neighborhoods. How the fada's engagement in community policing has shaped young men's quest for masculinity is the focus of this chapter. As an organizing principle, David Pratten (2008a:11) writes, security can become a central locus of creativity and improvisation. Rather than considering the fada's activities as an instance of how the community is redefined through vigilantism, I treat vigilance as an analytical lens through which to examine young men's reformulation of belonging at the intersection of gender and generation.

In tandem with the institutionalization of night watches, a culture of muscularity emerged at the fada, centered on young men's need to combat a general sense of impotence and forge a façade of toughness that would prove intimidating to outsiders. Inspired by tough cinematic heroes such as Bruce Lee, Jean-Claude Van Damme, and Arnold Schwarzenegger, whose exploits were disseminated via the circulation of videocassettes and, later, CDs, samari took to pumping iron. At the turn of the century joining a fada thus became an opportunity for building muscle. Lifting weights was a means of fighting the numbness of boredom as well as the image of apathy that clung to tea circles. Corporeal countenance was intimately related to moral standing. By forging new physiques, samari sought to transform themselves into a picture of discipline and moral rectitude. A whole ethos centered on the care of the body took shape that, in the absence of conventional modes of generating value, laid an alternative path to masculine dignity. With the development of body care, nutrition became a critical concern. Young men took to cooking *wake* (beans). Beans were cheap yet rich in protein. They proved to be a critical ingredient in the forging of a masculinity centered on corporeal pride.

A decade later fadas no longer served as open-air gyms. Bodybuilding had lost much of its appeal. It led to violent clashes between young men who ended up in prison, people said. Moreover many elders denounced fadas as breeding grounds for violence and crime. In their eyes, fadantchés who used force to resolve issues were no different from the *'yan banga* who terrorized neighborhoods under the guise of preventing crime. Such blanket condemnations obscure the diverse range of projects fadas have engaged in over time. Some fadas are simple conversation spots. Others function as NGOs, *tontines* (rotating credit associations), or training centers, earning their neighbors' respect. Yet others operate like gangs, relying on the sale of *hanna kwana* (lit., "prevent sleep," amphetamines), *wiwi* (marijuana), tea laced with tramadol (opioid pain medication), and stolen goods to survive. But trying to sort the "good guys" from the "bad boys" is problematic, Christian Lund (2006) contends, for it leads to tunnel vision. Those who operate in the shadows and are hard to nail down are just as significant in local politics as more virtuous organizations.

Fadantchés themselves are generally keen to demarcate themselves from "hoodlums" and lawbreakers. They stress the civic dimension of their engagements, whether they are "fighting crime," writing hip-hop songs, or discussing national politics around a pot of tea. Yet if we are to make sense of their activities, we must not overlook how the paths to viable futures have been drastically curtailed, immobilizing many samari or forcing them to pursue unreliable, opportunistic, and, occasionally, dangerous livelihoods. In Dogondoutchi one young fadantché I knew was a successful drug dealer. Many of his neighbors earned a living smuggling gasoline from Nigeria. The money earned from the sale of drugs and smuggled gasoline was what facilitated the sustenance of households and enabled these young men to become good providers. Soon after our first encounter, the drug dealer married a girl from a respectable family, and upon my return to town, I attended the naming ceremony held for their newborn daughter. This is not to say that fada projects and pursuits can be reduced to the logic of amoral pragmatism—a form of "making do" that operates beyond ethical boundaries because it is about surviving. Instead we must recognize that people everywhere have ideals (or what we may call "values") to which they aspire. Whether or not these ideals actually guide their daily lives, they are nevertheless indicative of what matters to people and what kind of persons they want to become (Robbins 2013).

In this chapter, I trace the workings of what I call "street ethics" by considering a range of practices of self-making through which samari forge moral orientations, at times explicitly, at other times less so. Focusing on the aesthetics and pragmatics of bodybuilding, I first examine how the fada initially constituted a vehicle of self-fashioning through which young men reinvented themselves as tough, muscular subjects in the wake of socioeconomic shifts that threatened the transition to adulthood. Drawing on the work of Bourgois (1996), Wacquant (2004), and others, I discuss the moral economy of weight work and bean consumption among young men for whom muscularity was synonymous with masculinity and cooking was as much about sociality as it was about sustenance. Second, I explore how, in the wake of growing disaffection with bodybuilding, fadantchés turned the fada into a space of civility. Whereas bodybuilding was primarily centered on what Michel Foucault called the "care of the self," the regulations and forms of engagement that followed have put the accent on how to live well with others. At some fadas, this is achieved through the cultivation of enforced rules of loyalty and silence, signs of belonging, and other regulatory practices—"small disciplines" (Das 2012:137)—aimed at promoting harmony and a shared sense of purpose. Security, I ultimately argue, is a fitting lens for exploring the forms that striving and improvisation take at the fada, for it is both a source of moral ambiguity and a path to rehabilitation.

Insecurity, Masculinity, and the Work of Sitting

In the wake of the disappearance of 'yan banga and their brand of swift, retributive justice, the presence of samari who sat together in the street was viewed as comforting by local residents. Note, of course, that the perception that fadas made the neighborhood safer did not happen overnight. Nor can we assume that all fadas are involved in crime prevention. A great deal of ambiguity surrounds the activities of some fadas, and from Niamey to Zinder, gangs of thuggish youth are a notable urban presence. All the same, people have warmed up to the fadas, their missions, and their methods. We might say that as an enduring feature of street subculture, the fada found its purpose. Jamilou, alias A.B. Man, told me people in his neighborhood were suspicious of him and his friends until one night, while sitting at the fada, they caught a thief who was running away and called the police. After the incident, neighbors were kinder and more respectful of their fada, with some occasionally bringing them gifts of tea and sugar. A.B. Man's case provides a blueprint for the way that fadas became integrated in the landscape of security. Recall that idleness, as a mode of passive inactivity that leaves one vulnerable to the devil's snares, is widely believed to lead to delinquency. By catching a thief and delivering him, unharmed, to the police, the young men demonstrated they were mature, dependable, honorable. Their feat earned them their neighbors' trust. It suggested that rather than being liabilities, fadas brought tangible benefits to their communities. In sum, sitting, once synonymous with impotence and idleness, has been rehabilitated as a form of work.

Fadas today are tightly associated with crime prevention in some urban neighborhoods that are less policed by an official security apparatus. Fadantchés relish the opportunity to publicize their exploits. They cite the number of thieves they captured as proof of their indispensability to the neighborhood. Mindful that beating suspected thieves could lead to legal unpleasantness, the large majority insist that they do not inflict violence on trespassers.[2] "A year or so ago, we caught a thief. He was trying to steal cell phones. We caught him but did not beat him," a saurayi by the name of Don't Panik explained. "Now, if you beat a thief, you get to pay for their hospital treatment." The young man sounded resentful, as if he missed the days when summary justice could be delivered with impunity. He nevertheless saw himself as engaged in the principled conduct that the fada, as a space of responsibilization, fostered. He was proud of the reputation his fada had earned in the neighborhood by keeping crime at bay.

Though credited with helping restore security, fadantchés are occasionally assimilated to the vigilantes who once spread terror under the guise of keeping order. Besides signaling how fuzzy the distinction between protection and predation can be, the conflation of fadas with violent militia reminds us that youth, specifically young men, are often perceived as a problem: far from being stable, the space they occupy in society is routinely contested. In light of the correlation frequently made between young men and violence, insecurity provides a fitting alibi for criminalizing disaffected samari. Take the case of Zinder, the country's second largest city, where members of youth organizations known as palais ("palace," local French translation of fada), are reportedly responsible for the rash of violence that has erupted in recent years. Like the fadas, palais are a product of growing disaffection. While the fadas first appeared in Zinder in the late 1990s, a trend Lund (2009) links to the launching of a private radio station,[3] the palais are a more recent phenomenon (Schritt 2015). What distinguishes them from fadas is supposedly their gang-like character. Chronic poverty and diminishing prospects have pushed many youths to the margins where they rewrite the rules of society, using sex and violence both as rites of passage and to singularize themselves. Whereas fadantchés are lazy and indolent in the eyes of law-abiding Zinderois, 'yan palais (palais members) are thugs—a threat to social order. Robberies, housebreakings, and physical aggressions are routinely attributed to 'yan palais. In the religiously conservative city of Zinder, the palais have emerged as the fada's doppelgänger— the evil twin—in public consciousness.

In the past decade the mobilization of palais by local politicians seeking to broaden their influence has unleashed new surges of violence, heightening the insecurity that has gripped Zinder since the retreat of the state (Le Sahel 2012; Motcho 2004). In December 2011, a protest march, which hundreds of 'yan palais were invited to join, turned violent, resulting in widespread looting and destruction across the city. The terror spread by rioting youths reportedly reached such levels that Zinder was dubbed by local commentators the "Benghazi of Niger," after the town in neighboring Libya in which the revolution that toppled Gadhafi's regime was born.

Following the interventions of civic and religious leaders and parents' associations, *'yan palais* and fada members formally organized under the umbrella of the Mouvement des Fadas et Palais pour la Promotion des Jeunes. UNICEF stepped in to provide training opportunities and create alternative venues for samari to settle disputes. For some Nigériens, however, the *'yan palais* are beyond redemption.

Beyond the question of whether fadas (or *palais*) can be assimilated to gangs, I should note once more that the impulse to criminalize these forms of sociality is largely rooted in the hedonistic images associated with them. In Niger the definition of manhood is predicated on having a professional occupation. Men have serious matters to attend to and no time for "play" (Gaudio 2009); from this perspective, fadas are *bata locaci* (a waste of time). For those for whom idleness inevitably conjures transgression and crime, the spectacle of young men chatting around a pot of tea signals not only self-indulgence but also waywardness. "They start with tea and cigarettes, and before long, they have moved on to drugs, and they must steal to get their fix," is how a civil servant and father of five put it. Samari struggle to overcome these stereotypes. As one high school student bitterly put it: "Elders do not like our fadas. They see you and think you're a *voyou*, a delinquent. They don't see that some of us, we are students, we come to the fada and we might be doing homework or taking a break from homework. All they see is that we sit. They think we do nothing. Some show us no respect." Paradoxically some samari actively draw on the "bad guy" stereotype as the "boastful centerpiece of a culture of compensation" (Gilroy 1993:85). Deploying images of criminality allows them to inhabit spaces of masculine fantasy. One group of samari called their fada Capitale du Crime. Another boasted their fada, known as Petit Couloir Danger (Small Corridor Danger), served as a road stop to "fleece passersby." Drawing from both local and imported repertoires of violence (Bin Laden and the Italian Mafia are popular sources of inspiration) allows young men to define the spaces they inhabit in terms of intensity, struggle, and endurance. They live in a world of conflict, and the fada, by helping them cultivate the capacity to prevail in this world, is a school of survival. Samari from Dogondoutchi unofficially recruited by the municipality to guard administrative buildings named their fada Attaque sans Pardon (Attack without Forgiveness) in a fierce assertion of their supposedly tough stance on crime. In Niamey some youths provocatively named their fada Hargiya, after the local chief of the *'yan banga*, while a stone's throw away, another fada emerged under the name Commando, after the 1985 action movie starring Arnold Schwarzenegger. While illustrating how the images of the fearsome watchdog and the special forces soldier are used to evince a sense of invincibility, these names also point to the close kinship between vigilance and violence.

Samari I spoke with insisted that the adversarial images they projected on the walls of their neighborhoods were a form of posturing, nothing more. They scoffed at the notion that fadas instantiated the unraveling of the fabric of law and order. Hence calling their fada Bin Laden did not prevent a group of samari from striving to be good citizens: they tutored local schoolchildren in French and mathematics (Youngstedt 2013). Eighteen-year-old Boubacar, alias Crimson, explained that despite its sinister name, Capitale du Crime, which he had joined four years earlier, was composed of "*des jeunes gentils* [kind youths] who don't do bad things and don't make trouble." Rather than dismissing Boubacar's statement as inconsequential, I take it as an expression of ethical stance. Boubacar was saying that he and his friends had chosen not to follow the so-called path of delinquency. They cared for one another and were mindful of the wider world in which they lived. By describing his fada as a place where young men not only engaged in leisurely activities (soccer mostly) but also served the neighborhood through occasional street cleanups, Boubacar deliberately positioned Capitale du Crime as a counterweight to "useless" fadas. To fend off criticisms that fadas promote idleness and parasitism, some samari now draw a distinction between fadas *utiles* (useful fadas) and fadas *inutiles* (useless fadas). Tea circles that serve no apparent purpose besides offering tea and conversation are useless fadas, while fadas such as Capitale du Crime, whose members aspire to do good things, are useful fadas that do not deserve the scorn that some elders heap on them.

Building Muscles

Anthropologists have widely documented how the body constitutes a privileged tool of self-improvement for those for whom avenues of social realization are severely limited. Wacquant (1998:345) described how impoverished boxers subject their bodies to rigorous training in their quest for a "transcendent, moral, masculine self." Sports, the anthropological literature has shown, constitute a mechanism for the integration of immigrant and other minorities into dominant society. By drawing athletes from the Global South to the Global North, they enable impoverished youths to enjoy tremendous recognition and material rewards (Besnier and Brownell 2012). Inmates resist the dehumanizing carceral universe to which they are confined by engaging in punitive weight-training routines and cultivating their bodily appearance (Cordilia 1983; Wahidin 2004). By putting on muscles, they retake ownership of their bodies when everything else has been seized from them; they literally expand in volume, thereby regaining the space that the penal institution deprived them of. "Prison makes you ugly" is how some inmates summarized the bodily degradations—including loss of teeth and hair—they suffered as a consequence of their impoverished diet and way of life (*Le Monde* 2009, my translation). By combating what Erving Goffman (1961) called the mortification of the self, weight lifting hides the penal system's damaging impact on physical and social identities. It makes possible the creation of "a very beautiful display window" (*Le Monde* 2009, my translation), as one inmate put it. When selfhood is effectively shattered by the carceral system, the body surface is charged primarily with identity function; it is there that the process of rescuing and displaying masculinity operates. By carefully redefining the contours of their bodies, inmates resist the prison's disciplinary gaze and regain some control over their diminished sense of humanity.

Just as prisoners latch onto the body as a means of transcending the dehumanizing restrictions of prison life, so idle samari channeled their youthful energies toward the creation of muscular selves, using weight lifting as an alternative conduit to proper masculinity. It was on their bodies that they displayed who they were—or more specifically, who they aspired to be. In his study of sport and class, Bourdieu (1978) wrote how sports shape bodies in ways that reveal the social position of those who inhabit them. Far from being a matter of personal taste, sports reflect sensibilities and aspirations that are directly linked to class. Thus, in sports such as boxing or rugby, one can discern, Bourdieu argued, an instrumental relation to the body that is distinctive of how working classes treat the body. Members of the working class choose sports that require a significant investment of effort as well as pain and suffering. In contrast, through their engagement in jogging or gymnastics, the so-called privileged classes produce a "body-for-others" (Bourdieu 1984:207).

Today no social theorist would contest the claim that bodies bear the imprint of class or that bodily capital (that is, the resources one inherits or acquires through socially approved diet, dress, and exercise regimes) plays a crucial role in the maintenance of social distinction. Yet in the wake of extensive socioeconomic transformations that have displaced work as a source of valuation, the connection Bourdieu drew between the physical attributes of particular sport activities and class habitus is not so clear-cut anymore. In the absence of secure employment, men, particularly working-class men, in Euro-America are increasingly treating the body as an end in itself in their attempts at self-reaffirmation. With the rise of "somatic society" (B. Turner 1984) in which large muscles no longer signal specific class identities, it is not the body as a working tool so much as its "to-be-looked-at-ness" (Mulvey 1975) that is a source of social capital. What this means is that athletic bodies are valued not for indexing a capacity for physical labor so much as for what they say about another kind of work: the workout at the gym (Klein 1993). So obsessive is young disenfranchised men's concern with their bodies in the Global North that Rosalind Gill, Karen Henwood, and Carl McLean (2005) write of the emergence of an extraordinary fetishization of muscles that coincides with the disappearance of traditionally male manual jobs in our post-Fordist era. Muscularity has become an armor covering up men's deep vulnerabilities.

The fashionability of muscularity has been documented in Africa as well. Jean-François Havard (2001), Sasha Newell (2012), and Katrien Pype (2007) thus document the appearance of an ethos of success associated with the cultivation of a muscular body in contemporary Senegal, Côte d'Ivoire, and the Democratic Republic of Congo, respectively. Under this new system of value, domination is no longer expressed through age or cast but through physical performance: the young man who, by winning the fight, demonstrates he has worked the hardest to get his body in shape is identified as the champion—at once an object of reverence and the rival others hope to defeat.

In the early 2000s samari lifted weights to defend themselves in case of an attack by a rival group. Relations with other fadas were sometimes tense, and fadantchés were quick to throw the gauntlet when their fada's honor was at stake. Bound up in the pride they shared with fellow members, they battled with rival fadas to wash out offenses with blood. Though not everyone participated in the fistfights (or cutlass battles) against opposing fadas, keeping fit nevertheless became a must in the struggle to preserve dignity. Like poor youths in Brazzaville who romanticized male violence through the register of the *yankee*, based on the heroic images of masculinity projected by Hollywood westerns (Bazenguissa-Ganga 1999), samari invested in the fashioning of muscular bodies frequently to provide an alibi for the performance of lawlessness and brutality. Drawing on popular culture, specifically the martial art images circulating via bootlegged video cassettes and later CDs, they recycled gritty narratives of masculine violence to fashion an ethos based on muscle, resilience, and fierce loyalty to the fada, which they routinely described as their second family. The names they gave each other, often based on physical characteristics or one's identification with a heroic action figure, spoke of their fascination with the images of hypermasculinity propagated by the cinematic industry.

At the fada great value was placed on courage and discipline. When he joined Gangasta Flow (*sic*), Oumarou, aka Tupac, started lifting weights regularly. He devoured large quantities of beans and rice enriched with canned sardines (he knew the value of a high-protein diet) and was disciplined about his daily workouts. Following a nasty street clash that left several youths wounded, he was designated as *l'homme de casse*, the breaker who led fellow fadantchés on the warpath when rival fadas challenged Gangasta Flow. Though it was not uncommon for the entire fada to show up armed with knives and sticks, he was nevertheless expected to fight the enemy's own "champion" one on one. "If there's a dispute, *l'homme de casse* is the one who fights," Ali, a member of Super Mafia Boys, explained. "He is the front man, he decides whether there's gonna be a fight. He is the champion. If someone *touche* [offends] us, we need to show him we're strong."

Contradicting the script that equates bodybuilding with thuggery, some former adepts described the practice as a form of ethical pedagogy, the cultivation of capacities oriented toward the goal of living well. Take the case of Hassane. The young man was a member of Black Warrior, a fada his older brother had founded years earlier with schoolmates. Although his brother no longer visited the fada, Hassane considered Black Warrior (or B.W. for short) his second family. The youngest of sixteen children, he grew up on the periphery of the Dogondoutchi urban district. Like many of his siblings, he was enrolled in school by age seven. By age fifteen he had quit school but was too proud to take a manual job (though he helped his father with the harvest). Shortly after joining Black Warrior, he discovered bodybuilding. At first, the saurayi lifted weights to fit in. Before long he noticed that the intense physical activity made him feel good. Soon he had included in his daily schedule a grueling routine of weight lifting and push-ups. In a matter of months, the previously shy and slender youth developed an imposing, muscular figure, which he learned to showcase through careful sartorial choices. At the fada where *gaillards* (strapping young men) are typically objects of emulation, he earned the nickname of *L'Homme* (The Man)—a tribute to his brawny physique. Having grown conscious of his diet, he routinely extolled to all who would listen the health benefits of certain foods while stressing the dangers associated with alcohol and other harmful substances.

By building muscle, samari not only built themselves up but also carved out spaces of self-expression, affording us a glimpse of how they imagined the good life, even in the most challenging circumstances. Tupac, Gangasta

Flow's former champion, relished the warm camaraderie he experienced during his daily physical training at the fada. The barbell he and his friends took turns lifting—a true piece of bricolage, created out of two cement-filled paint cans welded to an iron bar—was kept at his house. He brought it to the fada every day for he liked to work out in the company of fellow weight lifters. "I was in real good shape. In fact, on days when I didn't exercise, I felt light, like I was sick," he told me. For embodying the heroic masculine ideal disseminated by male action cinema (he was a devoted fan of Belgian martial artist and actor Jean-Claude Van Damme), Tupac was admired by samari for whom manliness was measured in terms of toughness and physical strength. At the fada, the maximization of body size through which young men created expanded versions of themselves was a prime instance of gendered performativity.

Initially I assumed that samari like Tupac and Hassane looked to local athletes, particularly traditional wrestlers, in their search for models of heroic masculinity. Niger is home to a vibrant culture of traditional wrestling.[4] The national wrestling competition held in Niamey every year draws enormous crowds. Many Nigériens watch it on television. Samari I spoke with each had their favorite wrestler, whom they described as a national hero and a "superman" of sorts.[5] Despite its immense popularity, however, traditional wrestling is not a source of emulation for fadantchés. Like the *sportifs* of Dakar (Havard 2001), the gorillas of Kinshasa (Pype 2007), and the *bluffeurs* of Abidjan (Newell 2012), fadantchés in search of role models have turned to foreign archetypes of tough masculinity. In addition to Jean-Claude Van Damme and Arnold Schwarzenegger, Asian martial arts heroes such as Bruce Lee and Jackie Chan are often idolized by fadantchés. Several samari I met practiced judo or tae kwon do and took up aliases inspired by the action figures of the martial art videos they watched together. Some of them would adopt the swagger and idiosyncrasies of their favorite cinematic hero. They belonged to fadas that bore names such as Dragon Rouge, Dragon Blanc, or Boss Karate.

Although martial arts have drawn the passionate interest of many samari, it is the world of hip-hop that constitutes the richest source of insight and creativity for young men in need of masculine models (see chapter 4). The fada lexicon is peppered with references to hip-hop culture. There are literally dozens of fadas named Weezy Baby, Killer Boys, Bad Boyz, Cash Money, Mad Boys, Sexion d'Assaut, or Soldja (or Soulja) Boys. One hears fadantchés who go by the names of Florida,[6] Snoop Dog, Nelly, or 50 Cent. According to Jesse Shipley (2013), the black US rapper embodies for African youth the contradictory legacy of the African diaspora as a space of both victimization and empowerment. As such he suits samari's aspirational sensibilities. To this day, he remains a critical icon of masculine agency as well as an instantiation of how "gender is the modality in which race is lived" (Gilroy 1993:85).

Mountari, a member of Master Boys, makes a persuasive case for why rap is such an important font of cultural referents:

> "Master," it's something colossal, something grand. It's about those who're at the very top. So, the Master Boys are the young men—the *boys*—who're the best. Most of the names we pick [for our fadas] are in English, because the fadas imitate American ghettos. The ghettos come from the US. We emulate Americans—Tupac and the other black Americans—rappers, revolutionaries who denounce the wrongs. The denouncers, they are socially committed. When you speak of social engagement, you mean black Americans. It is they who are the revolutionaries. We don't look to French rappers for inspiration in the same way. What we watch are images of American ghettos [in rap videos]. French rappers don't show us images of ghettos. But we samari, we're in ghettos.

Not only does American hip-hop constitute a vernacular for speaking about the reality of living on the margins of world society, but as Mountari suggests, it also provides a store of images that samari can appropriate to frame their own identities as black youth. The concept of the ghetto looms particularly large in the moral imagination of male youth eager to cast themselves as a poor, disempowered minority. Samari refer to their sleeping quarters as *ghettos*. In the US ghetto, the rapper represents both the threat of the male black thug and the potential of the artistic antihero struggling against injustice. His oversized, exaggerated masculinity functions as a counterweight to a life of privation—a compensatory mechanism that "self-consciously salves the misery of the dis-empowered and the subordinated" (Gilroy 1993:85). He is the iconic figure for young Nigérien men aiming to construct themselves as disenfranchised but self-aware, cosmopolitan subjects.

Add to this the fact that great value is attached to English and one can see why Mountari and many of his peers have embraced US hip-hop as the language of protest while declaring French hip-hop irrelevant. Despite the political pertinence of their message and the fact that they offer trenchant criticism of racism, imperialism, and the pernicious effects of globalization,

French hip-hop lyrics do not have the cachet of English rap. Granted, few Nigérien youths have mastered the rudiments of English. The words they hear are almost exclusively part of a "sonic discourse" (Levy 2001:138)— most make little sense. Yet the realities of black urban ghetto life and the Afro-centered performances of swaggering, muscular masculinity exercise a strong enough pull on fadantchés' imagination that US hip-hop remains the uncontested number one source of cultural influence for samari looking for compensatory models of manliness.

Beans

To build muscle, samari will tell you, the aspiring bodybuilder must first and foremost adopt a high-protein diet. Including meat in his daily diet is ideal since meat is synonymous with pure strength. Given its prohibitive cost, however, the overwhelming majority of samari turn to beans (*wake*) to meet daily nutritional requirements. Today dumbbells have largely disappeared from the scene, but beans remain an essential component of fada sociality. Because it is both an excellent source of protein and an affordable food item, *wake*—or black-eyed pea—is often referred to as *la viande du pauvre* (the poor man's meat). It has become a favorite staple in many urban households in times of austerity and privation. Also known among francophone Nigériens as *niébé* or *haricot*, *wake* grows well in poor soil. It doesn't require much water and is not threatened by irregular rainfall. When planted in conjunction with millet, the traditional staple food of Nigériens, the two plants grow in perfect symbiosis. *Wake* enriches the soil by manufacturing nitrogen, thereby promoting optimal millet growth, and it takes advantage of the shade provided by millet stalks once those reach a certain height. Moreover its leaves, once dried, provide valuable fodder for animals.

During his presidency, Seyni Kountché actively promoted bean cultivation as a means of diversifying crop production. His efforts were largely successful: today Niger is the second world producer of black-eyed peas after Nigeria. In 2008–9 Niger produced between 800,000 and 1,548,000 tons of beans, netting the country 750 billion francs, that is, twice the profits brought by uranium extraction (Institut National de la Statistique 2010). This success cannot be solely attributed to Kountché's vision of a self-sufficient Niger, however. The rising popularity of beans as a staple food must also be traced to the successive famines (1972–74 and 1984–85) that thoroughly transformed food production and food consumption in Niger (Luxereau 1998). As local crops were revalorized in contexts of food scarcity, *wake*—a staple urbanites previously snubbed because of its connotation as peasant food—gained progressive acceptance in urban markets. "Before Kountché, if you ate *wake*, you were nothing," is how one of Anne Luxereau's (1998:293) interlocutors aptly described the radical shift in value that brought "stardom" to *wake*.

Prevalent as *wake* has become in local cuisine in recent decades, it is nowhere as popular among the average Nigérien as among fadantchés for whom a meeting at the fada is practically synonymous with *marmite de niébés* (pot of beans). A saurayi explains how, by filling hungry bellies, *wake* contributed to the rise of fada culture (and the concomitant immersion in hip-hop): "The beans, at the fada, it all started with the hip-hop craze. We'd spend all night recording our music, drinking tea to stay focused. We were hungry, so we pinched beans and rice on the sly. Some of us have left hip-hop but we still cook *wake*. Now, it's shop owners who give us tea and beans so we keep watch on their businesses." One frequently hears fadantchés claim that they prefer beans to everything else and that "beans are the food of samari."[7] Beans are cheap, available everywhere, and also easy to prepare. Unlike millet, which requires a series of time-consuming steps (sifting, pounding, boiling, and so on) before it can be consumed, beans demand limited preparation. In fact, cooking beans is a straightforward process. All one needs, fadantchés will tell you, is a cooking pot, some oil, and a few handfuls of rice (rice is *wake*'s "best friend") as well as salt and hot pepper in addition to the beans. One can add sautéed onions and tomatoes as well as natron, if available. Since preparing a pot of *wake*—short for *wake da shinkafa*, rice and beans—is relatively effortless and does not require special skills (like pounding), many young men learn how to do it. In some cases, it is their claim to fame: samari like to brag that they cook beans better than women do.

Fadantchés often say that beans are the best "medicine for hunger" (*maganin yunwa*). Not only do beans fill you up, but they also "stick to your stomach." More than any other food, they are said to give people a feeling of satiation, especially if, as samari who rarely eat more than once a day are prone to do, they swallow two cups of water following the ingestion of *wake*: "After you drink water, the beans swell up in your stomach. You're completely full." Needless to say, the sensation of having *le ventre bien calé* (a densely filled stomach) has great symbolic purchase in a country routinely plagued by food crises. The fact that beans are protein-rich and supply energy to the body makes them especially valuable in the eyes of young men looking to strengthen their physiques. Beans are said to provide strength, which is why their consumption must be indispensably associated with the physical training young men undergo to build body mass. As one of them explained, "young men, next to the plate of *wake*, they put weights. [Once they're done eating] they do some weight lifting to see who is the strongest. *Le niébé* gives you *karfe* [strength, power, energy]. It sticks to the stomach."

Beans are the aliment of choice for male youth hoping to feed their aspirations for a better future by developing athletic, expansive bodies that emblematize power and success. Through their capacity to impart energy and their association with the fada's tight web of friendship, beans become the very definition of food for samari in search of both emotional nurturing and masculine affirmation. "I love beans," a member of Alcatraz told me, "I eat beans in the morning, I eat beans at midday, and I eat beans in the evening. It's my kind of food." So effectively constitutive of youthful masculinity are beans that a pundit writing of *le phénomène niébé* (the bean trend) observed that the pot of beans had now displaced the teapot as the emblem of conviviality and timepass at the fada (Maazou 2007).

When I asked a recently married young man why he preferred beans over *maka* (pasta), he responded: "When I go home, if my wife has prepared beans, I won't even look at the dish. It does not appeal to me. But at the fada, when someone prepares beans, I eat a ton of it." His friend added that he too tended to eat "only a couple of mouthfuls and I leave the rest" when beans were served at his home. At the fada, on the other hand, he ate "lots of it. It tastes great." Despite their many virtues, the two friends intimated, beans acquired their tastiness and emblematic status as the "king of food" only at the fada, where social bonds were built on trust, loyalty, and emotional closeness.

At the turn of the century, as samari aimed to make something of themselves, beans, thanks to their newfound association with urbanity and virility, became a central ingredient in the economy of muscular practices built on the cult of toughness. While a decade later life at the fada no longer revolves around weight-lifting routines, the pots of beans fadantchés prepare late at night continue to sustain the bonds they have built with one another. In the sharing of food, young men find a primary outlet for the performance of masculinity while configuring the fada as a second family—what Marshall Sahlins (2013) described as a "network of mutualities of being" (20).

From Fistfights to Dress Duels

I have suggested that through its role in the making of manly bodies, the fada once provided a stage on which male youth enacted the core values of a street ethos. This ethos, based on the valuation of honor, discipline, and muscular power, put a premium on loyalty. Samari were united in the shared sense of pride they felt in their fada. When a fadantché was insulted (or assaulted) by members of another fada, the fada's honor was at stake. Fellow fadantchés must defend it, by violent means if necessary. This is how a member of Smoll Boys (*sic*) described how he defended his fada's honor:

> If someone insults a fadantché, *alors c'est la bagarre* [then there is a fight], because we cannot let someone *toucher* [offend] one of us. First we decide on a place and a time. It'll be at night, in a faraway, isolated place since we don't want our parents to find out about it [*laughter*]. Now, it's absolutely forbidden to do that, of course. . . . If a member leaves the fada to join another fada, we send three *combatants* his way. The first one fights with him, then the second, and finally the last one. This is how it is done.

Fights that erupted between rival groups sometimes involved weapons: "There was a lot of competition between fadas. One fada would set up a meeting with another fada and show up with knives and machetes. Some got hurt."[8]

The days of avenging the fada's honor by physically confronting one's competitors are over—at least, officially. Today fadantchés speak of physical confrontations in the past tense. "When we were younger, we lifted weights. Our fada would compete with other fadas so you had to have strong champions who could fight. But we don't do it anymore" is how a thirty-two-year-old motorbike washer put it. According to a university student, "when we were young, we were agitated. We provoked each other, we fought, we hurt each other. Now we have left these things." Violence, these narratives imply, was the main avenue through which hotheaded samari solved disputes and salvaged dignity. But fadantchés have since realized the error of their ways; at least, this is how many of them put it when asked about how things have changed. I was told that the incarceration of a number of samari convicted of assault and battery and the severe remonstrances from Muslim religious leaders dissuaded a number of fadantchés from resorting to violence. The romanticization of past violence notwithstanding, the fact that many fadantchés speak of having given up fighting to embark on civic-minded projects or start jobs is a reminder that the fada, as a training ground, is folded into the life cycle. As fadantchés mature, they are expected to trade the impulsive, selfish conduct of youth for more mature occupations.

Some of my interlocutors cited parental pressure as a determinant factor in the reformation of fada culture. Tupac, Gangasta Flow's former champion, gave up weight lifting to please his parents: "The whole body-building thing is a way for people to compete. 'Look, my muscles are bigger than yours!' But it's not good, it changes your character. You become a *voyou* who only wants to pick a fight. You fight to see who is stronger than you. At the beginning, being in a fada was all about fighting with other fadas. We were *bandits* [thugs]. There was a lot of fighting. This is why our parents disapproved of our activities." A motorcycle taxi driver similarly spoke of how elders condemned his engagement with violence: "When I fought at the fada, my parents didn't like it. *C'est logique* [It makes sense]. Parents want what's best for their children. They worried about what was happening to their sons when they saw them fight. They thought we had turned into delinquents." As these testimonies suggest, samari must sometimes walk a fine line between filial submission and masculine glory. For one thing, they must imperatively submit to their parents' wishes. Anxious though they may be to shed the bad boy image inherited from their predecessors, they also yearn to make a reputation for themselves in the neighborhood. This is where the fada's name comes in. By naming their fada Gang of City or Mafia Boys, they project the coveted image of toughness without compromising their roles as obedient sons. Crimson thus described the members of Capitale du Crime as "kind youth" who did not do "bad things" to stress that self-fashioning at the fada was a moral project.

Fistfights and cutlass battles may be a thing of the past, but the cult of masculinity is far from over. Samari now compete with one another through what could be called dress duels. These performances take place during dance parties and shows, which fadas organize to impress their competitors and expand their reputation.[9] In the absence of other mechanisms aimed at confirming male adulthood, the body, particularly its surface (Featherstone 2000), remains a prominent vehicle of masculine empowerment. The goal of these events—which may take weeks to organize—is to *faroter*, show off, and amaze your audience with your style and elegance. Some samari display their toned, muscular bodies and impress guests with an overabundance of food in classical potlatch fashion to enhance the reputation of their fada. In Abidjan poor young men engage in the *bluff*, an elaborate performance—akin to a potlatch—aimed at projecting the appearance of success while also demonstrating cultural knowledge of foreign trends (Newell 2012). Like the Ivoirian *bluffeur* who confounds the distinction between illusion and authenticity through his masterful display of name brand products, samari are experts at managing impressions.

Some samari make a point of wearing revealing clothes: "slim jeans" and tank tops so that they can *rouler des mécaniques*, strut while rolling their shoulders. Accessories (such as sunglasses) help too. The idea is to gather admiration from young women while intimidating one's potential rivals. Far from being a stable, preexisting identity, masculinity is a never-ending process one is constantly working on. Samari's engagement in these "body projects" (Gill, Henwood, and McLean 2005:40) suggests that more than a simple site of self-styling, the male body is an object of gaze. Moctar, a member of Alcatraz who went by the name of Le Guerrier (The Warrior), explained he ate primarily beans and fish (which he caught in the river) before working out in preparation for a show. By using his body as a form of symbolic capital and literally flexing his muscles, he constructed himself as a "big man" who caught the girls' attention while intimidating other samari. He thrived on competition; in fact, it was when competing against similarly driven young men that he felt most alive. On an ordinary basis Moctar was tasked with enforcing discipline at the fada. He broke up fights and kept track of fadantchés who used crude language. Sociality at the fada is often regulated by a range of customs and rules. It is to these that I now turn.

Small Disciplines

Discipline is a central dimension of fada life: when joining a fada, recruits agree to adhere to the implicit (as well as more explicit) conventions members live by that make life together not only possible but also rewarding (this is why some fadas interview prospective members). Heeding Das's (2012:137) recommendation that we attend to the everyday dimension of ethics, I trace ethical practices at the fada in the "small disciplines" that members perform on a daily basis. These customs govern many facets of fada sociality from greetings to tea drinking to how to resolve a dispute or deal with a member's bereavement. Take the practice of serving tea, for instance. At some fadas, seniority dictates the order in which tea is served among fadantchés. Elsewhere tea is distributed on a first-come, first-served basis, or the glass is passed around in the order in which people are sitting. Sometimes the person who paid for the tea is served first so long as he stays while the tea is being prepared. If he leaves during the tea making, he may have to wait his turn, for as a young man put it, "le thé, ça se mérite" (tea must be earned).

Other seemingly inconsequential practices strengthen intimacy. By pouring the whole content of the teapot in a large glass from which samari sip one after the other, the tea maker reaffirms trust and closeness among the fadantchés, enabling us to appreciate "the delicacy of maintaining regard for others through the minutest of gestures" (Das 2012:133). While appearing casual, unrehearsed, the sip each person takes from the common glass is nevertheless measured—based on an evaluation of how much tea is left in the glass and how many individuals have yet to partake of the brew. Caroline Humphrey (2012) has noted how, in Mongolian hospitality, the distance between spontaneity and rules is buffered through tiny, strategic gestures aimed at producing an effect of measure and detachment. Like the emotional economy of hospitality in Mongolia, the affective economy of tea drinking at the fada is grounded in ordinary, minute acts that show us how ethical practices constitute what Das (2012) calls "the threads woven into the weave of life" (132).

Whereas older fadantchés follow largely tacit rules, embedded in everyday practice, junior fadantchés often take great pains to spell out fada etiquette. The rules they create to ensure harmony and amity at the fada are generally listed in a notebook kept by the secretary. At some fadas swallowing all the foam sitting atop the tea is not only rude but also transgressive and may result in a fine. New members are warned that misbehaving and flouting the *règlement* will result in penalties ranging from small fines to expulsion. A key principle of good conduct is respect for one's fellow fadantchés. When the fada holds a meeting, for instance, it must be informed when a fadantché won't be able to make it "so your friends know you are not disrespecting them." At all times members are enjoined to show consideration for other members and refrain from selfish or offensive actions. They must learn to exercise restraint in their dealings with others in keeping with the norms in place at the fada. Through the stress placed on good manners, thoughtful conduct, and polite language, the fadantchés undergo a kind of apprenticeship in the art of living. To paraphrase Wacquant (2004), the fada is a "school of morality" (15) in the Durkheimian sense: as a social institution, it is designed to produce the spirit of discipline, loyalty, self-respect, and respect for others required of ethically minded subjects. Pointing to his friend, a saurayi told me that he was *le marabout* (Muslim ritual specialist) *de la* fada, charged with providing moral advice when needed. The so-called *marabout* had attended Qur'anic school for a number of years. Aside from helping to address thorny ethical questions, he reportedly monitored the rightness of members' conduct.

At the fada, behaving respectfully toward other members begins with avoiding gossip and offensive, hurtful language. Words have power and "hot speech" can be dangerous; as one grows up, one learns to measure the power of one's words in social settings. The fada, which was once described to me as *un cadre de formation*, an educational environment, often puts great emphasis on language as a tool of civility. New fadantchés are made aware that *hululu* (idle chatter) easily turns into gossip—or lies. Rules are not always followed, however, and jealousy and unfulfilled expectations occasionally saturate relations among fadantchés. A pious saurayi left the fada he founded because he could not reconcile the acid tittle-tattle he was routinely exposed to with the nurturance and support he wished to receive from fellow Muslims.

To curb foul language and discourage swearing, many fadas levy fines on members caught using censored words. A fadantché is assigned to police the speech of fellow members, thereby ensuring that social interactions remain within the boundaries of courteous behavior and that a climate of amity permeates daily gatherings. Predictably, fighting at the fada is frowned upon. To enforce the rules, some fadas appoint a *taxeur* (or *tax-man*) who levies fines ranging from 100 to 1,000 francs on fadantchés caught behaving insolently and fighting with one another. A young man explained how it was done at his fada: "If you insult someone or you say something insulting about his mother, you will be fined. For this kind of transgression, you will be fined one *shai* [100 francs' worth of tea], one *sucre* [50 francs' worth of sugar], and one *charbon* [50 francs' worth of coal]."[10] At another fada fighting earned you the burden of having to prepare the pot of beans for the late evening meal. Elsewhere the fada's president decides how to sanction fighting between members. Leaving the fada may be punishable by up to 10,000 francs. While fada leaders recognize that individuals may leave because they don't get along with others, they nevertheless want to minimize attrition. The steep fine is meant to discourage members who might be thinking of quitting on a whim.

Once fined by the *taxeur*, fadantchés must pay the fine if they wish to remain members in good standing. Ignoring the fine may result in being denied entrance to the fada. Jamilou alias Alex[11] explains: "If you do not bring the money you were fined, if you do not bring 50 francs' worth of both coal and sugar and 100 francs' worth of tea, you will be further penalized: it is the *mise à pied* [suspension]. You cannot talk to your friend until you pay your fine. They won't let you come to the fada." While fadas may impose tough sanctions for violence, foul language, and insubordination, some reportedly provide assistance to fadantchés known for resorting too quickly to blows or insults. They designate counselors tasked with offering advice to those who are prone to quarrel. Others appoint someone to act as a mediator between the warring parties and help them develop an appreciation for the importance of respect and civility. By devising a whole array of checks and balances aimed at deflecting tensions and promoting harmony and by helping members develop the capacity for trust and empathy, some fadantchés appear to take seriously the notion that, as Paul Ricoeur (1992:172) put it, ethics is largely a matter of living well with others or for others.

While not all fadas require their members to wear a uniform—in fact, few actually do—a minimum of sartorial care is nevertheless required of fadantchés. A member of Big Boss Two put it this way: "You cannot just wear anything you want. If you show up with a *culotte* [shorts], the *amendeur* will send you home. You have to dress properly." Note, of course, that every fada has a sartorial code of conduct and that what is deemed to be acceptable attire may vary widely from one fada to another. Not every fada banned *culottes*, for instance. Moreover there is a fine line between acceptable and unacceptable dress. At Big Boss Two the shin-length pants worn by rappers and known locally as *baggy coupé* were acceptable, but shorts above the knee were not. In the early 2000s ripped jeans passed muster at most fadas since they signified fashion savvy, not failure to maintain one's wardrobe. On the other hand, wearing a worn T-shirt whose tears were not part of the look would lead to sanctions. At La Belle Vie des Jeunes Garçons, a *contrôleur* monitored hygiene and tidiness. Members who showed up unwashed or in torn clothing were (in theory, at least) sent home. As the founder of La Belle Vie des Jeunes Garçons implied when he stated that a good life was predicated on "do[ing] things that please people," it was by producing principled young men who led orderly lives, behaved considerately, and complied with social expectations that the fada earned respect from elders. This is not to suggest that life at the fada is confining. Moral practices are not simply the result of following rules and regulations. They can be tacit, grounded in agreement. In the way ethics entails exercising judgment and making decisions, it is about being "invested in a way of life" (Keane 2016:12). As such, it is less about constraining people than about enabling them to act and creating goals for them.

Keeping Watch

The fada, I have suggested in this chapter, provides a window into the ethical forms that self-fashioning takes among samari. It is where samari refine what I have called street ethics. Aside from reminding us that the values shared by samari find their most vivid expressions in the back streets and alleyways of Nigérien towns and cities, the concept of street ethics is meant to call attention to the moral ambiguity of certain fada-centered projects, such as bodybuilding, that have tested the boundaries between crime and community in times of insecurity. Through a discussion of the fada's technologies of ethical development ranging from weight work to small disciplines, I have explored how samari cultivate (or try to cultivate) moral discernment and practical wisdom as well as self-esteem. The social benefits of this moral development are most starkly instantiated at night when fadantchés become watchmen. In addition to recognizing fadantchés as decent young men to whom they can entrust their property and their security, grateful residents ply them with tea and sugar as "payment" for services rendered. Since samari stand watch at night while everyone else is sleeping, tea keeps them awake, and alert to any possible threat. Tea and sugar—key ingredients of fada conviviality—thus become the "tools" of the security trade, suggesting the extent to which surveillance is tangled with sociality. At another level, fadas' tactical involvement in crime prevention signals how samari faced with limited social mobility "deploy their very marginality to their own advantage" (Pratten 2008b:70). Rather than signaling idleness, sitting is now part of the "work" samari do to combat crime.

To be sure, by serving as informal night watchmen, samari are not securing a livelihood that will take them beyond the immediate future. Nevertheless, these forms of engagement help us see how, far from nurturing unattainable fantasies, fadas are more accurately described as sites of hopeful striving. By countering the crushing banalization of everyday life, the fada offers a unique arena for fostering self-esteem and restoring dignity. Despite being described by many fadantchés as a passing fad, bodybuilding figured critically in local redefinitions of masculinity at a time when the path to manhood was thwarted by reduced job opportunities. Much like the sports that men pursued in ancient Greece, physical training at the fada points to the role played by the body in the realization of the self. As such, it is part of what Foucault (1988) called the "technologies of the self," methods of modification employed in the pursuit of ethical (trans)formation. This form of ethical cultivation gives direction and purpose to one's life. But that is not all. It may, in some cases, even enhance one's employability.

When rising crime and social unrest led to a heightened concern with security in the 1990s, several actors stepped in to compensate for the gap in state service provision. Patrolling intensified in the streets of the Nigérien capital and elsewhere (Göpfert 2012). While some samari joined the 'yan *banga*, others were hired by private companies as security guards. They proudly became what Nigériens call *porteurs d'uniforme* (uniform wearers), thereby joining the large cohort of upwardly mobile Nigériens who made a living as soldiers, policemen, and national guards. More than simply translating as financial stability, the uniform brings status and prestige to its wearer (Debos and Glasman 2012). In the way it highlights the uniformed individual's role as a defender of the peace, it contributes to the heroization of life. As the trend for private protection took hold, samari hoping to capitalize on the security industry's growing need for fit bodies arduously trained at the fada. The aspirations of impoverished male youths dreaming of prosperous careers in one of the world's most destitute countries are easy to dismiss for being out of step with reality. The recent anthropological focus on hope as an animating force that provides orientations toward possible futures should nevertheless inspire us to take seriously marginalized people's projects of self-fashioning, no matter how improbable they seem (Miyazaki 2005).

Hope, as a form of affect implying an active state of becoming (Bloch 1995), may be grounded in the very physicality of the bodybuilder's body. When academic diplomas and other forms of qualification have lost their value, the muscularity samari deploy in the defense of personal prestige and communal interests (for not everyone, it seems, has set aside the barbells) reminds us that the body serves as a privileged source of capital. From this perspective, pumping iron is more than the simple pastime of idle youth. In the way it harnesses the body to actualize life projects, it can become a means of generating the credentials needed to get a permanent job. After despairing whether he would ever find stable employment, Hassane, Black Warrior's former champion, was hired as a security guard. The young man longed to start a family. The girl he was courting would not seriously entertain the idea of marriage until he had a steady source of income, however. I lost touch with Hassane, but I like to think that having secured a decent livelihood, he was able to break the condition of enforced presentism he was trapped in and that he is now heading his own household.

SIX

Dress and the Time of Youth

Style . . . is the currency of social recognition.

—Brad Weiss, *Street Dreams and Hip Hop Barbershops: Global Fantasy in Urban Tanzania*

Samari often declared to me that they yearned to be valued for who they were rather than for their appearance. Many of them deplored the older generation's disapproving stance toward their fashion choices—particularly the way that Muslim preachers singled out their "American" (i.e., hip-hop style) outfits as concrete instances of their impious conduct. As far as they were concerned, dress was a matter of personal choice, not something that should be dictated by religion, politics, or parental expectations. "Wearing an outfit is about desire. It's a personal thing" is how Moussa, a nineteen-year-old high school student from Dogondoutchi who favored slim jeans and body-hugging T-shirts of Western provenance, put it: "I might want to wear a certain type of dress that isn't going to please everyone. Let's say I enter the mosque with my T-shirt and I pray. I may not be wearing a *jaba* [locally tailored, long-sleeved tunic] but as long as I have a shirt on, my prayer will be accepted. What's unacceptable are T-shirts with designs that attract your neighbor's attention. Instead of concentrating on his prayer, [your neighbor] will focus on the picture on your shirt." Moussa, a member of Kensas City, was well aware that his appearance, popular as it might have been among many of his peers, was likely to generate criticism from pious Muslims, particularly reformist Muslims who made a point of wearing long sleeves and ankle-length pants as an expression of their religious commitment. He had often heard Izala preachers warn samari whose trouser cuffs dragged on the ground that the filth they collected on their clothes invalidated their prayers. Yet he refused to adopt the bare-ankle look and other sartorial conventions prescribed by reformist Muslim leaders simply to blend in. Moussa grew up in a large polygynous family. As the youngest in the family, he had been his parents' favorite child. Their displays of affection had prompted his siblings to lash out at him. He endured a lot of abuse on their part for much of his childhood. Then his father died, and life became even more difficult. He took a small job so he could buy his own clothes. When he was seventeen, one of his brothers invited him to stay in Lomé for the summer holiday. The young man remembered that time as the best of his life. His brother gave him money to buy clothes, and while perusing the city's numerous shops, he developed a keen interest in fashion.

Moussa believed that God did not discriminate between His followers on the basis of their appearance and that He accepted all prayers as long as they were genuine expressions of personal faith. Like many of his peers, he did not view dress as an index of religiosity. Nor did he think that being Muslim should entail restrictions regarding sartorial choices, for as long as one remained a youth. Determined to wear whatever clothes he fancied, he insisted that samari should feel free to experiment with dress without having to incur parental disapproval, or worse, condemnation from Muslim religious authorities. There would be time later on to embrace conformity and adopt a more mature style of dress.

When Izala reformists started making sartorial corrections to Muslim garb in the early 1990s, they urged women to cover their bodies and enjoined men to shed their voluminous *babban riga* (open-sleeved, flowing male gown, known in French as *grand boubou*, that Muslim men throughout West Africa often wear to attend the Friday prayer and other religious and ceremonial events) in favor of the less pricy and ostentatious *jaba*, a long-sleeved tunic worn over matching pants. The modesty of a true Muslim man's attire was a measure of his virtue, they tirelessly proclaimed as they grew beards and replaced their embroidered hats with turbans. While shortened pants (so as not to collect dirt), lengthy beards (trimmed to a fistful), and watches worn on the right wrist (to emulate the Prophet, who wore a ring on the right hand) signaled men's uncompromising commitment to Izala, the *hijabi* (veil) constituted visible proof of women's newfound piety. Over the years growing numbers of Muslims have taken to heart Izala's call for sartorial reforms and embraced, through dress and deportment, what now passes in many Nigérien households for universalistic expressions of Muslim piety. Others, however, have remained deaf to the reformist injunctions to dress modestly. Among the younger generation, in particular, an overwhelming number of male youths are resolutely eschewing Islamic attire to adopt clothing of Western inspiration. Invoking the well-known adage *L'habit ne fait pas le moine* (clothes don't make the man), they confidently affirm the right to dress as they see fit. They are no less Muslim, they maintain, because they don't wear their religion literally "on their sleeves."[1]

Paradoxically, many samari take great care to cultivate their appearance so as to project a certain image of who they are. Even as they bid others, elders in particular, "not to judge a book by its cover" and be more tolerant of youngsters' sartorial choices, they are mindful that clothes communicate a great deal about a wearer's identity and that they can serve as an effective mode of self-promotion, in the absence of stable employment, for instance. "You dress a certain way because that's who you are," explained a recent high school graduate who prided himself for being the fashion plate of the neighborhood thanks to the clothes his paternal aunt, a successful *commerçante*, regularly brought back from Benin: "You see, I put on my *jean poilu* [lit. "hairy jeans"; jeans with frayed trims and stiches] and Sebago shoes when I want to dress up. I like to look stylish." A university student from Dogondoutchi known to the members of his fada as Ronaldo often wore a yellow jersey that publicized his great fondness for the Brazilian national soccer team. "I took the name Ronaldo after my favorite player in my favorite team—Brazil," he told me. "My friends and I watch a lot of soccer. So I wear the team's jersey, it's who I am." By regularly donning Brazil's yellow jersey (of which he owned three identical versions), the young soccer aficionado did more than display his devotion to the *Seleção*, Brazil's national team. He also crafted his own identity as "Ronaldo," thereby ultimately demonstrating the centrality of dress in young Muslim men's practices of self-fashioning.

To sum up so far, on the one hand, samari often deny that their dress can be read as an expression of identity. On the other, many of them—at times, the very same young men who dismiss the indexical dimension of dress—contend that they dress the way they do to express who they are. How do we reconcile these seemingly inconsistent claims about the relation between dress and identity? Are these claims contradictory or do they complement each other? Under what conditions does dress become legible? And how do dress practices figure in the navigation of the life course? In this chapter I address these questions by considering how young men negotiate life stages through their tactical engagement with style, seizing upon emblems of seniority or self-sufficiency and drawing upon the performative elements of age-indexed statuses and relationships.

Clothes constitute part of the "social skin" (T. Turner 1980) that acts as a filter between self and society. The two-sided quality of dress—the fact that it simultaneously touches the body and faces outward toward others—is what enables it to participate in the formation of both individual and collective persona. The fact that clothes are simultaneously worn and viewed creates the potential for considerable ambiguity as to what dress actually achieves. Through its capacity to index both the personal and the social and, in the process, absorb history, condense biography, and fashion identity, dress is a powerful vehicle of experimentation and contestation. How samari harness this capacity to suit their own agenda is what I examine in this chapter.

Recall that the boredom pervading the lives of many young men is known as *zaman kashin wando*, a prolonged period of sitting that causes the bottom of their pants to wear out. This suggests that the anxious wait for jobs rubs away the threads of connection—material and otherwise. Like wealth, its antithesis, poverty, is often signified in sartorial terms. To my question about what it meant to be poor, an elderly man responded, "wearing mismatched flip-flops." The fact that samari translate their sense of ennui in sartorial terms further hints at the role of dress in social experience, including privation. For young men trapped by job scarcity, the pursuit of stylistic trends offers a means of countering the harmful effects of what I have called *désœuvrement*. In some contexts, many samari dress so as to position themselves as part of a global youth culture whose aesthetics they see as having originated in the Global North. In other contexts, they appear to be more future-oriented, adopting the uniform of social maturity in anticipation of their transition into adulthood. As a means of escaping the inertia that "burns" holes in their pants, dress practices instantiate not only spatial but also temporal mobility. Understanding the place of dress in the lives of young men, many of whom are unable to move up the generational ladder in conventional ways, thus entails a consideration of the spaces as well as the temporalities of youth. This chapter is an exploration into how samari navigate the fraught territory between youth and adulthood, claiming and contesting age statuses by relying on the performative quality of dress.

In considering the linkages between youth and globalization, scholars have tended to privilege spatial relations over temporal dimensions in part because their understanding of space is tangled up in ideas of mobility, marginality, global flows, and "scapes." Despite the fact that temporality is an important aspect of globalization, their analytical focus has largely been directed at the ways that young people move across literal and metaphorical spaces through their engagement with media, politics, and consumer culture. Recently, an emerging body of literature has put the accent on time as a critical dimension of youth, suggesting that global flows have to do with the reworking of time as much as the reworking of space. Some scholars have drawn attention to the way in which the temporalities of youth unfold, prefiguring, intersecting with, or, conversely, calling into question future adulthood (Christiansen, Utas, and Vigh 2006; Dalsgård et al. 2014). Others have complicated the neat trajectories of progressivist models of human development and pointed to the ways that age status is often situational and, in some cases, reversible (Meiu 2015). In what follows I consider how young Nigérien men situate themselves in time through their engagement with global fashions. Taking my cues from Jennifer Cole and Deborah Durham (2008), who argue that youths produce new cultural geographies in the way they embody locally fluctuating relations to time, especially the future, I discuss how samari draw on the power of dress to not only reshape relationships across space but also tentatively position themselves in the life cycle. As a platform for sharing ideas and experimenting with trends, the fada offers a supportive space where samari can speak about fashion and try on new styles without fearing opprobrium.

Although the temporalities of youth tacitly point toward the prospect of adulthood, it does not mean that Nigérien youths are necessarily and uniformly eager to experience social maturity and take on the responsibilities that come with it. In fact, many young men use dress to cling to their youth rather than escape it. Understanding how dress serves as a practical medium for enacting aspirations and securing identity thus requires a consideration of how samari's engagement with fashion is implicated in the configuration of youth as both a life stage and a lifestyle marked by particular forms of inclusion and exclusion. In this chapter I explore how young men use dress to cultivate a range of improvisational personas so as to plot concurrent alternative life trajectories, attempting to access adulthood yet also claiming the space of youth.

Dress and Consumption at the Fada

Samari are sharply aware of the centrality of dress in social life. In urban Niger, every social event is an occasion to dress up. New outfits are must-haves for wedding and naming ceremonies, even if it means buying cloth on credit or borrowing money from moneylenders. During religious and national celebrations cash-strapped adult men may be seen wearing a crisp, new *babban riga*, the costly robe traditionally worn by political elites to assert their *girma*, bigness. Up to 2.5 meters wide, the flowing, richly embroidered gown endows its wearer with regal bearing. Through its association with *alhazai* (pilgrims from Mecca), it connotes piety, wealth, and respectability, making it the de rigueur dress on Islamic holidays. Some women are known to go heavily into debt—or pressure husbands (or suitors) for cash—for the sole purpose of engaging in public displays of prosperity and outshining peers at social functions. Young men too occasionally borrow money from kin or earn the necessary cash to purchase costly attire. They share an intense preoccupation with clothes and invest much of their resources in the acquisition of stylish outfits. At the fada, they take photos of each other dressed in fancy outfits and post them on social media. The clothes, the dress performances they enable, and the photographs that are produced can be said to constitute a "prestige economy" (Fuh 2012:501) that is a vibrant, if competitive, dimension of fada life.

In Dogondoutchi and even more in Niamey, samari have access to a wide panoply of dress styles whether they commission outfits from local tailors, buy secondhand imports at the *fripperies* (secondhand stores), or acquire more expensive knockoffs at fancier boutiques. For the large majority of them, keeping up with fashion means buying clothes of foreign provenance. With the emergence of rap in the mid-1990s many of them adopted the baggy pants, oversized T-shirts, neck chains, and baseball caps of their favorite hip-hop artists. The ghetto life peddled by African American rappers in their music videos loomed large in the imagination of samari who saw themselves as a disenfranchised population fighting for visibility. Black hip-hop artists were potent symbols of raw, unapologetic, assertive masculinity. In the way it instantiated samari's membership in the global hip-hop nation, *l'habillement MC* (MC dress; MC stands for *maître de cérémonie*) materialized the dual process of self-making and being made by power relations—including garment import policies—that define the modalities of belonging and recognition.

A decade or so later, *coupé-décalé*, a style of Ivoirian provenance (skin-tight jeans, body-hugging T-shirts, and fancy high-tops) rapidly conquered the local fashion market (see chapter 4). After watching *coupé-décalé* performers on television incite their audiences to enjoy life, samari wanted to look like them. "We dress like Ivoirians," a member of Zorboto, a fada named after a *coupé-décalé* song,[2] told me, "it's what's cool now." If figure-hugging clothes are all the rage among the younger generation, rap shorts (that fall below the knee) nevertheless remain a staple together with the ubiquitous sunglasses and baseball caps associated with black US culture. Recently, Wizkid, a new look named after the hugely popular young

Nigerian pop singer Wizkid and composed of T-shirts and pants with striking, yet somewhat generic, black and white graphics, has surfaced among
samari. Meanwhile the Rasta look (dreadlocks, Rasta caps, and T-shirts or
bandanas featuring the red, gold, and green colors of the Ethiopian flag)
associated with reggae music and Jamaican cool remains well entrenched
among young men who identify with the message of Bob Marley and Ras-
tafarians disseminated by radios and glossy magazines. Popular as well is
the classical look favored by urban dandies: dark pleated trousers, white or
pastel dress shirt, and dress shoes.

Although not all fadas put the accent on fashion, a number of them are
known for their exclusive style through their membership's entanglement
with particular aesthetic subcultures (hip-hop, Rasta, etc.). A few of them
even advertise their members' fondness for clothes through the names
they choose for themselves. Members of Me Kowane Aja Bariki (Everybody
Dresses Up [and shows off]) may not routinely show up at the fada in their
best clothes, but they nevertheless invest a great deal in their appearance
so they can *faire le show*, impress others with their elegance and sartorial
savoir faire at competitive events they put on. During its heyday, La Fada
des Sapeurs brought together young men who liked to dress in designer
suits. Directly modeled after La Sape—a movement initiated by Congolese

youth who acquired expensive, high-end clothes in Paris and became celebrities upon returning to Brazzaville by translating their elegance into signs of wealth and success (Gandoulou 1989)—the fada was known in the early 2000s for the chic clothes worn by its members. Meanwhile the members of Top Star Boys, Gangasta Flow, and other rap-oriented fadas were known for keeping their finger on the pulse of hip-hop fashion. They picked their personal fada names from the vast repertoire of hip-hop personalities, becoming known as Tupac, 50 Cent, Snoop Dog, and so on. Abaje, Glissement Yobi Yobi, and Seka Seka, fadas whose names referenced *coupé-décalé* songs, were made up of fans of *coupé-décalé* aesthetics, while members of Babylone professed a preference for reggae music and what might be called Rasta style (such as Bob Marley T-shirts and crocheted caps). In such settings, style is the self-evident expression of group identity, and clothes can be said to constitute a kind of uniform that affirms fadantchés' sense of belonging by making visible the stylistic norms of the "guild" to which they pledged themselves.

The carefully planned competitions fadas stage to display through dress and other means their cultural mastery of the signs of success afford us a sense of how they envision the good life: a life filled with material wealth and comfort as well as flair and elegance. Young men who through sartorial investment and strategic performance distance themselves from what they define disparagingly as "tradition" are known as *branchés* (plugged in). They are attuned to emerging fads and display this awareness through the way they dress, speak, and carry themselves. *Branchés* samari are "in the know," uniquely embedded within the social trajectories of new things but without appearing to work hard at it. According to a member of Glissement Yobi Yobi known to his friends as Dayle, after the popular Taiwanese motorcycle company Daylong, a *branché* person "eats well, dresses well, attends parties, and then returns home to do nothing." Dayle's definition of being *branché* nicely captures the experience of young men who remain unemployed rather than seek poorly paid, insecure employment that does not reflect their educated status because they view this kind of work as degrading, even stigmatizing. As they wait for an opportunity to come their way, they keep themselves informed about everything and anything. Significantly, the *branché* young man who returns home to "do nothing" may well be perceived by the older generation as lazy and unproductive, but in the eyes of his peers, he embodies the very essence of coolness through a combination of ostentatious consumption, leisure, and style.

The fadas young men such as Dayle belong to often become a primary forum for the cultivation of their *branché* reputation. Recall that the fada

Me Kowane Aja Bariki was created for the purpose of providing young men who enjoyed dressing up with a platform for showing off. *Aja bariki*, which is the Hausa equivalent to the French "faire le show," can be roughly translated as "to bluff" or "to show off." The expression is rooted in the resonant imagery of the *'dan bariki*, a term that, like its French equivalent, *évolué*, was loosely applied to lettered Nigériens who spoke French, dressed like Europeans, and adopted a Europeans lifestyle during the colonial period. While the *'dan bariki* belongs to a privileged class, *aja bariki* is but a performance, a bluff, in which critical resources are spent to create the illusion of wealth.

Like the *bluffeurs* of Abidjan who spend without restraint on costly foreign brand-name clothes, cell phones, and nightlife entertainment to impress their peers, being *branché*, Dayle further suggested, hinges not on financial stability so much as on the "display of potential" (Newell 2012:1). It sometimes consists in conjuring, if only momentarily, the grand lifestyle one would enjoy if one had a steady source of income. As Newell (2012) argued, in the world of *bluffeurs*, looking fashionable is not a sign of success; it is success itself, produced through "the magical efficacy of clothing" (165). In the face of a chronically depressed labor market, the *branché* young man's strategy is to spend all his money on a few expensive items so as to appear to be doing well. Many samari obtain consumer goods, including clothes, hinting that they enjoy a standard of living they cannot afford in reality. In this context, a young man's new Adidas sneakers and fancy watch may suggest that he has resources when, in fact, he is jobless. While operating in seeming defiance of the logic of economic rationality, he displays a stylistic savoir faire enabled by his grasp of the world "out there." It is, in fact, by demonstrating his cultural knowledge and aesthetic sensibilities that he earns his *branché* reputation. As a cell phone repairman vividly put it: "When a young man walks by, people will say: 'Look, he is not a *petit*.' [This is because] they look from top to bottom at what he's wearing. He wears at least 100,000 francs or perhaps even 150,000 francs [worth of clothing]. His shoes cost 50,000 francs. Everything he wears looks expensive even though he has nothing."

In describing the *branché* lifestyle, Dayle also implied it was because they had a home to return to after spending wildly on fashion and entertainment that samari earned reputations as *branchés*. Claiming to be a youth and remaining dependent upon elders are for some young men a more viable option than asserting social maturity. The *branché* tactics thus emerge as a product of marginalization as much as a mode of participation—a way of navigating the structures of possibility and impossibility that have arisen in contexts of religious reforms, political liberalization, and economic restructuring. Put differently, in contexts of joblessness the *branché* is the substitute for the successful man whose wealth is measured in people.

(E)valuating Clothes

Clothes lend themselves to creative manipulations and countless permutations. They are an ideal medium for positioning oneself in the social landscape whether one seeks to blend in or set oneself apart from others. By communicating information about a wearer's identity, clothes constitute a legible screen for the discerning eye. The clothes a saurayi wears may signal that he is a member of the civil service, the world of hip-hop, or the *umma*. They may suggest he is an urbanite or a villager. They may also hint at how prosperous he is, given the extent to which wealth is typically signified through lavish sartorial displays. Aware that people (including potential girlfriends) assess them on the basis of their appearance, many samari rely on the semiotic power of dress to cultivate particular looks.

In the wake of Niger's economic liberalization the expanded availability of garments of different provenance on local markets has pushed the diversification of tastes in multiple directions while also facilitating the emergence of new consumptive practices and stylistic trends among the younger generation. It has contributed to the popularization of global brands, especially among male youth who have learned to evaluate consumer goods according to a global hierarchy of social values. By putting on recognizable brand-name clothes (such as a Fila T-shirt or Adidas shoes) to attend an event or go dancing, a young man draws on the performative potential of dress to enhance his appeal but risks exposing himself to his peers' discriminating gaze. Friends and rivals as well as young women will "read" his outfit to determine his worth and relate to him accordingly. Youths are proficient in the language of fashion. They scrutinize each other's outfits to evaluate how much money was spent. A young man once enumerated for me the value of the clothes his friend wore at a party: the khaki fatigues cost 6,000 francs, his long-sleeved polo shirt could be had for 3,500 francs, and his imitation Gucci glasses sold for 2,500 francs at a local market.

Although people often speak of clothes in terms of their market prices, the value of a particular item is also encoded in other potentially less stable but no less significant properties such as place of origin, pattern of circulation, and age. The crispness of a fabric, its sheen, and the novelty of a style are clues that people read as signs of "pecuniary standing" (Veblen 1994:16). They signal the wearer's financial capacity to purchase clothes frequently enough that his wardrobe retains the aura of newness.[3] While clothes "made in China" often cannot stand much wear, making it hard for owners to maintain a neat appearance, a distinct challenge facing some consumers is that the secondhand clothes they purchased may look washed out from the very beginning, as this fadantché's testimony makes clear: "Jeans, you want to buy them new. Not everyone does, of course. Say you wear new jeans that are still dark and your friend wears secondhand jeans. You can tell from the faded color. So you're going to make fun of him. You're going to tell him: 'Your jeans, a white man wore them!' [*laughter*]" While joking and jesting are important means through which young men relate to one another at the fada, this allusion to the ribbing taking place between samari is a reminder that the empathy they have for one another is often tinted with competitiveness. Dress can be a focus of intense rivalry between young men because, aside from exposing social inequalities, it may determine who wins the attention of a *budurwa* (unmarried girl) for whom the prosperity of a suitor is a critical measure of eligibility.

Clothes are things that matter, "artifacts" (Miller 2005:4) with texture. Through their sensuous materiality, they shape bodies and affect persons, at times, in unexpected ways. Insofar as social relations are realized through our material worlds, the significance of dress emerges out of our sensual engagement with clothes. That is, the value of a garment, its capacity to touch us, does not inhere in the item itself but arises in the context of social interactions and through its embeddedness in circuits of consumption and social reproduction. When they move between persons, clothes "anticipate, acknowledge, constitute, recall, and memorialize relationships" (17). In their folds are condensed the relationships they weave through their circulation as new commodities, secondhand purchases, gifts, and so on. The biographies they accumulate and the valuations they give rise to are inescapably tied to these histories and trajectories. A reputedly "good-for-nothing" young man who stole a bag of rice from his mother before disappearing from sight returned a few days later wearing brand-new sneakers. Having heard his mother complain about the theft, residents of the neighborhood where he lived readily suspected the saurayi of having bought the shoes with money obtained from the sale of the stolen rice. Rather than gathering approval, his sneakers elicited contempt from neighbors. Thus, not only do the meanings of clothes remain open but the evaluations they prompt may point to "unrealized futures" (Keane 2005:193). Insofar as the gifts of cloth, shoes, and jewelry a *budurwa* receives from a suitor can be read by her family as a measure of his suitability as household provider—it is a Muslim husband's duty to clothe and feed his wife—they may instigate wedding preparations, but they do not determine the outcome. Ultimately, the value assigned to a particular item of clothing is neither stable nor rigid, contingent as it is on ever-changing combinations of performances, audiences, and contexts.

The Work of Dressing

Samari often invest a great deal of labor in their sartorial projects. In contexts where many of them are scrambling to get by, they have learned to buy with an eye to maximizing their purchasing power—even if that implies occasionally pinching cash from the parental purse. Acquiring the right item of clothing for the right price takes skill, especially when the item in question is in short supply—as was the case for the heavy neck chains some young men coveted when the rapper look was popular in the late 1990s and early 2000s. Buying new clothes is best because, given how the sheen of new garments is taken as a sign that the wearer is flush with cash, they are likely to attract attention. Some samari obtain clothes from suppliers in Niamey or buy them directly from traders returning from Tripoli or Dubai, thereby eliminating the middleman. Others buy their clothes at full price from local shops. Those who cannot afford new clothes (referred to as *qualité*) purchase secondhand clothes. Secondhand clothes are known as *bosho* (from Boston), *yugu yugu* ("shake the dust off" in Bambara), or *France au revoir* (goodbye France). Local *fripperies* sell a range of *bosho* clothes from ski jackets to jeans and gangsta-style shorts to dress shirts in addition to offering items such as the stuffed teddy bears that have become de rigueur gifts to girlfriends on Valentine's Day.

Originally *bosho* clothes were known as *kayan matatu* (dead people's things). Like hair extensions thought to be dead people's hair, they were largely spurned by local consumers. With the loosening of restrictions on used clothes imports and the continued impact of economic reforms, *bosho* items gained popularity among Nigériens whose purchasing power had dropped: "You can find nice *tissu* (gabardine-type fabric) pants for 750 francs at the *fripperie*, but the same ones will cost you four times as much if you buy *qualité*," a young man pointed out. Replenishing one's wardrobe by visiting *fripperies* often entails carefully sifting through large heaps of clothes to find what one is looking for. In short, it requires dedication. Buyers are motivated by the prospect of finding a deal. There is the added possibility one might find something valuable in the pockets of the item just purchased. A young man explained: "Someone has an accident and dies. The family gets rid of the [deceased's] clothing, it's sent to Africa and sold as *bosho*. If you don't mind wearing a dead person's clothes, it's good value. On top of it, if you're lucky, you'll find money in the pockets." The prospect of finding cash in a *bosho* garment illustrates how the value of clothes, far from residing stably in their visual appearance, emerges as "bundles" (Keane 2005) of qualities, contingently bound up with one another.

Young men are well aware that being well dressed opens doors. Yet their sartorial ambitions are often constrained by their purchasing power. As much as they aim to elicit *daraja riga*, the respectability attached to well-dressed individuals, by dressing smartly, they must also preserve their best clothes for as long as possible. Good clothes may be reserved for special occasions: a wedding, a Muslim holiday, or a visit to a local official. "Sure, I wear a pair of pleated plants with dark leather shoes for *vins d'honneur* [wedding receptions]. But, at the fada, nobody bothers me if I wear an old pair of pants and flip-flops. These are my friends," Boube, the jobless graduate and member of Bienvenue, once noted, pointing to a group of samari huddled under a shelter. The fada was a refuge from constrictive social norms—a place where he need not cover up his poverty under layers of fancy clothes. For everyone else at Bienvenue, everyday dress reflected a compromise between stylishness and practicality. The exception was a young man known as RastaMan who usually showed up at the fada wearing a crocheted cap in the colors of the Ethiopian flag and a T-shirt featuring reggae icon Bob Marley. RastaMan took pride in being the only fadantché whose dress reflected an investment in Rastafarian culture.

"Clothing competence" (K. T. Hansen 2004:174) is not restricted to an ability to select items from a vast array of stuff of differing origin, quality, and value. It is also predicated on proper garment care—knowing how to preserve the immaculate appearance of an item of clothing so as to keep it looking new for as long as possible. The problem is that some fabrics lose their sheen after a few washes, and the soles of sneakers that are cheap knockoffs come unglued or fall apart. A *kabu-kabu* driver from Dogon-doutchi complained to me about the cracked leather of the shoes he had recently bought. Despite regular applications of shoe polish, his socks were beginning to show through the tear. He figured the cobbler could repair the shoe but worried about what the patch-up would look like. Staying sharply dressed, he implied, was a constant struggle.

As they carefully select the clothes they will wear for a special occasion, samari are not averse to borrowing items from each other to enhance their looks. "I borrow a cell phone from a friend at the fada, and on occasion I have borrowed their shirt. But I don't wear other people's shoes. That's how you get fungus," Boube from Bienvenue explained. Renting a motorbike for an evening is another common strategy for impressing the young woman one is courting. Not only do some *budurwa* pay attention to men with "fancy wheels" but they reportedly rank suitors according to the brand they ride. Although none of them ever put it to me that way, young Nigérien men would probably agree with their Zambian counterparts that dressing for self-enhancement is "hard work" (K. T. Hansen 2009:118).

Learning to Inhabit Clothes

More than referring simply to the time and effort invested in the acquisition and care of garments, the work of dressing encompasses what Janet Andrewes (2005) describes as "bodywork." Through their enduring presence on the body, clothes leave their imprint on the body's muscular structure and on the way it moves across, and makes use of, space. Put differently, clothes prompt the body to move in particular ways, producing specific bodily demeanors that ideally should (but occasionally don't) accord with social expectations of how the dressed body should perform. Garments that stay close to the body may limit mobility and how far the body can extend into space, while loose, flowing garments demand that the body "make some use of the fabric that covers it" (33). Take the heavy and cumbersome *babban riga* worn by some Muslim men. As a flat-cut garment, it does not constrict the body as tailored clothes do. Instead it obliges the wearer to move in a deliberately slow and dignified manner, as every gesture is amplified by the voluminous folds of cloth. By insisting on the formative function of clothes, on the way they mold the body and position it in a social field of power, the notion of bodywork calls attention to the performative dimension of dress practices.

The capacity to translate dress into bodily presentation is not instinctive, however. It is the outcome of a learning process through which body and dress are brought together as situated bodily practice through what Joanne Entwistle and Elizabeth Wilson (2001) call "embodied competence." This competence relates to the skills with which people wear clothes so as to produce desirable embodied identities. During this process a whole set of postures, movements, and gestures are progressively sedimented as routine embodied practice so that the knowledge of how dress is to be displayed on the body eventually becomes intuitive.[4]

By signaling the distinction between dress and bodiliness (or body sense), certain modalities of dress draw attention to the process of naturalization entailed in the acquisition of embodied competence. The sight of a woman unaccustomed to wearing high heels tottering awkwardly in her new stilettos helps us appreciate how dress works—and occasionally rubs—on the body. In fact, dressing uncomfortably—in the physical sense (wearing an itchy sweater) or in the social sense (dressing casually at a formal event)—leads to the development of what Umberto Eco (1986) describes as an "epidermic self-awareness" (192). By focusing her experience on the boundaries of her body, uncomfortable or inappropriate clothes impose a distinct demeanor on the wearer: instead of enabling her to be "at home" with her embodied self (Craik 1994:10), they have an alienating effect. This alienation is a reminder that our bodies are a means through which we express ourselves and make our place in the world.

Dressing as a youth is no different from putting on a *babban riga* or walking in high heels. It similarly requires the incorporation of a "clothing habitus" that fuses body and dress so that one's youthfulness exudes from not only the fabric, cut, and style of one's garments but also the manner in which these garments are worn by the body. Consider the visceral shame that seventeen-year-old Salifou, from La Belle Vie des Jeunes Garçons, experienced following an unexpected encounter with his aunt as he was walking down the street in sagging pants. The fashion of baggy (and more recently skintight) pants riding below the hip in seeming defiance of gravity is known locally as *check down*. As any samari will tell you, to carry baggy lowriders properly, the wearer must spread his legs apart so as to maximize the tight fit of the fabric around his upper thighs and prevent the garment from sliding further down. In short, there is an art to wearing lowriders. Having recently acquired the lowriders, Salifou was still perfecting his gait when his paternal aunt, a pious *hajiya* (Muslim woman having accomplished the pilgrimage to Mecca) who kept an eye on the neighborhood's youths, confronted him. Caught off-guard by her caustic comment on his appearance, Salifou straightened up. His pants instantly slid down to his ankles. The mild embarrassment the young man had experienced upon being scrutinized from head to foot by an elder (who disapproved of "Western" fashions) gave way to a burning feeling of humiliation for having been literally caught with his pants down.

In the process, Salifou exposed more than his nudity. He was a greenhorn, the loss of coverage implied, still struggling to master the "visual vernacular" (Ewen 1988:73) of hip-hop style. The low-slung pants did not fit him in the sense that, aside from being oversized in relation to his thin frame, they had not been fully incorporated in the dress performance he wished to produce. Ideally one learns to inhabit one's clothes so that they come to feel like a social skin and enhance one's self-definition. Insofar as the construction of identity through dress requires the deliberate cultivation of "techniques of the body" (Mauss 1973), Salifou's exposure spoke of an incomplete fusion of dress and body. "I forgot," is how the young man explained what caused his pants to slip down, implying that what we could call the *check down* habitus had not been fully stored in his body as a site of social memory. Far from being effortless and intuitive, translating youthful dress into youthful performance—a performance in which body and garments are one—is a learned practice that requires the cultivation of particular sensibilities, skills, and strategies.

Salifou's loss of confidence in the presence of his aunt (and the subsequent mortification he experienced when his dress literally failed him) also signal how self-conscious he already was about not meeting the standards governing the sociomoral context in which he navigated. Embarrassment, Thomas Hansen (2012) notes, has to do with public behavior and "an imputed gaze upon one's conduct as a stereotyped category" (79). Having been conditioned by this external gaze, Salifou was made painfully aware by his aunt's disapproving stare that his dress practices were not only socially inadequate but also morally deficient. The widespread popularity of *check down* notwithstanding, young men remain constrained by local codes of dress and demeanor that dictate how male bodies should be dressed. To appreciate the depth of Salifou's shame, we must recognize the extent to which men, including young men, are affected by moralizing discourses aimed at containing male sexuality, especially when they come from strict Muslim households. In this context, shame (*kumya*) extends beyond the mere notion of embarrassment to encompass a proper sense of modesty.

Only outside the regulatory space of school (where many of them wear uniforms) and away from the parental gaze do samari such as Salifou dare to wear lowriders. The relative privacy the fada affords makes it a safe place for them to engage in sartorial experiments. Fadantchés are quick to catch on to new styles and new trends. In all likelihood, Salifou did not remain long the only member of La Belle Vie des Jeunes Garçons to strut around in lowriders. When samari wear *check down*, it is often with a mix of trepidation and self-conscious glee; they are aware that by bringing attention to their undergarments (which stick out in plain sight) and what lies underneath, lowriders risk offending elders. Paradoxically, it is precisely the sartorial style's subversive potential—the fact that it violates local standards of propriety and modesty—that enhances its appeal in the eyes of many young men.

The maximization of body size I described in chapter 5 is another instantiation of the cultivation of the body-dress habitus. In considering how bodybuilding results in the production of an appropriately masculine look, one cannot separate muscularity from dress, for the two are inter-twined dimensions of the façade of toughness many young men con-structed up until recently as part of their self-realization. By donning tight clothing that accented their muscularity, bodybuilders demonstrated how clothes wear the body as much as the body wears the clothes. Or as Jen-nifer Craik (1994) put it, "clothes are activated by the wearing of them just as bodies are actualized by the clothes they wear" (16). Enhanced by both weight work and dress, young men's bodies acquired a social existence—what Maurice Merleau-Ponty would describe as corporeality—that stabi-lized their vulnerable selfhoods in the absence of opportunities to engage in the kind of labor that traditionally demonstrated male worth. Body-work in such contexts refers to not only the dressed body as a performative practice but also the physical labor (weight lifting, push-ups, and so on) that produces the kind of body that will "wear" skintight garments prop-erly. Whether or not samari describe youth as a period of experimentation, the dress practices they engage in are often experimental. Tentative though these practices may be, their success hinges on the cultivation of bodily techniques that make it possible for young men to inhabit their clothes both comfortably and confidently. What I have called the work of dress-ing thus encompasses a range of tools and technologies that produce a fit between body and dress such that the wearer is fully at home in his social skin.

Fun and the Time of Youth

Household heads are—in theory at least—responsible for providing cloth-ing for their dependents. Typically, male youths receive money from their parents (or an older sibling) to update their wardrobe, especially if they at-tend school and do not draw a regular income. During adolescence, young men are nevertheless expected to demonstrate increasing self-reliance by finding ways to pay for their own clothes, especially if they come from a large family with a limited income. Many of them take odd jobs, earning the cash required to buy items—expensive shoes, a fancy sports jacket—their parents are unable or unwilling to pay for. It is not unheard of for a young man to spend weeks hauling goods for a patron so he can buy the Adidas high-tops or the Sebago dress shoes he covets. In fact, this is a typi-cal way of claiming youthfulness. "I buy lots of clothes for myself. That's what youth do," is how a young man put it, implying that once he married, his purchasing pattern would likely shift.

For samari who cannot rely on kin support, keeping up with fashion is costly. Among other things, not being able to dress fashionably may diminish their romantic prospects. A young man confided to me the torments he once endured when the girl he loved rejected his overtures because he could not compete sartorially with his peers. He was only thirteen when his father's business failed and the family's income plummeted. From that moment on he was forced to pay for his own clothes. An older sister occasionally gave him a little cash, but he could not rivalize sartorially with other youths whose consumer practices were fully subsidized by their parents. He remembered a number of occasions when he had been deeply ashamed of not having the "right" clothes. These memories were particularly embittered by his failure to measure up to a girl's exacting standards of successful masculinity owing to his inadequate wardrobe.

Though many parents sympathize with their sons' struggles and approve of their fada-centered initiatives, others suspect that samari engage in illicit activities to win the affection of young women. A Qur'anic teacher told me the pressure to appear fashionable may lead young men "to do improper things." From his perspective, the fadas amounted to the devil's workshop where temptations abounded; rather than enabling young men to follow the straight path, they were hotbeds of crime and corruption. That is, not only did young men fall in with "bad company" and become corrupted by their association with drug dealers and other "delinquent" types, but they also adopted immodest, foreign fashions, which pious Muslims saw as the expression of moral deviancy.

Recall that fadas are frequently vilified for promoting a culture of hedonism and idleness that stands in direct contradiction with conventional ideals of masculinity based on steady work, a stable income, and the fulfillment of familial obligations. Young men, critics argue, spend their time drinking tea and playing games at the fada while others toil. Just as worrisome, they are fixated on fashion; they talk endlessly about what to wear and how to wear it. They dress in fancy outfits and take countless selfies which they disseminate through social media. Young men's obsessive preoccupation with dress is seen by detractors of the fada system, elders in particular, as yet another reason for discouraging these forms of sociality; far from contributing to the public good, they breed vanity, irresponsibility, and daydreaming. They also impose burdensome sartorial requirements on their members. "Your friends wear nice clothes. So you have to wear nice clothes. You don't want to be made fun of" is how the Qur'anic teacher put it, using a high-pitched, ironic voice to parody a young man describing peer pressure at the fada. In a society where social recognition is contingent on conspicuous expenditure and where dress practice is a "potent form of wealth" (Bastian 2013:15), such criticism may seem out of place. It never-theless signals that some elders perceive young men's sartorial practices as self-indulgent, wasteful, and immoral—a threat to Islamic values.

There is, of course, nothing remarkable about these intergenerational tensions. Elders typically accuse youths of forgetting their traditions. They frequently disparage young men for being heedless, selfish, and dissipated when they can no longer siphon off their juniors' income—as is the case when young men migrate in search of waged labor. Meanwhile samari re-sent the social control elders exert over them through their tight grip on leadership positions. In contexts of protracted economic stagnation and high unemployment rates, these tensions only intensify. Yet within the tangle of powers relations in which they are embedded, youth enjoy cer-tain rights and privileges—notably the right to be provided for. As Durham (2004) reminds us, claiming to be a youth is "a political, or pragmatic, act" (592), positioning individuals so as to maximize their access to resources, material and symbolic. In return youth are expected to demonstrate defer-ence and obedience to the older generation. Given how processes of social reproduction structurally oppose young people to elders, we should not be surprised when young people feel prompted to lash out at the old, chal-lenge established hierarchies, and spend their money as they see fit.

Samari themselves frequently invoke their youth in the defense of their pastimes and pursuits. "We are juniors," they retort in the face of com-plaints that they squander resources on flashy consumer goods or get so absorbed in card games that they don't hear the call to prayer. Samari's actions, these claims imply, are removed from consequentiality and fateful-ness. If mistakes are made, there will be time in the future to repair them. Young men's lack of piety, for instance, is not as consequential as grown men's. Once they marry, they will make up for lost time by praying five times a day. Since a married man's prayer is worth more than a bachelor's, they will earn numerous blessings—enough to gain entry into paradise. By deferring to their youth, samari also suggest they are not ready to make the commitment that social adulthood requires. Such commitment hinges on both a steady income and the moral agency required to serve as a role model for the next generation.

Ideally the immaturity that is assumed to be the hallmark of the young is a temporary stage one eventually outgrows. By rejecting the mantle of adulthood, samari signal that however restrictive juniority may be, it is also a means of asserting certain privileges, such as having fun. In a general sense fun points to "improvised, spontaneous, free-form, changeable, and thus unpredictable expressions and practices" (Bayat 2007:434). It signals a temporary departure from daily obligations and a rejection of social norms. As such it is said to typify the activities of the younger generation, which liberal Western tropes of youth characterize as impulsive, unconventional, and "nonserious." The fact that the baseball caps worn by samari fond of hip-hop were nicknamed *hanna salla* (prevent prayer) by *malamai* hints at the subversiveness of youth fashion and its potential to contest the authority of elders. Baseball caps were un-Islamic, Muslim religious specialists claimed, because the vizor prevented their wearers from touching the ground with their foreheads during worship. To such claims, samari would flippantly respond that they wore their caps backward—like the US rappers they saw on television.

Bayat (2007) has singled out young people as key practitioners of fun; they are thought to be more adventurous, more likely to experiment, and more inclined to embrace change than other segments of society. Bound as it is to practices of self-fashioning and consumerism, dress provides an especially vivid exemplification of this process of experimentation. Moussa, for whom dress was about "desire," once proudly showed me the sandals with the name Obama written on the sides he had just purchased. Though they were overpriced, he had not hesitated: "When I saw them, *j'ai craqué* [I was unable to resist]. I don't know Obama but I love him. We share the same blood." Aside from reminding us that consumerism aims to connect samari to a global order of values they feel otherwise excluded from, Moussa's purchase points to the joyful, impulsive, and adventurous dimension of youthful practices. "I am young, I buy clothes," the young man said, as if to suggest he was a typical saurayi and that his behavior, far from being unique, was emblematic of how youths claim their place in the world.

Whether they play backgammon, attend a hip-hop concert, or simply enjoy a round of water pipe with friends at the fada, samari bracket their activities from the world of adults and its consequences. They often point out that because they don't play for money, their card games are harmless. Firmly located in the "here and now" and seemingly unburdened by a sense of the future, fun emerges as a mode of improvisational practice that situates youth away from the domain of organized power, adulthood, and responsibility. Youngstedt (2013) writes that after being berated by a Muslim teacher for letting a soccer game distract them from religious duties, some young men countered in their defense that soccer was fun. By bracketing soccer (or any other form of engagement) as play, samari claim license to do what they might perhaps condemn in other circumstances. They are aware that *malamai* disapprove of many of their activities and that worship should take priority over soccer or card games. By suggesting that their pastimes are not part of *la vie sérieuse*, young men highlight the provisional, transient, and inconsequential nature of these practices.

More than one young man I spoke with justified his pastimes with the contention that "this is what youth do," implying that when they married, produced children, and became saddled with obligations, they would leave their youthful pursuits behind. Only by flouting the rules during their immature years did they learn to respect them later in life. Not letting *samari* momentarily rebel against tradition has its price, for as a local saying goes, "A youth who does not enjoy his youth will make up for it in old age." A married man once showed up at his *fada* with his eighteen-month-old son riding in front of him on his motorbike. At the sight of the toddler, wearing baggy jeans, a baseball cap, and tiny black high-tops, everyone (including the anthropologist) laughed heartily. "Ah, look at the old man wishing he was young again!" one *saurayi* exclaimed. Despite the recognition the young father enjoyed as a household head, everyone understood that he missed his youth. Dressing his son in the clothes he once wore allowed him to relive—if only vicariously—some of the fun associated with his "old" life and momentarily forget the sartorial strictures of adulthood. Because the rebelliousness of youth is an indispensable prelude to the pursuit of seniority, some parents do not chastise their sons for refusing responsibility. If they consider *samari's* pastimes as part of the normal order of things, they nonetheless worry that their "dissipated" lifestyles might bring about the collapse of their moral world, as reformist Muslims insist will happen if these practices are not promptly abandoned.

Figuring the Future

I once asked a young man if he owned a *babban riga*. He shot me a look of mild astonishment before sheepishly responding that he was a *petit*. He evidently found the question ludicrous—everyone knew that the *babban riga* was the dress of elders, a garment that connoted Islamic piety, wealth, and respectability. Yet he also felt obliged to remind me that he was only a youth, that is, someone whose wardrobe did not include a *babban riga*. Granted, the garment's prohibitive cost (each *riga* calls for several meters of expensive cotton damask and intricate embroidery around the collar) limits its obtainability for those who, like my interlocutor, have yet to find "real work."

There are other reasons the *babban riga* is worn exclusively by elders. The gown is a potent index of power and maturity, unsuitable for young men who have yet to marry and father children. As noted earlier, it hinders exertion, requiring its wearer to move in a slow, deliberate, and dignified manner. The open sleeves of the minimally tailored garment must be continually folded over the shoulders to prevent the outer edges from falling down and gathering impurities. Before taking a seat, the wearer must wrap both sides of the gown over his knees to keep them from spilling on the ground. When stiffly starched and accompanied by a *hula* (embroidered cap), a turban, or both, the *babban riga* endows its wearer with stately bearing and a commanding presence. Like the Herero dress that "intertwines a moral aesthetic of fatness and a sartorial sense of mass" (Durham 1999:392), it requires a certain kind of body to be activated. That body belongs to the mature, well-fed, and financially secure household head who occupies space in a measured, yet expansive and confident way (both in a physical sense and through his command of others). As embodied practice, the *babban riga* is the physical manifestation of respectable, agentive maturity.

The fact that young men typically reject the *babban riga* as unsuitable attire "for now" does not mean they do not look to the future. Indeed the future is very much on their minds, as the popular practice of *s'habiller en responsable* (dressing as a responsible man) suggests. In a general sense to be *responsable* is to enjoy financial security and to be fully implicated in the care of one's dependents. For children and youth, the path to adulthood is secured by making contributions to the household—in cash and kind—rather than acquiring more autonomy as might be expected of their Western counterparts. Growing up implies increasingly taking on responsibility for others. Recall that it is by securing a stable income and becoming a provider to his wife that a saurayi typically crosses the threshold of adulthood. Once married, a young man must not only act like an adult but dress like one. If he used to wear high-tops, baseball caps, and baggy pants, he must give them up to adopt a more conservative style more in keeping with his future role as a father to young children who will look up to him for guidance (though these changes do not happen overnight). One could argue, of course, that young men act as providers long before they are married since they typically shower the *'yammata* they court with gifts. The expenses they incur to attract young women and keep them happy thus foreshadow their future responsibilities as household heads. By dressing as *responsable*, that is, by adopting what a young man described as *un habillement décent* (decent, respectable dress) that typically excludes skintight garments, oversized hip-hop gear, and ripped, fringed, or acid-washed jeans, samari effectively subvert the temporalities of aging and project an image of prosperity that often contradicts the precariousness of their actual circumstances. Whether or not these practices actually enable young men to slip in and out of youth, they must be understood as forms of aspiration, that is, as concrete manifestations of the capacity to project oneself against a temporal horizon and imagine the future.

Those who select the *jeune cadre* (young executive) style from the available sartorial repertoire wear the locally tailored, multipocketed shirt and matching pants worn by civil servants. Key to this particular look is the display of several pens in the breast pocket: the pens signal both one's educational status (literate elite membership) and one's profession (civil servant). "The *jeunes cadres* have jobs" is how a young man pithily answered my question about what made the outfit desirable for samari, who typically enjoyed trendier fashions. Those who adopt the clean yet pricier look of cosmopolitan dandies (pleated pants, leather belt, and a buttoned-down shirt of Western inspiration) to show they have means are said to *s'habiller en boss* (dress as a boss). Meanwhile the related *tonton* (lit., "uncle"; prosperous elder) look insists on square-toed shoes and a perfectly ironed shirt. Through their capacity to materialize the future (however distant it may be) for those who hope for a better life, the various looks of the *responsable* repertoire remind us that young people's endeavors, in particular their dress performances, take place at the intersection of multiple inspirational and aspirational registers. Rather than stick to one performative script, some young men shift from among several available performances (*tonton*, "Muslim," "relaxed," and so on) depending on the context. A young man may adopt "Muslim" attire to celebrate the end of Ramadan, dress *en responsable* to attend a wedding party, and wear MC dress (hip-hop style) to visit his girlfriend. By situating samari within distinct social fields through the mobilization of diverse signs and techniques, these embodied performances are closely implicated in the deployment of multiple, coexisting, yet persistently hazy future horizons. To return to the questions I raised at the beginning of this chapter, they help us understand how samari can dismiss dress for not indexing their "real" selves yet also claim their style of dress reflects who they "truly" are.

Recall that in the eyes of reformist Muslims, young men wearing *tuffa-fin zamani* (modern clothes) of Western inspiration act in disregard of Qur'anic teachings. Earrings, adhesive facial bandages (a craze that took off after young men saw a video of rapper Nelly wearing a Band-Aid to honor a jailed friend), braided hair, and sagging pants were the object of particularly virulent criticism in the first decade of the twenty-first century. Given the oppositional stance many elders have taken toward prevailing youth fashions, young men wishing to earn some measure of respectability take pains not to dress like rappers or *coupeurs-décaleurs*. I once asked a young policeman in training what he wore when he did not wear his uniform. He explained: "When I was younger I dressed as an MC with baggy jeans and chains. I even wore an earring. Now that I am a *gendarme*, a *Monsieur*, I cannot dress like that. When I go out, I wear a three-piece suit. I must look respectable." Dress was an inescapable dimension of the social mobility the young man wanted to project now that he was gainfully employed. When I offered to buy a recently married friend a pair of jeans as a goodbye present, he refused, saying that he wanted his students to respect him. He too was well aware that youthful performances were scripted by a "politics of fun" (Bayat 2007:433) that contradicted the kind of responsible personhood he wished to embody. Although he could barely sustain his wife and baby daughter on his salary as a *contractuel*, he strove to project through dress and deportment an appearance of propriety in keeping with his new status as a mature person. Like the young Zambian men close to finishing secondary school who refuse to wear jeans for fear of being mistaken for street vendors (K. T. Hansen 2010), the policeman and the schoolteacher did not wish to curtail their career aspirations by looking like struggling youths. As these cases suggest, clothes, the techniques they require, and the practices they enable are complexly implicated in the negotiation of youth and maturity.

Dress and the Boundaries of Youth

Youth studies have drawn attention to dress, leisure, and consumption as vital sites of youthful practice, but until recently they rarely questioned the category of youth itself (Cosgrove 1989; Hebdidge 1979). Meanwhile, save for some exceptions (Durham 1999; LeBlanc 2000; T. Turner 1980), the anthropological literature on dress has not critically considered how youth, age, and generational status are negotiated through sartorial means and dress performances. Critical analyses of dress, I have suggested, might be enriched by a consideration of how people navigate the life course through the cultivation of skills such as dress habitus or fashion sense. By the same token examining how dress is implicated in the naturalization or contestation of age and maturity might contribute to youth studies by pointing to the relations of power and dependence in which youth is entangled or the aesthetic economy that young people navigate to access potential futures.

Samari's dress practices unfold within two distinct yet intersecting temporalities. The first is what we might call contemporaneity. Insofar as fashion is a matter of timing, to be fashionable is to have a sense of the "now" of fashion. Youths are often assumed to act as the vanguard of an emerging consumer culture. In the Nigérien context young men's pursuit of fashion aims to establish a contemporaneity with the world "out there" and forge connections so as to establish some sense of belonging. Significantly, these references to time often resonate with local understandings of what development is insofar as they imply (leaving tradition behind and) moving forward. The second temporal dimension that samari's dress practices mobilize, and that I have discussed in this chapter, is futurity. Dress and the work required to pull off a successful embodied performance, I have suggested, provide a window into how samari anticipate, realize, or, alternatively, delay their adult futures. As a platform for experimenting with styles and cultivating fashion sense, the fada is a critical site for exploring the role of dress in the temporalities of youth.

Much of the value of being fashionable, Joanne Finkelstein (1991:143) notes, rests upon successfully eliciting respect, approbation, and envy from others. Nigérien young men who, through dress, articulate desirable social identities would probably concur. As they wait for adulthood and its attendant rights and responsibilities, they often use dress as a personalized mode of conveying who they aspire to be, mapping out desired itineraries from un(der)employed citizens of the world's poorest country to *branchés* consumers. Yet even the local horizons of hope and desire opened up by *coupé-décalé* or hip-hop must enter in conversations with other, more conservative designs for the future. By dressing as *responsable*, young men play with the boundaries of youth, anticipating their future as household heads while also attempting to guarantee that future for themselves. At a time when traditional mechanisms of social reproduction are threatened and consumption is the most visible mode of self-enhancement, exploring how youth, age, and maturity are staged and performed through fashion-centered practices at the fada and elsewhere is critical to our understanding of how young people construct and contest their position in a world that is not of their own making.

SEVEN

Zigzag Politics: Tea, Ballots, and Agency

There is no rest for who pursues the whirlwind.

—Hausa proverb

The events of February 9, 1990, are now enshrined in popular memory as a pivotal moment of the nation's history. On that day students from the University of Niamey held a peaceful demonstration to denounce the Nigérien government's adoption of a structural adjustment package intended to defund secondary and higher education. International donors no longer saw education as a priority of development. Countries such as Niger that depended heavily on loans from the International Monetary Fund and the World Bank were forced to implement drastic cutbacks in education.[1] University students, especially those who relied on government funding for their livelihoods, would be substantially affected by these financial reforms.[2] The march was intended as a protest against the predicted worsening of living conditions and educational training. As the demonstrators crossed the Kennedy Bridge on the River Niger, the armed forces mandated to keep order fired on them, killing three of them and wounding dozens more. The tragic event, which would henceforth be referred to as the Kennedy Bridge massacre, shocked the nation. The state's subsequent failure to investigate the students' deaths, occurring in an increasingly embittered social climate, unleashed a wave of civil unrest that gathered momentum and culminated in a change of government and the establishment of liberal democracy.[3]

The irruption of youth in the political arena is often described as a refusal of the places assigned to them by political power (Diouf 2003). It is because they feel relegated to the margins that the young take to the streets, erecting barricades, burning tires, and destroying property. Regardless of what serves as the catalyst spurring them into action, protesting youths share the view that their prospects are blocked by those in authority and it is only by opposing governing elites that they will secure a future for themselves. By upstaging the older generation or, at the very least, threatening their hold on power, they aim to provoke changes that will translate into improved an economic outlook for their generational cohort. A lanky, bespectacled agronomist from Dogondoutchi recalls his own participation in the countrywide protests that followed the Kennedy Bridge massacre:

> I was in *seconde* [sophomore year of high school] at the time. When we heard that *nos grands frères* [our big brothers] had been killed—it wasn't clear how many victims there were, some people mentioned as many as thirty-two casualties—we were outraged. We took off and destroyed everything in our path. We looted shops, we trashed schools, breaking all the tables in the classrooms. We took all the vegetables from the [communal] gardens. We even entered the police station and put policemen in prison! [*Laughter*] We thought of setting the police station on fire but, in the end, decided not to. In retrospect, I'm ashamed of what we did. All this destruction, it wasn't warranted. But then we felt that since the path was blocked for our older brothers [university students], it would be even worse for us. We were angry. No one could stop us. No one dared oppose us. We went on strike. That is when we started the fadas.

While the murder of three university students at the hands of security forces was the spark that set the Nigérien youth world ablaze, schoolchildren's realization that their own future was imperiled, the agronomist's testimony suggests, was also a critical factor, helping mobilize the "younger" youth against a government widely believed to be indifferent to their generation's plight. For the protest movement did not end there. On February 16, 1990, a week after the fateful event, a massive demonstration was held to commemorate the killings and demand justice for the victims. The fact that the demonstration was attended by all Nigérien civic associations—including the Nigérien Student Union—signaled the extent to which Nigériens of all ages and stripes felt alienated from the political process and ready for change. Thereafter labor and student unions coordinated a series of general strikes that ground the local economy to a halt. Colonel Ali Saïbou, who had succeeded Kountché at the helm of the country, eventually gave in to both internal and external demands that he initiate the democratization process. He agreed to hold a national conference that would lay the foundation for a new political order. By paving the way for multipartism and democracy, the National Sovereign Conference that took place in 1991 marked a turning point in Niger's political history.

The transition to democracy sparked by the ill-fated student protest ushered in an era of public debate that witnessed the emergence of new expressions of citizenship and new spaces of belonging. With the boycotting of classes, students faced overnight with the problem of what to do with their time sat together drinking tea and discussing "politics." These informal discussion groups, which later came to be known as fadas, profoundly reshaped the logics of sociality and civic engagement. As meeting places where young men could openly exchange ideas and "discursively construct" (Gupta 1995:375) the state, they provided a critical alibi for the elaboration and deployment of a whole repertoire of practices through which young men claimed public space—a territory previously off limit—as theirs. Today these early fadas are described by former fadantchés as incubators of political careers. It was there that young men who later became prominent political figures allegedly met one another. It was also there that they started working together to articulate their vision of a democratic society.

Today it is still at the fada that many samari become initiated into the world of politics. Given Niger's large youth population, individuals running for office must cash in on the demographic dividend in order to win elections. Fadas are therefore obligatory campaign stops for any political candidate hoping to marshal youth support in forthcoming elections. Certain fadas turn themselves into a party's de facto headquarters during electoral campaigns. They hang banners on their *rumfa* (thatched hangar) to signal their political affiliation.[4] During their visits to fadas campaigning politicians distribute gifts (tea, radios, T-shirts, and so on) to secure young men's political allegiance. Some young men use their fada as a platform to mobilize support on behalf of a political party, creating visibility for the fada in the process. Political allegiances are shifty and unpredictable, however, and the euphoria generated by a victory of the favored candidate at the polls can quickly give way to widespread discontent if the government is perceived to take unpopular measures. As the face of the opposition party, fadas may put pressure on governing elites, though they also make convenient targets for those who seek to foment violence that can be blamed on political rivals. When President Mahamadou Issoufou came to Zinder (a hot spot of political opposition), to inaugurate the country's first oil refinery in November 2011, his presence sparked violent protests on the part of disenfranchised youths. Manipulated by the local opposition, who remained loyal to his predecessor, Mamadou Tandja, *'yan palais*, who had assembled in *comités de défense*, took to the street to protest the high price of oil. Like many others, they reasoned that gasoline should be affordable for everyone now that Niger was an oil producer. In a competitive climate where political debates often unfold "by proxy" (Schritt 2015:52), the mobilization of youth around the fraught question of oil points to the ways that social grievances are exploited for political ends. It also signals how fadas and *palais*, as reservoirs of human energy, constitute a formidable resource for politicians looking to enhance their visibility or consolidate their base.

Significantly, when politicians travel in search of votes, talk of their platforms and programs is reduced to a minimum. Political programs are not a priority during electoral campaigns (Makama Bawa 2015). Instead, at issue are the concrete projects candidates promise to bring to their constituents (schools, roads, and so on). What this also means is that joining a political party is no longer a matter of political convictions—if it ever was. Young men often get into politics to gain access to the favor of a power holder—and with the expectation of rewards—and not because they share that party's vision of how to improve society. As we shall see, they may well abandon one party for another if their aspirations of social mobility are not fulfilled. Given the exigencies of survival, they have no qualms about switching political allegiances when an opportunity arises.

Craig Jeffrey and Jane Dyson (2013) have suggested that in the Global South, where young people seize opportunities as soon as they appear and shift directions whenever necessary so as to canvas the whole landscape of possible options, "life has become an exercise in 'zigzagging'" (R2). Rather than engage in conventional forms of economic transactions, youths navigate a treacherous landscape of fluctuating opportunities and risks that requires them to be continually on the lookout for new prospects at the same time that it hampers any long-term planning. Jeffrey and Dyson call this new type of entrepreneurship (or hustling) that is emerging in contexts of deep economic uncertainty "zigzag capitalism" (R1). Drawing on their insights, in this chapter I discuss how the political trajectory of Tahibou, a young man who negotiated his way in the treacherous landscape of Nigérien politics, exemplifies what I call "zigzag politics." The rise of zigzag politics in Niger, I suggest, signals how the rules of the game have changed even if at some level they replicate the networks of patronage and clientelism that have long structured the local field of accumulative politics. As a form of both provisional and future-oriented action that generates social benefits, zigzag politics recognizes the contingencies of political identities and the shiftiness of social positions.

Tahibou's tactical navigation of the political landscape and, in particular, his search for a patron point to the ways that, contrary to liberal commonsensical notions that progress lies in the elimination of dependence, relations of obligation are the principal mechanism for achieving full personhood in Niger. Inspired by recent studies (Scherz 2014; Ferguson 2015) that unsettle emancipatory liberal models of agency, I argue that when access to resources are scarce, actively inserting oneself in webs of dependence must be seen as a form of "provisional agency" (Jauregui 2014) rather than an expression of passivity and victimhood.

The Fraught World of Politics

More than one young man I met in Niger told me that they planned to be politicians (*'yan siyasa*) when they grew up so that they could become rich. While most of them imagined themselves as *députés* (members of the National Assembly), a few of them made it clear they had higher ambitions: they wanted to be elected as the country's president.[5] These youths were for the most part students or former students, whose aspirations, fueled by expanded education, urbanization, and exposure to consumerism, found no traction in the current context of economic stagnation, slippery career opportunities, and precarious livelihoods. "I want to live in a large *villa* and drive a Mercedes so I'm going to run for office," Saley, a young Niamey resident who wore ripped jeans, red sneakers, and a modish haircut responded when I asked him how he envisioned his future. In the absence of secure jobs in the formal sector, a career in politics seemed to him to be the surest way he could fulfill his aspirations of upward mobility. "Everyone is into politics," some young men told Aoife McCullough and his colleagues (2016:3), to stress that politics was the way to make money.

Among members of the younger generation Saley's ambitions are far from exceptional. Facing similarly uncertain futures, a number of young men I met have joined political parties and attend the party's meetings with the hope of ingratiating themselves with an influential politician and securing favors, resources, and even jobs. A tall, gangly high school student who went by the name of Sarki ("king" or "chief") told me he had made contact with the youth wing of the Mouvement National pour la Société de Développement (MNSD), the party of former president Tandja, and planned to become more involved during elections because "the only way to earn money is to be in politics." He further explained that "as a member of the government, you can earn some real money running an import-export business. Since you enjoy diplomatic immunity, no one can touch you." Like other young men I spoke with, Sarki saw politics more as a form of entrepreneurship than as public service. He understood that elected leaders abused public power for personal gain and were rarely held accountable for their actions. Indeed, it was precisely because politicians did not have to account for abuses of power (they enjoyed what Sarki called "diplomatic immunity") that they were able to generate such profits from their economic activities. Once in office, Sarki implied, he would evade custom duties to boost his earnings from international trade.

In Niger corruption is generalized and conspicuous. It is public knowledge that prominent politicians accumulate large personal fortunes by siphoning state funds while securing their positions through investments in clientelistic networks. Although ordinary citizens may not be aware of the actual mechanisms through which political elites amass their wealth, they routinely witness the outward signs of prosperity and privilege (lavishly appointed homes, luxurious cars, and so on) among the well heeled. Sarki was well aware that some political leaders used the state as their private commercial syndicate. He also knew that only those who mattered politically benefited from the redistribution of public resources; they were rewarded for their services or, conversely, bought off to prevent them from agitating as the voice of the opposition.

The processes through which weak states in Africa have contributed to the hyper exposure of corruption in high places while also ensuring that high-ranking civil servants can operate with total impunity has been well documented (Blundo and Olivier de Sardan 2006). So widespread and routinized are fraud and profiteering that analysts speak of the "moral economy" (Olivier de Sardan 1999) of corruption. The embeddedness of corruption in "'logics' of negotiation, gift-giving, solidarity, predatory authority, and redistributive accumulation" (Olivier de Sardan 1999:25; Smith 2008) effectively guarantees that a large number of individuals benefit to some extent from corruption. Consequently even as they deplore its existence, ordinary citizens do little to prevent corruption. Corruption, as far as they are concerned, is what others do.

Samari routinely denounce the corrupt practices of political elites who are robbing the country of its riches and doing little to provide job opportunities for youth. Yet, like Sarki, some of them aspire to insert themselves within patrimonial networks—what Jannik Schritt (2015) calls political machines—so that they too may enjoy the spoils of political power.

In the climate of economic uncertainty in which they live, they surmise, only fools would forsake opportunities for enrichment. It might not be far-fetched to say that they see themselves as victims of patrimonial neglect, who just cannot afford to ignore politics. Indeed the imperative to survive dictates that they grab whatever profits they can get their hands on. As Daan Beekers and Bas van Gool (2012:25) note, making ends meet in conditions of neopatrimonialism often calls for, paradoxically, direct participation in, rather than outright rejection of, neopatrimonial politics. The gifts young men receive from politicians, the misappropriation of public resources, the nepotism, and the siphoning off of special funds for private use thus find legitimation in the precarious circumstances in which they find themselves, as they must provide for the dependents they acquired (or will soon acquire) along the way.

Like many of his peers, Sarki saw the MNSD (the party in power at the time of our conversation) as a conduit for *bouffer* (eat in French slang), that is, for accessing public resources for his personal benefit. Joining the party was the first step of the political career Sarki envisioned for himself; once firmly situated within the corridors of power, he would have multiple opportunities to enrich himself. Before he could make money from his political clout, however, he would have to insert himself into networks of patronage and learn to become indispensable to the party's political elders. For young men like Sarki, who must continually adopt new survival strategies in the face of a quasi-inexistent job market, politics was a means of positioning oneself favorably within the field of economic competition so as to extract a maximum of resources. In sum, it was a business, the success of which hinged primarily on securing wealthy patrons.

It is worth noting that young Nigérien men are greatly ambivalent about the state. On the one hand, most of them confess to being often skeptical of the campaign promises uttered by political candidates. Yet, even as they distrust the state, they also come to see it as an indisputable source of potency and value. Mbembe (2001) has described the relations of disdain and complicity between ruler and ruled in Africa as a "politics of conviviality" to stress that these relations cannot be easily reduced to either resistance or subordination. People's ambivalence toward state power, Mbembe argues, manifests itself in simultaneous inclinations to admire and avoid the state. The overindulgences and dirty tricks of oligarchs are savagely criticized, yet paradoxically they are also celebrated and emulated. Julien Kieffer (2006) suggests that rather than focusing on the apparent contradiction between denunciatory discourse and deferential approbation, it is more productive to attend to the role of the political imaginary that valorizes, even glorifies, the shrewdness and resilience that political figures emblematize. Power, Mbembe and Kieffer submit, is revered even when it is seen as corruptive.

When I asked Samir, a twenty-two-year-old artisan, if he was impressed by the fanfare, glitter, and pageantry through which campaigning politicians promoted themselves, he responded tartly: "Obviously! [Politicians] must show they have money and power if they want us to follow them. If they did not have big cars, it would be useless to come and ask us to vote for them. We only listen to people with big cars." As far as Samir was concerned, politicians, reviled as they may be, nevertheless were models of social success in the absence of alternative pathways to prosperous livelihoods. Only political candidates with deep pockets can afford to get elected given the resources they must mobilize to encourage people to cast their votes for them; those who are stingy with their resources tend to have short political careers. As a mayor from the Maradi region put it, "what interests [voters] is what you are going to give them" (McCullough, Harouna, and Oumarou 2016:6). Nana Aïchatou Issaley and Jean-Pierre Olivier de Sardan (2015:263) report that during an electoral campaign in 2004, villagers attending a meeting sponsored by a political party complained when no money was distributed: "It was not good. There was nothing but talk."

Tea and Ballots

In the music video for "Fada Flow," a song by the hip-hop crew Kaidan Gaskia 2, a wealthy middle-aged individual (whom audiences immediately identify as a politician) emerges from a car to bring tea and money to a group of young men sitting by the side of the street. The young men, all members of the same fada, want none of the politician's gifts, however. Before the politician can protest, they throw the money back in his face. Phéno B, Kaidan Gaskia 2's front man, sings: "We don't want it. We don't vote. Leave us in peace. You think of us only when elections are near. We understand that now." The song denounces the manipulative ploy of campaigning politicians who secure votes by showering young men with gifts but do nothing to help them once they have become the country's leaders.

The older man in the video is campaigning for office; he drives from one fada to another with the aim of persuading fadantchés to vote for him by distributing gifts (tea, money, radios, and so on). A familiar sight during political campaigns, he symbolizes the corruption of a system in which votes can be supposedly bought for a few packets of loose tea. The video is more than a critique of the political system, however. Insofar as it is pitched at hip-hop aficionados, it also sounds a warning to the younger generation: young people, Kaidan Gaskia 2 stresses, should not make deals with politicians. Put differently, youth can continue to be part of the problem, by accepting gifts in exchange for votes, or they can become part of the solution, by rejecting bribes and holding elected officials accountable at election time.

Vote buying is a common campaign tool in Niger. In fact, it is one of the most widely practiced strategies of political mobilization. Party systems have experienced high levels of electoral volatility. Once popular, ideologically based political parties are no longer viable. What drives partisan attachments in contexts of poverty and joblessness is the promise of immediate material rewards. Rather than attract voters with ideological or programmatic appeals, political parties attempt to win them over by offering them goods (food, clothes, and so on) or small amounts of cash.[6] This is where the fadas come in. Ordinarily ignored by politicians, fadas become a focus of political attention during political campaigns. In a country where youths above eighteen constitute a significant swath of the total population, mobilizing this demographic (and securing their vote) is key to success. Political candidates thus turn to the fadas, bringing gifts with them. "Political parties have understood that the fadas are an important element of the political terrain. They can't win an election without us" is how the president of a fada put it. According to another young man, "all political parties pay attention to the fadas. To expand their electorate, they must come in contact with [fadas]."

Widespread as the practice of plying fadas with gifts may be, it does not guarantee political loyalty. I was told by some samari that candidates requested that fadantchés turn over unused paper ballots. Such a strategy ensured that their vote-buying strategy paid off: Voters are given a set of ballots, one for each candidate, in an envelope before they vote. Before a recent law made it illegal for them to do so, voters could thus leave the voting booth with their unused ballots. Requesting unused ballots was a way to ascertain through a process of elimination which ballot each voter had slipped into the ballot box. This suggests that if youth distrust politicians, the reverse is also true. Politicians know they are engaged in a fool's bargain, yet they have no choice but to participate in this gift-for-vote economy. Hardly foolproof, the procedure requiring fadantchés (and other voters) to return unused ballots was also labor intensive. According to samari I spoke to, political parties ultimately gave up testing the loyalty of their electorate in such a manner. Harnessing the power of mobile technology, they developed a new strategy: they collect the phone numbers of fadantchés so they can use mobile communication to keep in touch with their constituents and mobilize them on election day.

Fadas also constitute a source of human labor and social capital. They are useful points of entry for gaining access to youths who might not otherwise develop an interest in politics. Although each fada is an independent social unit, politically engaged youths can activate their fada networks to secure additional votes for their party. "We know what young people want, what matters to them," a young member of the Nigérien Party for Democracy and Socialism (PNDS) explained before concluding, "we know how to talk to them." As election campaigns unfold, fadas emerge as veritable extensions of the political apparatus. "You can hang the slogan of the political party you support at the fada," a young man told me. His friend added, "every fada has its party." The reality is a bit more complicated. It is true, of course, that some fadas visibly support specific candidates. Indeed some registered fadas have allegedly received substantial sums of money for mobilizing their social networks in favor of a candidate. Many fadantchés nevertheless insist that their fada does not dictate political allegiance; everyone is free to vote according to his conscience. A young man stated that "during Tazartché ["Continuation," Mamadou Tandja's controversial program for a third presidential term] we were divided at the fada. Some of us were in favor of Tazartché, the others were against it. But we were still friends. We didn't let our political differences divide us." Elsewhere a fadantché insisted that political identity had little to do with fada membership: "Ultimately since we're a democracy, members vote for who they want."

Despite efforts by politicians to capitalize on the fadas' human potential, many fadas are apolitical. They proudly claim to have no party affiliation and refuse gifts from politicians. The list of rules and regulations at certain fadas contains a clause stipulating that members are barred from accepting gifts in exchange for votes. Though samari have absorbed notions of liberal democracy and frequently pepper their conversations with references to human rights, they have grown wary of the gap between the rhetoric of good governance and their own experience of government. Forced to recognize that far from constituting an object of genuine concern on the part of the state, youth is just a tool of political propaganda, they often describe politicians as liars and profiteers whose sole ambition is to get elected. More than one young man told me that as far as they were concerned, politics was a "dirty game" their fada wanted no part of. "Politics doesn't interest me" is how some of them put it.

The disengagement of youth from politics is reflected in the voting record. A large number of samari supposedly don't bother to vote. According to Elisabeth Sherif (2015), the largest party in Niger is the abstentionist party, which currently counts more than half the registered voters. Nigériens' abstentionism suggests how widespread the perception is that politics constitutes a universe of intrigues and deceptions that honest citizens should shun altogether. A young man claimed that "everything [had] gone downhill" since the advent of democracy and that what the country needed was a man of the moral stature of Seyni Kountché, the military leader who, after ousting Hamani in 1974, pursued his vision of a more orderly Niger with single-minded ruthlessness until his death in 1987. Echoing other testimonies I collected over the years,[7] such a pronouncement signals a citizenry's struggle to understand why, contrary to expectations, political democratization unleashed waves of criminality and blurred the boundaries between legality and lawlessness (Comaroff and Comaroff 2006).

"The problem of Niger, it's the politicians!" is how a fadantché explained the swelling tide of corruption, while his friend added for good measure: "The true crooks, they are all in politics." Implied in such statements is the notion that corruption is a problem of scale. While *la débrouille* is a mode of "making do" that finds legitimization through the language of "provision and possibility" (Jauregui 2014:78), the so-called corruption of politicians is excessive, immeasurable, and ultimately wrong because it is driven by greed rather than the exigencies of survival. Young men often complained to me that members of the government were too busy engaging in *magouilles* (dirty deals) to care about ordinary citizens.[8] By abstaining, young men acknowledge their mistrust of the political process while also reaffirming the fundamental difference between the contingent nature of their tactics of economic survival and the rapaciousness of political elites. Note again that the opposition between corruption and the provisional modes of making do known as *débrouillardise*, far from static, tends to shift in tandem with the positionality of observers.

Among reformist Muslim activists who believe Islam should play a much larger role in the political life of the country, there is a widely shared conviction that multiparty politics has brought nothing but lawlessness and immorality. Arguing that secularism has relegated the Qur'an and its teachings to social irrelevance, a number of Muslim reformists insist that using Islam as the source of political values is the only way to guarantee good governance in Niger (Sounaye 2009). While not all young men see the implementation of sharia (Islamic law) as a solution to Niger's economic woes, many of them nevertheless share a distrust of institutional politics, with a few going as far as identifying members of the government as "the principal enemies of Niger."

As shown in the Kaidan Gaskia 2 video, gifts of tea figure prominently among the tactics used by politicians to secure the youth vote. "The one who wants to steal from his country, he brings tea to youth," the rapper Raz Gaz observed. "And what's the purpose of giving out tea? It's just so that youth sit and look at the street!" For the young artist, who aimed to awaken the consciousness of the younger generation through the songs he penned and performed, tea was a poisoned gift: by placating youth, it contributed to further entrench the current leadership. Once elected, politicians forgot their promises to improve education, expand training programs, and create jobs for youths. A group of fadantchés told me they had recently received a visit by leaders of a political party: "They wanted us to vote for them. They know we can mobilize people. But each time it's the same story. Once the elections are over, they forget about us. When we try to contact them, they have changed their phone numbers. When we visit their ministries, they are nowhere to be found. They give instructions not to let us in. We can never meet them." Ironically, critics of the fada system similarly bemoan the use of tea by political elites to pacify the disenfranchised, who "forget their miseries once they are addicted to the stuff." A high school teacher once likened tea to opium. It made young men content so that instead of "rebelling against the system," they just sat, waiting for things to improve. The young man had vowed not to become corrupted by political power: "I systematically refuse the politicians' gifts." He wanted real opportunities for his generation, not a few handouts aimed at mollifying jobless samari while preserving the logic of patronage that maintained a privileged few in power. These reflections about the corruptive effect of tea and the empty promises of politicians are far from unique. Consider this fadantché's statement collected in Niamey by Boyer (2014): "In Niger, youth are caught like animals day and night; when politicians wake up, they ask young people to help them gain power and they promise that once elected, youth will no longer suffer. But once elected, they forget the youth. That's even the case of the current president [Mahamadou Issoufou]. He made promises to youth but nothing. Those who govern have no pity for us. Youth suffer, there's no work, no food" (14, my translation). Although young men are warned by the likes of Phéno B that by accepting gifts of tea and money, they are selling their souls and further contributing to political corruption, many of them have few qualms about accepting donations from local officials. Some see themselves as navigating a wide patrimonial network where trickery and trust, loyalty and resentment jostle for prominence. For others, redistribution is a moral imperative. The handouts they accept enable those with resources to fulfill their duty. This is a reminder, as Ferguson (2006:85) notes, that popular legitimacy in Africa rests on the perception not only of "good government" (that is, of institutions that perform efficiently) but also of a government that is "good," that is, committed to protecting citizens and improving their lives. A young man who built a shelter for his fada with material received from a campaigning politician said he had not bothered to vote. The politician's gift, he argued, was owed to him because "leaders have responsibilities. They must take care of the little ones." I was told a number of times that people expected gifts from campaigning politicians but little else. Indeed some fadantchés are rumored to move from fada to fada when politicians are campaigning just so they can enjoy some of the financial rewards fadas receive from candidates. Claims such as these further support Olivier de Sardan's (1999) thesis that within the moral economy of corruption, predation and redistribution are two sides of the same coin.

In the wake of the demise of the providential state, there is a sense of urgency about mobilizing alternative relations of obligation to create pathways to full personhood. To be sure, with each presidential candidate that rises above the fray with a compelling message of change, there is renewed hope that the newly elected leader will act in the name of "the people" and devote his time in office to improving Nigérien youth's access to education and employment. During his presidential campaign Mahamadou Issoufou promised youth he would take care of them. Young people were hopeful. After being elected, Issoufou launched an ambitious development program with the aim of jumpstarting the economy through large investments in education and other domains, but the much-touted initiative has created few jobs. The current government's failure to expand the employment market has been met with great disappointment from those who believed things would improve with the PNDS's victory at the poll.

Joblessness is the single most urgent issue the younger generation expects the country's leaders to tackle. The measures implemented by succeeding governments to create additional jobs have been derisory. Despite their continued insistence that solving the unemployment "crisis" is the state's responsibility, many young men have stopped counting on the government for support. In the face of the state's failure to provide for ordinary citizens, an alternative is to enter politics and attach oneself to a politician. By securing patronage one accesses resources in the form of cash, employment, educational scholarship, and so on. In Niger strategies of self-fashioning often involve acquiring patrons and weaving networks of dependency, not fulfilling some Western liberal ideal of autonomy and self-reliance. As we shall see, being a dependent is a key step toward social mobility and the fulfillment of youthful ambitions.

The Lizard's Cry Is in Its Heart, or How to Succeed in Politics

Consider the case of Tahibou, a gangly young man who nurtured serious political ambitions. After graduating from secondary school, Tahibou, who grew up in a small town, moved to Niamey to enroll at Abdou Moumouni University and pursue his education. Although he was caught in the social agitation of the late 1990s and early 2000s, when students routinely boycotted classes and took to the streets to protest substandard housing conditions, insufficient food, and shrinking educational opportunities, he eventually received the equivalent of a master's in social work. After returning home, he was hired as a *civicard* to teach physical education in a local high school. Hoping to expand his range of professional expertise and augment his income (even as he applied each year for permanent teaching positions), he initiated a number of business ventures and routinely took additional work assignments. He founded a small NGO aimed at fighting unemployment and poverty among youth. When the World Health Organization took on the challenge of globally eradicating polio, Tahibou signed up to participate in polio vaccination campaigns. He traveled to distant villages armed with an insulated box filled with vials of oral vaccines, earning an additional 5,000 francs a day. He opened a music shop, bought seeds and hired laborers to cultivate a couple of land parcels his father lent him, and even tried his hand at commodity speculation.

In 2002 Tahibou joined the youth wing of the PNDS-Tarayya, led by Mahamadou Issoufou. Within a year he had acquired visibility within the organization in his hometown. Thereafter he campaigned actively for Issoufou, going out of his way to spread the presidential candidate's vision for the future and his plan for addressing the problems facing Nigérien youth. He loudly criticized President Tandja and entrenched political elites, stressing their supposed lack of education and competence.[9] Issoufou had a program that would improve opportunities for youth, he told me at the time. In the 2004 presidential elections Issoufou placed second behind incumbent Mamadou Tandja. In 2011, after campaigning for the fifth time in a presidential election, Issoufou was finally elected president. Tahibou was predictably elated by his champion's victory at the polls. By then he presided over the local youth wing of the PNDS—a strategic but largely honorary position. He had also managed to secure permanent employment as a high school teacher.

Despite the substantial raise his recent promotion entailed—he now earned 148,000 francs per month and received an 18,000 francs travel stipend—he was still struggling financially. Having recently married, he now had a wife to support. While he could dismiss most of his younger siblings' demands for financial assistance, he had to contribute to his aging parents' upkeep. He had given his mother a large sum of money so she could reimburse a loan she had taken for her business, but his father was also counting on him to pay for a new roof on the family's house. Tahibou had previously agreed to finance his wife's last year of training as a teacher. Unfortunately, his recent business ventures were resounding failures. He was forced to close the CD shop he owned after realizing it would never be profitable; the leftover merchandise was sold at a loss. Following a botched attempt to make a profit by buying beans at harvest time and exploiting the price differences opened up by food shortages a few months later, he was scrambling to repay the money he had borrowed at high interest from a local moneylender.[10] His attempts to obtain funds from international donors to breathe new life into his now defunct NGO had been unsuccessful, and the chicken farm he had recently invested money in had yet to generate a profit. Meanwhile, his video camera stopped working, so he could no longer count on the money he once earned by videotaping weddings. He hoped the PNDS victory at the polls would translate into some sort of personal windfall. Recall that presidential elections are coopted in patronage logics; those who run for office promise to provide access to resources in exchange for political support.

In the months following Issoufou's investiture as president, Tahibou waited in vain for a sign that he would be justly rewarded for his loyal services. On January 1, 2013, unwilling to wait any longer, he showed up at the PNDS headquarters and confronted the local party leader, demanding to know what kind of appointment he could expect to receive in recognition of his loyal services. The man's response stunned him: "He told me: 'Who do you think you are? You are nothing, you have nothing, you can't mobilize anyone.' He kept saying I was nothing. He insulted me. I was terribly hurt. I'll never forget this. You know, I worked so hard for them. At that moment I thought, the PNDS is destroyed in [this town]. 'Go to hell, you people of the PNDS!' I said to myself. But out loud I said nothing. I was totally crushed." Dejected and disillusioned, Tahibou returned home vowing to have nothing more to do with the PNDS. In fact, he stayed away from PNDS events and cut all ties with the party's representatives. He was convinced that a jealous competitor had thwarted his ascension in the party. "People are very mean, here. They'd rather see you fail than succeed," he observed before invoking a popular proverb that compares people to cassava, a drought-tolerant, virtually pest-free shrub that doesn't let other plants prosper in its vicinity.

Several months later, Tahibou received a phone call. The regional president of the youth wing of the PNDS told him he had just been given a spot on that year's pilgrimage to Mecca. Far from appeasing him, the phone conversation with the PNDS official left him fuming. He refused the offer: "They thought they could throw me a crumb? I told him I was no longer a member of the PNDS." The offer to go on pilgrimage had been extended as an olive branch (before the quota set for Niger gets filled by ordinary Muslims, the state allots a number of hajj spots for dignitaries), but Tahibou perceived it as an additional insult. For one thing, he was still seething over his humiliating meeting with the local party leader. More important, he was Christian, something his former colleagues had evidently not bothered to remember. The fact that no one appeared to have noticed his absence in the past months was further confirmation that he mattered little in the overall scheme of things.

Though he felt hurt, Tahibou kept his feelings bottled up. He still had enough pride left to hide his distress from the world. "The lizard's cry is in its heart," he concluded after recounting his ordeal to me. By drawing once more from his stock of proverbs, Tahibou gave expression to his feeling of angst while finding in a traditional cultural collective the justification for not speaking out about what had transpired with the PNDS official. Individuals commonly demonstrate their aptitude as public speakers through their mastery of proverbial speech. I suspect Tahibou was trying to impress upon me the loss to the PNDS that his absence represented.

Tahibou had another motivation for licking his wounds in private. He had recently joined Lumana or MODEN-FA, the Mouvement Démocratique Nigérien pour une Fédération Africaine (Nigérien Democratic Movement for an African Federation), headed by Hama Amadou, then president of the National Assembly and Issoufou's main political opponent. "I wasn't getting anywhere with PNDS. So I decided to switch to Lumana" is how he put it. Now that he belonged to an opposition party, Tahibou did not hesitate to openly criticize the president's performance. He spoke of how Zaki ("the lion," one of Issoufou's epithets) had not kept his promises: the lives of Nigériens had not improved since he had been sworn in as president. In fact, Tahibou claimed, things were worse. Along with the rest of the opposition, the young man complained that the president spent too much time abroad and did not sufficiently engage with the country's most pressing domestic problems, such as youth unemployment. The numerous trips Issoufou made to Europe had earned him the sobriquet of Kaina Turey (My Head in Europe)—the expression used by Hausa speakers to refer to the headless frozen chickens of European provenance currently flooding West African markets. The 50,000 jobs Issoufou had promised to create for youths each year as part of his Programme de Renaissance (Revitalization Program) had not materialized. "Now many youths realize he was just bluffing," Tahibou said.

Tahibou's new political affiliation energized him. He spoke confidently of Hama Amadou's chances of winning the 2016 presidential elections (though it was still years away). He was so certain of his own capacity to mobilize the youth vote that he once bragged about being ready to hand Amadou the town. A Lumana victory in 2016 would help him secure a position in the local administration, Tahibou thought. In the meantime he would tap into his networks, mobilize local fadas around key issues, and reach out to youths in the countryside by distributing tea and soap. What crystallized Tahibou's sense that his political future was with Lumana was the visit he made to Hama Amadou's home in April 2013. He was excessively proud of the fact that the "big man" himself had welcomed him to his private residence: "It was such a beautiful house and Hama was so kind to me." Tahibou was particularly touched that Amadou, despite his presumably busy schedule, had chatted with him for almost an hour and graciously posed for photographs. He was convinced that the connection he enjoyed with Hama would translate into substantial rewards once his new patron was elected president: "This was the biggest house I ever saw. A real palace." By providing a measure of how prominent political figures lived, the opulence he had witnessed in Hama's home made him readjust his own political aspirations. He vowed to quit his teaching job and move to Niamey, wife and children in tow, as soon as possible to pursue his political ambitions and enjoy the lifestyle he felt he deserved.

A few months later Tahibou's career took yet another unexpected turn. The young man quietly left Lumana to reintegrate into the PNDS fold. He had been offered a prominent position in the *préfet*'s (district head) administration. Initially, he kept mum about his nomination; he knew from experience that the position could be taken away from him should a more "meritorious" candidate unexpectedly surface. Once the appointment was made official, however, he celebrated with great fanfare. Kin and acquaintances were invited to the investiture ceremony, new clothes for himself, his wife, and the children were ordered at the tailor's, and abundant food was served to the many guests who came to offer congratulations. Tahibou was pleased with the way things had turned out. The appointment came with an official residence. With the new salary he would earn, he anticipated he would soon be able to replace his aging automobile. He had other plans as well, which he hoped to set in motion once he was settled in his new position. In sum, he was now a successful man able to provide for dependents, including his aging parents.

When I asked Tahibou how he could rejoin the PNDS after critiquing so violently the party's leadership and throwing his support behind Amadou, Issoufou's archrival,[11] he told me with a grin that he had never intended to jump ship. Crossing over to Lumana and then crossing back to Tarayya had been a *feinte* (feint) aimed at shaking things up to his personal advantage. "I never really left the PNDS," Tahibou further clarified. "It was a political diversion." Having played his cards well, he was duly rewarded for his dedication to the party. In hindsight it probably made sense for Tahibou to argue that his political moves were premeditated and that he had never intended to leave Issoufou's camp. For one thing, by claiming his heart had remained with the PNDS all along, he could assure colleagues and higherups of his indefectible loyalty.

Zigzag Politics

Though Tahibou claimed his moves had been part of a deliberate maneuver, I want to suggest that far from being calculated, they were an example of what I call zigzag politics, a pattern of political engagements characterized by an improvisational approach, short-term horizons, and frequent goal recalibration. An emerging anthropological literature has documented how young people negotiate uncertain economic contexts by broadening their repertoire of income-earning activities, adapting to changing conditions, and engaging in incessant hustle. Operating within unpredictable time frames and limited horizons, these young entrepreneurs do not make long-term plans. Instead they secure "interstitial livelihoods" (J. Jones 2014:223) through tactics of improvisation, ruse, and pragmatism. Put differently, the income they earn by simultaneously engaging in a wide array of small projects—some licit, others less so—acts as a buffer against destitution, allowing them to get by even when some of these projects do not succeed, as is often the case. Atto Quayson (2014) observes that surviving in the informal economy requires a steady capacity to switch between tasks and job positions such that "the same person may today be a vulcanizer, tomorrow a barber, and the third a porter" (245). Given the uncertain outcomes of these enterprises, their once-and-for-all dimension, and the general instability of the economy, youth are always on the lookout for new opportunities. As forms of "provisional agency" (Jauregui 2014:76), these various techniques and tactics of improvisation cannot be reduced to simple amoral pragmatism that find justification in the logics of survival. Rather they must be seen as a "transformative mode of 'can do' sociality" that may ultimately secure more stable, dignified livelihoods.

Henrik Vigh (2006) describes how in the absence of clearly marked out trajectories, young men in Guinea-Bissau manipulate social and political structures through a combination of wit, craftiness, and flexibility that allows them to confront the fluctuating present while positioning themselves toward alternative but uncertain futures. The process of extricating oneself from restrictive structures and relations—avoiding obstacles that appear on one's path combined with the attempt to map out a course into the future—is what Guineans refer to in Creole as *dubriagem* (Vigh 2006). *Dubriagem* leads to a form of social navigation that entails simultaneously moving across a constantly shifting economic landscape and planning future trajectories in the absence of a clear-cut horizon. In Zimbabwe young men have responded to the lack of jobs and opportunities by engaging in similar tactics of zigzagging, which they call *kukiya-kiya* (J. Jones 2014). Because ordinary rules no longer apply, they must adopt new mindsets and develop new forms of savoir faire to survive. In the world of *kukiya-kiya*, Jeremy Jones (2014) writes, one is constantly pursuing short-term opportunities from a variety of angles while being pulled in new directions by future projects because the ground one operates on is inherently unstable and things can shift at any moment and in unpredictable ways.

The tactics of economic survival young people in Guinea-Bissau, Zimbabwe, and elsewhere have developed and the spatial images they have adopted to describe these tactics are helpful for making sense of Tahibou's political moves. When he first joined the PNDS, Tahibou naively assumed that his political trajectory was all mapped out. The work he did for the party at election time, he thought, would soon give him access to state-centered opportunities. Jean-François Bayart (1979) has shown, however, that youth occupy the bottom of the sociopolitical pyramid built on relations of clientelism and dependency. As social cadets, they do not enjoy the prestige and visibility needed to attract the attention of influential politicians through whom resources (jobs, money, and so on) are channeled. When the rewards he was anticipating did not materialize, Tahibou realized that his upward mobility within the party was far from guaranteed. To succeed he would have to search aggressively for where the action was and find ways to become part of that action.

Like the young Guinean or Zimbabwean men who constantly move about, dodging obstacles while concurrently plotting new paths, Tahibou learned to navigate the local political terrain by appearing to simply go about his business within the PNDS while remaining on the lookout for new opportunities. When the occasion to join Lumana presented itself, he seized it, hoping it might translate into a more immediate and stable political future. The alternative path, in the form of a career with the PNDS, remained partially open, however. He passed on the first opportunity to rejoin Issoufou's party when he was offered the trip to Mecca, judging it inadequate when weighed against the potential risks involved, especially given his Christian identity. When, several months later, PNDS officials approached him again, this time with a far more tempting offer, he jumped at the chance to rejoin his old party and ascend the political ladder.

This kind of zigzagging between PNDS and Lumana required a flexible outlook, a capacity for adaptation, and a gift for improvisation. For no matter which party he represented, Tahibou had to appear loyal, engaged, and trustworthy, and when he gave a speech, his words had to sound true (in the sense that insofar as they participated in the construction of a shared reality, they were recognized by those who were committed to that definition of reality). I have argued that the notion of subterfuge (or *feinte*) invoked by Tahibou in hindsight to rationalize his moves only imperfectly accounts for what actually took place because it implies long-term planning rather than continual improvisation. The fact that he saw himself as a trickster suggests instead that the political game he played resembled the tactics of zigzagging young Guineans and Zimbabweans engage in to guarantee both immediate survival and future profits. In this world of uncertainty, there is no space for the straightforward strategies of yesteryear. Successfully navigating the shifting landscape of Nigérien political affiliations now involves a combination of "moving and simultaneously planning movement" in relation to both the present and a remote, indeterminate future (Vigh 2006:128).

Agency and Dependency

In this chapter I have discussed how a junior politician pursued his ambitions in the absence of clearly marked out trajectories of social mobility. Through the use of what I have called zigzag politics, that is, by engaging

in tactics of improvisational pragmatism, Tahibou negotiated and renegotiated his political affiliation so as to position himself advantageously in
relation to a shifting landscape of opportunity. This tactical mode of remaining on alert even as he appeared to be resting (or retreating) required
flexibility and cunning, not to mention endurance and an ability to wait
for the right moment before making the next move.

Although Tahibou often spoke in a way that suggested he was in control of the situation at all times, he was nevertheless aware that he owed
much of this success to providence. Empowerment is typically defined by
mainstream development agencies as a destination, but Tahibou's story
is a sobering reminder that in the poor's struggles to secure livelihoods,
chance and contingency may play as much a part as deliberate choice,
and the pathways to social mobility are pitted with obstacles (Cornwall
2016). Toward the end of his account, Tahibou shot me a derisive glance
and remarked, "*Nous, les pauvres* [we, the poor], must constantly be on the
move" before invoking the well-known Hausa aphorism "there is no rest
for who pursues the whirlwind" (*babu hutawa ga mai kora guguwa*). By situating himself within a marginal constituency—the poor—Tahibou implied
that despite his improved financial situation, he still saw himself as merely
subsisting. He further suggested that the pragmatics of survival demanded
that he engage in some form of political hustling. Other youths have mentioned to me how they were themselves lured (or at least tempted to cross)
to the "other side" by the prospect of one-time financial rewards: "There
are people who try to make you switch parties. So they will say: 'Come!
Leave the MNSD and join the PNDS and we will give you 5,000 francs or
1,000 francs!' It happens all the time." Entire fadas are known to switch
their political allegiance on the basis of the rewards they are promised by
candidates. Scholars have characterized Nigériens who campaign for a political candidate as "transient activists" (McCullough, Harouna, and Oumarou 2016:3), so fickle is their party loyalty. As one campaigner put it
evocatively, "if they fill our stomach, we shall follow them" (3).

The proverb Tahibou cited implies that to survive one must continually
be on the move. Just like "pursuing the whirlwind," pursuing short-term
opportunities is an arduous process: not only must the pursuer run to catch
a whirlwind, but (since the whirlwind proceeds erratically in one direction
and then the other rather than move in a straight line) he must also continuously adjust his course. Imitating the zigzag pattern of the whirlwind
also means he never knows where he will end up. In this respect, young
men such as Tahibou who engage in political zigzagging are the antithesis
of the *flâneur*, the casual wanderer whom Benjamin (1999) described as an

emblematic figure of nineteenth-century Parisian modernity. Whereas the *flâneur* (who is essentially a man of leisure) idly strolls through the streets of Paris, taking in the sights, smells, and sounds the city has to offer, because he has no fixed objective, poor young men like Tahibou must change directions swiftly and incessantly in order to maximize their encounters with opportunity while simultaneously keeping their options open.

At another level my discussion has been an attempt to grapple with what Ferguson (2015) calls our "discomfort with dependency" through an exploration of the role of relationality in processes of self-making. In liberal progressive thought, making one's way into the world necessarily presupposes the successful elimination of dependence. In Niger, far from hindering social mobility, relations of dependence enable it. Understanding how strategies of self-fashioning hinge on hierarchical dependence has implications for our conceptions of youth and adulthood. As a social category indexing critical relations within and between generations, youth often emerges as a rallying point for debates on agency, authority, and autonomy. Anthropologists, Durham (2008) has noted, have a tendency to assume that youthful agency is adversarial, firmly set against conventions, hegemony, and predictability. Their conceptualizations of adolescence have been so influenced by classic theories of human development and romanticized narratives of coming of age that they rarely entertain the possibility that youthful agency might presuppose an alternative to independence and individualization. This scholarly preoccupation with youthful agency has resulted in a surge of studies on young revolutionaries, fighters, gang members, and other ostensibly heroic actors; the qualities (resilience, ingenuity, and so on) they display are often uncritically assumed to typify youth. Meanwhile, ordinary and presumably less interesting youth are relegated to invisibility—and the agency entailed in seeking out a patron (or pressuring the government for increased student allowances) is ignored altogether.

Take the recent protest movements that resulted in the overthrow of longstanding regimes in Tunisia, Egypt, and elsewhere in Africa and the Middle East. Even though most of these movements did not succeed in their aim to establish democracy and improve livelihoods, the revolutions they spawned have been widely celebrated as instantiations of youthful agency, creativity, and boldness. For some scholars, the fact that young people inspired by the revolutions in North Africa have organized street demonstrations elsewhere to protest economic inequalities, political corruption, and the lack of prospects for youths is further confirmation that this generation is standing up for itself (Honwana 2015). In Niger no such youth-led movement took place in the wake of the Arab Spring. To be sure, young people did try to intervene in the political process. In 2009 many of them mobilized to oppose President Tandja's attempts to run for a third term, but their mobilization did not coalesce into a national movement.[12] After the Constitutional Court declared his bid to extend his power unconstitutional, Tandja dissolved the parliament and started ruling by decree. A referendum gave him the popular support needed to void the existing constitution and introduce a new constitution that would do away with presidential term limits. On February 18, 2010, the army staged a coup, thwarting his plans. A military junta was appointed to run the country until democratic elections could be held. Later that year, the first wave of youth protest unfolded in Tunisia, culminating in the ousting of President Zine El Abidine Ben Ali and the dissolution of the government.

Despite their violent opposition to Tandja's authoritarianism, Nigérien youths failed to oust the man from the political scene. Their political engagement did not attract the attention of analysts. In contrast to young Egyptians who battled the police in Tahrir Square or Internet-savvy Senegalese students who mobilized the nation's youth behind their Y-en-a-marre movement, they were not seen as standing up for themselves. In the aftermath of the Arab Spring, samari I spoke with often deplored the apathy of their generation, attributing it to poverty. "For revolution to happen, we must overcome our food problem," a student, who had actively opposed Tandja together with other members of his fada, told me. The "search for food" (that is, the quest for survival), my interlocutor implied, took time and energy, preventing youth from mobilizing in the defense of the common good.

In response to the romanticization of youth agency, I would argue that young Nigérien men who secure patronage, go on strike to demand better living and studying conditions, or receive radios in exchange for votes are no less agentive than their more noticeable counterparts who push for social change by marching in the streets or taking up arms. Along the same lines, Jessica Winegar (2012) asks what makes the domestic routines of Egyptian housewives who cared for children, cooked for protestors, and stood in line for food in anticipation of shortages less revolutionary than the more visible and arguably more dramatic actions of defiant young men in the streets of Cairo. In considering the deployment of youthful agency in Niger, Egypt, or elsewhere, we should not lose sight of the ordinary facets of young people's lives. Nor should we ignore the paths to social mobility these young people take because they do not correspond to modern liberal strategies of self-making. Tahibou's story is a reminder that in Niger personhood, rather than existing outside of relations of dependence, is constituted by them. Far from signaling an inability to grow in his own power, Tahibou's persistent efforts to secure political patronage must be seen as an agentive mode of engagement with the world. Though he complained about having to "pursue the whirlwind," Tahibou was proud of the ingenuity he deployed through his engagement in zigzag politics. We could say that his activation of political networks into sources of social capital exemplifies the virtuous nature of provisional agency. It is also a reminder that social reproduction is tied to politics, as the political significance of "wealth in people" demonstrates. By securing political connections—on the basis that powerful men look after their followers—Tahibou was able to secure a decent income and look after his family. And by demonstrating his capacity to act as a good provider, he proved he was good at being a man.

Conclusion

Waiting, for many young men confronted with a dearth of formal-sector employment, is something of a pervasive condition in urban Niger. They have created spaces specifically for waiting, and they repair to those spaces daily in their efforts to cope with the boredom, hardship, and anxiety of being out of work. In this book I have mapped out the territory of waiting that samari navigate in their quest for sustainable livelihoods. What emerges from my exploration of the fada is that while waiting may be a suspension of time, it is rarely a suspension of activity. Life at the fada translates into routinized activities through which samari become absorbed into the "thick" of time. Waiting has long meant engaging in informal discussions around a pot of tea or attending agenda-driven meetings. For a while it also took the form of weight work. Today it often translates into keeping watch at night while other people sleep. In short, waiting is never just one "thing." Moreover it is often tactical. Because opportunities (in the forms of jobs, scholarships, and so on) disappear as suddenly as they appear, samari must be ready to snatch them as they wait for them. During a university strike, a student told me he was back home, waiting for the strike to end. In reality he was working for a former patron—because "one just can't stay idle." He took the job knowing he would quit as soon as the university reopened its doors. Far from being "wasted time," his wait was a mode of engagement that allowed him to remain attuned to the strike. No matter what expression it takes and what temporalization it generates, waiting is often work. In this respect, the fada as a place of and for waiting is a workshop—a place of training and experimentation where skills are honed, selfhoods are crafted, and the art of waiting is cultivated in a lighthearted atmosphere that (except for the occasional bickering or fistfight) promotes mutual respect, civility, and hope.

Sitting and Moving

According to Mbembe, the idea of Africa casts doubt on the manner in which social theory has thus far reflected on the problem of the collapse of worlds. Social theory, Mbembe (2001) claims, "has failed also to account for *time as lived*, not synchronically or diachronically, but in its multiplicity and simultaneities, its presence and absences, beyond the lazy categories of permanence and change beloved of so many historians" (8, emphasis in original).

In this book I have tried to answer Mbembe's call to account for the living of time by attending to the ways in which time is lived at the fada "in its multiplicity and simultaneities, its presence and absences." For those who have no jobs (or only intermittent jobs), time is often described as an excessive, alienating presence—a burden—that overwhelms attempts to carve out spaces of belonging. It can also be felt as an elongated stretch of experience or an emptiness that one seeks to fill. Time is never experienced as pure burden or boredom, however. Life is structured not by rhythm (or tempo, period, and duration) operating singly but rather by a complex meshing of many concurrent—and frequently conflicting—temporalities that actors must continually manage as best as they can. Moreover, waiting happens in time but it also creates time in the sense that it produces its own temporality. In this regard, the concept of waithood on which much of the scholarship on youth depends is inadequate to account for the multiple forms, pulses, and patterns that samari's anticipatory temporalities take in urban Niger, for by reducing the wait for jobs and prosperous futures to a specific temporality sandwiched between the safety of childhood and the certainties of adulthood—a kind of life stage—it flattens out the complexity of time as lived. As lived experience, waiting and the multiple, intersecting temporalities associated with it require a more nuanced understanding of the heterogeneous temporal trajectories and imaginings that constitute the experience of young Nigérien men confronted with uncertain futures. Through an exploration of the grammar of quotidian practices at the fada, I have sought to grasp not only the experiential fabric of male sociality in urban Niger but also the texture of temporalities that samari craft through daily regimens and predictable routines, through bold visual statements and tentative sartorial performances, through weight work and teatime, and through the myriad ways in which they turn their lives into what Foucault (1985) described as an "oeuvre" that holds distinct aesthetic values and meets distinct stylistic criteria. Fada with names such as Les Américain or Territoire des Milliardaires thus speak to the kind of futures to which samari aspire. By relying on the magic of words to bring hoped-for worlds into being, young men are effectively "naming the future" (Meinert and Schneidermann 2014:170). Let me stress once more that ideals should not be written off merely because they are beyond reach, for they stir imagination and make striving possible. Waiting as living at the fada or elsewhere requires that we take seriously the kind of work that waiting does, if only as a work of imagination, for without imagination, there can be no viable future.

Fadas are derided by many elders as places where samari just sit idly. Samari too occasionally deploy similarly unflattering stereotypes that capture the crushing weight of boredom and the sense of helplessness it produces. Paradoxically they are also "busily" engaged in diverse projects that escape the narrow time frames of stasis and boredom. Put differently, the notion that fadas are spaces of inactivity and passivity is frequently contradicted by the ways many samari turn their fadas into forums of creativity, resourcefulness, and disciplined work. It is this apparent contradiction that I have addressed in this book through an exploration of the temporalities of masculine sociality and the modalities of waiting as social action. Stasis and mobility, waiting and working, engagement and deferment, I have argued, must be understood as co-constitutive rather than polar opposites. Consider the experience of sitting. In the way it bears witness to the rise of youth unemployment, sitting at the fada is often equated with idleness and indolence. It seems incompatible with zigzagging, a mode of social navigation demanding constant movement and good timing. But as I suggested in my discussion of night watches at the fada, sitting must also be seen as a tactical mode of being in the world at the intersection of agency, constraint, and impotence. Samari who keep watch while others sleep—and turn sitting into a form of labor—can do so only because they have nowhere to go in the morning. It is by deploying their social immobility as an asset—a mode of alertness to nocturnal threats—that they insert themselves into the shifting landscape of crime prevention. Sitting, rather than betraying structural liminality, becomes part of an informal apparatus of nighttime surveillance and a tactical expression of civic engagement.

These tactical "moves"—samari's surreptitious invasion of public space, the night watching they engage in, and so on—exemplify the "makeshift, adaptive pulse of the city" (Simone and Pieterse 2017:38) as well as the younger generation's willingness to experiment. But let us not forget the continuities with older forms of sociality. To be sure, many samari engage in practices—sartorial and musical experiments, for instance—that can be read as instances of generational affirmation, even rebellion. Their fadas emerge as a platform for showcasing consumerist excess in direct contravention with the models of competent adulthood that hinge on men fulfilling their role as providers. Nevertheless, the aspirations that animate masculinity at the fada (marrying, fathering children, and so on) are decidedly ordinary. Much of what happens there is part of samari's sustained attempts to comply with (rather than defy) social expectations of mobility—even when they "play" at being youth. Put differently, the fada is a critical tool of social reproduction, helping samari both predict the future and prepare for it (though not everyone succeeds at balancing the burden of daily survival with loftier ideals). It offers a valuable sense of stability—something like permanence in the face of the collapse of old certainties.

Dwelling

Rather than paint disenfranchised young men as victims, unable to fulfill expectations of social becoming, or hoodlums who target more vulnerable others, I have examined them as striving subjects who imagine, try stuff, and mess up, yet also exercise practical judgment. I have discussed the values they share, the practices they engage in, and the narratives they deploy as they tentatively assemble pieces of the good life they aspire to. Contradicting reports of their involvement in violence, crime, and thuggery, most samari strive to project a positive vision of the fada, as an organization made of principled individuals that deserves the respect of others. To this end, adolescent fadantchés put the accent on civility through the cultivation of discipline and decorum. Words, actions, and bodies are checked against the stylistic norms that fadantchés have vowed to uphold, reminding us that the good life, more than merely about economic survival or success, is about what Aristotle called flourishing. That is, it depends on the cultivation of a form of ethical discernment that, beyond the enactment of rules and regulations, enables young men to shape themselves as good persons—virtuous citizens who enjoy social recognition. Insofar as the good life is a "life worth living" (Mattingly 2014:9), the fada, as a moral laboratory, constitutes the space of apprenticeship where members learn the art of living.

Living in Niger is living with people. Above all, the fada is a place of friendship and conviviality. It is an infrastructure of solidarity based on the principle that precarity must be confronted collectively. By joining forces, its members can generate the conditions for opportunities leading to social mobility (through rotating credit associations, for instance). Nowhere is the fada's role as a ground for collective action better illustrated than in L'Union Fait la Force (Unity Makes Strength), the name some samari chose for their fada. Now a name typically emblematizes the "spirit" of a fada—its values and its vision of the good life. By naming (and emplacing) the fada, samari not only make themselves visible in a social universe where juniors have no voice, but they also carve out a space of belonging, attuned to itself and to its occupants. As we have seen, fadantchés pick mostly aspirational names for their fadas. Yet even occasionally denigrating stereotypes, such as L'Internationale des Chômeurs—deployed by insiders at their own collective expense—constitute idioms of identity formation. The name Manger Dormir Recommencer (or MDR), self-deprecating as it may be, similarly signals a kind of "cultural intimacy" (Herzfeld 2005). As a source of shame, disenfranchisement and dispossession elicit among the MDR membership a "rueful self-recognition" that conjures common ground or what Herzfeld called "assurance of shared sociality" (3). Whether they provide a forum for collective action, a place for sitting and commiserating about life's hardships, or simply a spot to enjoy some tea in the company of friends, fadas are spaces for, and modes of, dwelling—in Heidegger's sense of both building and care—where rather than merely surviving, one can live a dignified life, a life worth living.

ACKNOWLEDGMENTS

The debts incurred in the making of this book are greater than I can acknowledge in print. To everyone in Niger who offered help and support, I offer my gratitude and respect. Research there would not have been possible without the generous assistance of Salifou Hamidou, Adizatou Akaki, and Mahamadou Noma. I also thank the Moïse family, especially Fati Moïse, Sue Rosenfeld, and Henriette and Gabriel Mayaki, as well as Ibrahim Garba and Ali Mahamane Dade. I am particularly grateful to the numerous young men who welcomed me to their fadas and regaled me with stories, philosophical arguments, jokes, songs, and, of course, tea.

A number of scholars have offered critical advice on selected chapters. I thank in particular Hussein Agrama, Misty Bastian, David Berliner, Beth Brummel, Jennifer Cole, Jean Comaroff, John Comaroff, Line Dalsgård, Filip De Boeck, Bernard Dubbeld, Deborah Durham, James Ferguson, Mayanthi Fernando, Karen Hansen, Anne Haour, Marloes Janson, Jeremy Jones, Robert Launay, Lotte Meinert, Nancy Munn, Sasha Newell, René Otayek, Deborah Posel, Michael Ralph, Benedetta Rossi, Benjamin Soares, Abdoulaye Sounaye, Kabir Tambar, Sharika Thiranagama, Ilana Van Wyk, Brad Weiss, and Luise White. Allison Truitt offered key comments on a draft of chapter 2. At the University of Chicago Press, Priya Nelson has been wonderfully supportive. Since our collaboration on a previous editorial project, she has taught me some invaluable lessons about how to make the books we write more readable. Special thanks to Dylan Montanari and Kristen Raddatz for their expert assistance in the final preparation of the manuscript. Susan Tarcov copyedited the manuscript with great care and improved it immeasurably. I am very grateful to the two anonymous reviewers for their extraordinarily meticulous and incisive comments. The book is (I hope) much improved by their suggestions.

Funding for research upon which this book is based was provided by the Newcomb College Foundation, the Research Enhancement Fund, and the Glick Fellow Grant, all at Tulane University, and by the Netherlands Ministry of Foreign Affairs. Much of the writing was done over the course of research leaves funded by the John Simon Guggenheim Memorial Fellowship, Tulane University, and the Award to Louisiana Artists and Scholars. Thanks to the Aarhus Institute of Advanced Studies for its support in the last stages of this book's production. I am grateful for the support I received from these institutions. I benefited from invitations to present some of this work at the Catholic University of Leuven, the Free University of Brussels, the University of Chicago, the University of Florida, Michigan State University, Harvard University, Stanford University, Oxford University, the University of Bordeaux, the Centre for African Studies in Leiden, the University of Liverpool, Northwestern University, the University of Birmingham, the University of Cape Town, and the University of Aarhus. I also presented parts of this book at the School for Advanced Research in Santa Fe, the conference "L'Afrique des laïcités" in Bamako, and the colloquium "African Ritual and Religion" at Satterthwaite, UK, as well as the 2008 Symposium on Contemporary Perspectives in Anthropology organized by Brad Weiss. I thank these various audiences for the invigorating feedback they provided.

Finally, my family. As I write these words, Julia, our youngest daughter, is graduating from college. And Margaux and Eleonore have embarked on exciting careers. It's been thrilling to see all three of them chart distinctive paths that suit their personalities, passions, and aspirations. Thank you (really) to all three of you for reminding me, in your own ways, that books are not the world—they are simply about it. And to Bill. Thank you for your unwavering support of this project, especially for putting up with my crazy work hours. And for assisting me in small but critical ways when I was searching for the right word and when I was trying to organize my thoughts or get out of a conceptual rut I'd dug myself into. But mostly, thank you for making a life with me.

Some of the material in chapter 1 appeared previously in "Teatime: Boredom and the Temporalities of Young Men in Niger," *Africa* 83, no. 3 (2013): 470–91. Portions of chapter 6 appeared in "The Mouthpiece of an Entire Generation: Hip-Hop, Truth, and Islam in Niger," in *Muslim Youth and the 9/11 Generation*, edited by Adeline Masquelier and Benjamin F. Soares (Santa Fe, NM: School of Advanced Research Press, 2016), 213–38; copyright 2016 by the School for Advanced Research, Santa Fe, New Mexico; all rights reserved; reprinted with permission. Permission to publish this material here is gratefully acknowledged.

GLOSSARY

babban riga: flowing, open-sleeved robe worn by mature men; pl. *manyan riguna*

baccalauréat (or bac): examination capping high school education (French)

bosho: secondhand clothing, term derived from "Boston"

branché: connected, in the know (French)

budurwa: literally "virgin," unmarried girl of marriageable age

check down: style of pants, lowriders (English)

cikakke mutum: full person, adult

civicard: volunteer of civic service (French)

contractuel: worker with limited contract job (French)

coupé-décalé: Ivoirian musical culture (Nouchi)

'dan bariki: city slicker, *évolué*

discothèque: CD shop (French)

fada: chief's council, young men's discussion group, tea circle; pl. *fadodi*

fadantché: member of a fada

farotage: act of showing off (Nouchi)

faroter: to show off (Nouchi)

fripperie: secondhand clothing shop or stall (French)

gaskiya: truth, honesty, sincerity

ghetto: unmarried young men's sleeping quarters in the familial compound, cheap rooms rented by migrants (English)

intellectuel: learned person, university graduate (French)

jeune diplômé: young graduate (French)

kabu-kabu: motorcycle taxi

malami: teacher, scholar, Muslim religious specialist; pl. *malamai*

palais: equivalent of fada, street gang (French)

qualité: new clothing (French)

responsable: responsible, dress style of successful male urbanites (French)

saurayi: adolescent, young unmarried man; pl. *samari*

shai: tea

shaiman: tea maker (combination of Hausa and English)

shinkafa: rice

taxeur or taxman: tax collector at the fada (French/English)

tchatcheur: sweet-talker (French slang)

teaman: tea maker (English)

titulaire: permanent employee (French)

tontine: rotating credit association (French)

wake: beans, black-eyed peas

'yan banga: vigilantes, neighborhood militia, street gang

'yarinya: girl, young unmarried woman; pl. *'yammata*

yaro: boy, young man, unmarried man; pl. *yara*

zaman banza: sitting idly

zaman kashin wando: sitting until your pants are worn, condition of the unemployed

NOTES

1. Implemented in 1986, the first structural adjustment program led to the liberalization of the agricultural sector, the privatization of the public sector, the informalization of the economy, and the shrinking of state resources. The second structural adjustment program was initiated in 1996.

2. Approximately 80 percent of schoolteachers in Niger are currently temporary hires.

3. Displacement here implies not physical dislocation so much as dispossession. It refers to a range of transformations affecting people's ability to earn a livelihood and find their proper sense of place in the world (J. Jones 2014:20).

4. Although the plural of *fada* in Hausa is *fadodi*, in the media it is often frenchified as *fadas*. To stress the cosmopolitan aspirations of these conversation groups, many of which are composed of French-educated young men, I have opted to use the French plural form.

5. All the testimonies in this book are translated from French or Hausa.

6. The Human Development Index is a measure of health, education, and living standards.

7. Young Nigérien women too are victimized by unemployment. In this book, however, I focus my attention on the predicament of male youth.

8. The older generation of civil servants recalls the strict surveillance they were under at all times. Kountché himself allegedly made surprise visits to government offices, catching people unaware. By bursting in on high-ranking as well as lowly administrators, the late president, who is remembered as a man of impeccable rectitude, guaranteed discipline and productivity in the administration.

9. Lund (2001:859) attributes the rise in petty crime to the fact that following the Kennedy Bridge massacre during which three students were fatally shot in February 1990, the police and military were discredited and kept a low profile.

10. Following the 1999 presidential election of Olusegun Obasanjo, demilitarization, the lack of effective police security forces, and a sharp increase in armed robberies further exacerbated political conflicts, fueling the formation of what the Nigerian media referred to as "vigilantes" (Sen and Pratten 2008). Among such formations, the predominantly Igbo Bakassi Boys in eastern Nigeria, the militant wing of the Yoruba Odua'a People's Congress (OPC) in the south and southwest (Akinyele 2001),

and the *'yan daba* in northern Nigeria turned geographical affiliation, ethnicity, and religion into fetishized cultural codes people identified with (C. Casey 2008).

11. Paradoxically, some people remember this period fondly: "During the time of Tchanga, there were no thefts." Troubling facets of the *'yan banga*'s modus operandi are swept under the rug to help maintain the validity of this brand of justice.

12. Ousseina Alidou (2005) states that "Hausaness," which reportedly includes half of the Nigérien population, has always been a multiple and shifting identity. It is a socially constructed category that encompasses groups of different ethnic and geographic origin. Barbara Cooper (2010) notes that Hausaness cannot be reduced to a fixed set of practices but must be seen as an ongoing process of negotiation, reform, elimination, and mimicry.

13. A few fadas in Niamey bring together youths of similar regional or ethnic background, especially among the university student population.

CHAPTER ONE

1. All amounts are in West African CFA francs.

2. The *samarya* was modeled on the traditional Hausa youth association. Traditionally this association brought together young men and women into local organizations whose purpose, while primarily social, included village "public works." The *samarya* differed from the Hausa association in that it was directed by adults and given its marching orders by external authorities rather than local youth leaders. Participation in the *samarya* came to be seen as a test of loyalty to the regime (Charlick 1991). The *samarya*, which had a presence in all villages, engaged young people in theatrical festivals, athletic events, cultural competitions, and collective village works, among other things.

3. Mali Yaro is the leading musical artist in the country. Boureima Disco is another successful musician. Both are known for their distinctly Nigérien brand of popular music.

4. The name of certain fadas hint at the role of radio in the lives of fadantchés. A group of friends thus named their fada Top Étoile (Top Star) after a show aimed at youth audiences on Radio Dallol.

5. In 1950s Kinshasa young unemployed Congolese men known as the Bills emulated the look and lifestyle of American cowboys. A key trope of adventurous masculinity, the made-in-Hollywood cowboy was a suitable model for male youth in search of manhood (Gondola 2009).

6. In Ougadougou, unemployed Burkinabe youth "speak so that they don't forget to exist" (Mazzocchetti 2009:54). At the fada, it is similarly through their engagement in discussions that samari assert their existence in the absence of alternative processes of valorization.

7. The solidarity uniting fadantchés occasionally guide their choice of fada names: Oneness; Les Amis Soudés (United Friends); Unité (Unity); Jeunes Amis Solidaires (Young Friends Who Stick Together); Hangar des Amis (Friends' Shelter); Fraternité (Fraternity).

8. Benjamin's (1999) description of the boredom of modern times is eerily similar to the vision entertained by MDR. He notes, for instance, that events that punctuate time, or what he calls "thresholds," have dissolved to the extent that falling asleep and waking up have become "the only such experiences that remains to us" (O2a,1).

9. According to Anderson (2004), boredom "settles in precisely when an impercep-

tible extra, the 'more' does not occur under a condition of reiterative 'bare' repetition" (745).

10. The centrality of tea in Tuareg life explains why the heavily sweetened tea is referred to as Tuareg tea.

11. In Mali young men who routinely enjoy the energy boost provided by green tea call the drink "African whisky" (Marchand 2009).

12. Because of how tea sustains social ties, it is compared to kola nuts, a stimulant and the traditional offering to guests.

13. Although tinged with anxiety, samari's hope is clearly rooted in their faith in development and a sense of entitlement inherited from the brief period of prosperity Niger witnessed in the 1970s and early 1980s.

CHAPTER TWO

1. Tazartché (Continuation) refers to Mamadou Tandja's program for a third presidential term. Although third presidential terms are unconstitutional, Tandja planned to continue running the country (see chapter 7). AFC stands for Alliance des Forces du Changement—the presidential party of the Third Republic established in 1992.

2. Kilombo is a Brazilian town featured in two Brazilian telenovelas, *Isaura* and *Mademoiselle*, that were popular in Niger.

3. In the scholarly literature there is a predominant focus on large public spaces that can hold public demonstrations. In this regard the occupation of public spaces such as Tahrir Square in Cairo or Zucotti Park in New York sent a powerful political message to local authorities. The kind of occupation I discuss here is more modest but no less political.

4. Simone (2004) writes that African cities are made of rootless and provisional meeting points between residents—flexible nodes that function despite the fact that no blueprints exist to provide guidance for how the city should be used. These intersections rest on people's capacity to combine objects, spaces, persons, and practices, thereby generating infrastructure. Achille Mbembe and Sarah Nuttall (2008:7) have similarly noted that the main unit of infrastructure is the human body.

5. The "rights to the city" literature has been criticized for emerging out of a humanist philosophy about rights rather than being grounded in real spaces in the city. Annette Miae Kim (2015) thus argues that it "misses the location and tactics of the battle over public space" (19). Lefebvre (1991), Certeau (1984), and others have accused the state of supporting corporate interests by using tools such as land use mapping and zoning that transform place into abstract space. While recognizing that these tools are part of the arsenal of controlling space, Kim notes that by eschewing grounded analysis and focusing instead on abstract space, critical theory ironically replicates the very tactics it condemns.

6. Some fadas display their names on canvas banners. They make their presence visible by using disposable signage.

CHAPTER THREE

1. Telenovelas are an important source of insight for samari looking for instructions as well as training in the language of love (Masquelier 2009b).

2. When flush with cash, samari may purchase expensive handsets so they can resell them in times of need.

3. Such a practice is not as novel as it may seem. Young men have long delegated their best friend to the house of the girl they wish to court. The friend acts as the

go-between, ensuring that the norms of propriety are followed. By enabling samari to contact *'yammata* directly via text messaging, cell phones have radically transformed the geographies of romance.

CHAPTER FOUR

1. Fada Attayo / Fada Attayo / Fada Attayo / Hé mon ami / Si tu veux voir les fadas / Tu n'as qu'à descendre / Dans les rues de Niamey / Capitale du Niger / Tu verras des fadas / Où le thé est le roi

2. "Wa ga ba mu da aiki?" in the original version.

3. The original Kaidan Gaskia dissolved after one of the members, upon being invited to perform in the United States, decided to remain there permanently.

4. According to Phéno, Seyni Kountché was "a patriot. In our ways we wanted to immortalize his name, this man has done so much for our country" (Ras-Idris 2005).

5. Wassika (or Wassika New Posse) was one of the earliest Nigérien hip-hop groups.

6. Identifying as *jeune* implies one is a French-speaking youth. It is also a means of asserting one's modernity and cosmopolitanism.

7. The commitment to "realness" is not specific to Nigérien hip-hop performers. A strong link to "real life" is part of rap's very essence. Rap artists and devotees everywhere put a premium value on unmediated, authentic performances (Krims 2000; Mitchell 2001).

8. "We [rappers] are not empty-headed," a young man said, implying that crafting words involved sustained labor and that the lyrics they wrote had substance and soul.

9. According to a rapper, "youth would arrive at a studio, saying 'Make me an R-Kelly sound!' or 'I want to make a single!' Some didn't even speak French. They knew nothing. It was all a fad."

10. Few rappers succeed in achieving the fame that will translate into financial profits. A prominent rapper told me his family had financed the production of his first CD. Afterward, whatever money he made selling his music had to be reinvested in the production of his next CD.

11. It is the exceptional morality of Ramadan—a month during which religious obligations are more strictly followed—that gives norms and ethics legitimacy during the rest of the year (Schielke 2010).

12. Young men told me a number of times that although they liked the sounds of hip-hop and enjoyed dancing and striking "gangsta" poses, it was the words that really mattered.

13. *Coupé-décalé* lyrics are often metacommunicative: the performers themselves provide cues for how their utterances should be understood (McGovern 2010). They might thus refer in their songs to the money they are throwing at the DJ ("look how much money!") or the clothes they are wearing ("look at those pants!").

CHAPTER FIVE

1. The term *'yan banga* is a Hausa adoption of the English word *vanguard*. *'Yan banga* first emerged in northern Nigeria where they were employed as "thugs" to do the biddings of politicians (C. Casey 2008; Last 2008).

2. Brutal beatings still happen. Indeed some fadantchés brag about using violence as a deterrent against potential trespassers: "Thieves cannot pass in our street. We deal with them. Usually, we beat them up before taking them to the police station," hinting that even thugs have their own intricate form of moral order.

3. Under the tutelage of a charismatic radio host, Zinderois youths were encouraged to organize themselves, engage in civic activities, and report "good deeds" on the radio. In a matter of weeks, the first radio-clubs or fadas were born (Lund 2009).

4. In precolonial times, wrestling was a ludic and festive performance that marked the end of harvest season. Competitions opposed samari from different villages in the chief's court or some alternative public arena. After ingesting copious amounts of new millet, youths would defy each other to the sound of the *gunduwa*—a drum used exclusively during wrestling competitions (Ruszniewski and Bali 2005). During the colonial period, wrestling was relegated to the status of folk tradition by French administrators reluctant to recognize it as a legitimate sport. Only after independence did it regain prominence to become Niger's national sport.

5. Success has only partially to do with the wrestler's vigor and agility. More important is the mystical strength he possesses. All great wrestling champions are believed to have signed a pact with spirits. Like wrestlers, fadantchés occasionally enlist the services of *malamai* to protect themselves against blows and knife wounds.

6. Weezy Baby is one of Lil Wayne's nicknames; Cash Money is a record label that markets hip-hop music. Cash is also a symbol of wealth in hip-hop culture: carrying money in a "rubber band bank," just like bling or designer clothes, is a concrete manifestation of success; "Bad Boyz" is the title of rapper Shyne's most successful song; Sexion d'Assaut is a French hip-hop group; Soulja Boy is a rapper best known for his song "Crank Dat (Soulja Boy)"; Flo Rida is a hip-hop artist from Florida whose most famous song is "Flow."

7. "Millet doesn't work for samari. It doesn't fill you up. Salad and rice are fine for girls but boys like beans," a young man explained.

8. Youth-orchestrated violence was not restricted to the fada. The Commission d'Action Sociale et d'Ordre (or CASO), a student organization aimed at protecting student interests, functioned like a militia. Under the guise of defending students, its members, many of whom lifted weights or were trained in karate or tae kwon do, spread terror in schools.

9. In a bachelor's compound or a rented house, fadas host dance parties and provide *sucreries* (soft drinks). Young men typically pay an entrance fee, but admission is complimentary for young women.

10. As the necessary ingredient for what I have referred to as teatime, tea, sugar, and coal capture a critical sense of value, so much so that they become the currency of some fadas. As interchangeable units of value, the *shai*, the *sucre*, and the *charbon* are imbued with a moral dimension that money lacks.

11. Alex, a devoted fan of Jean-Claude Van Damme, took his name from the actor Alex Daniels, who performs with the Belgian actor and martial artist in the martial arts action film *Cyborg*.

CHAPTER SIX

1. Their frequent allusion to the proverb is an indirect criticism of the *'yan riga* (lit., "wearers of the robe") or *musulmans de façade* (Nicolas 1975:59), who dress as Muslims but do not follow the teachings of Islam by praying, fasting, and so on.

2. The actual name of the song and dancing style is Zoropoto. Its author is Ivoirian singer and composer DJ Arafat.

3. In contrast, worn, faded clothes signal destitution or, at the very least, an inability to translate one's social connections into access to cash and commodities.

4. Andrewes (2005) describes how footwear (or the absence of it) so thoroughly and

distinctly affected the gait of animist, Muslim, and Christian villagers in southern Senegal that she was able to recognize which community people belonged to based on the way they walked.

CHAPTER SEVEN

1. To meet the draconian requirements of the SAPs, the Nigérien government resorted to severe budget compressions in education. Annual student stipends were slashed. In 2003 the cafeteria at Abdou Moumouni University provided one thousand meals for 6,000 students each day while campus dormitories accommodated 1,230 of the 5,000 students in need of housing. Rooms built for two persons were often occupied by four students. Many students lived with as many as thirty roommates in large rooms referred to as *ghettos, tavernes,* or *sanzala.*

2. Young men often told me how they were personally affected by educational budget cuts. Some of them spoke of the hunger, squalor, and misery they experienced when, as students at Abdou Moumouni University in Niamey, they were forced to survive with limited means and in highly inadequate conditions.

3. The head of security forces was eventually discharged for having allegedly permitted the use of real bullets (instead of the rubber bullets typically used to repress civil unrest), but no one was ever charged for the deaths of the three students.

4. The gathering at a party's hangar is a strictly a male affair. Women's participation during political campaigns largely revolves around welcoming visiting delegations and preparing meals and spectacles (singing and dancing) for guests. The mobilization of female labor is not tied to political allegiance, however. It is by tapping into local female networks that women's participation is secured at such events.

5. There are educational requirements to become national deputy: to be eligible, one must pass the *baccalauréat* or its equivalent.

6. Some campaigning politicians are known to hand over bags of rice to every household to buy their loyalty. There are gifts for everyone. Women, for instance, see the clothes and food that are distributed during presidential campaigns as their due. I once witnessed a senior woman vouch she would vote for the PNDS candidate upon finding out that she had missed out on the distribution of tailored tops by local officials from MNSD, the party she had previously supported.

7. Some Nigériens believe Kountché was a model president and that his mode of governance, problematic as it was from a humanist standpoint (among other things, he jailed political opponents and fired civil servants for absenteeism), kept corruption in check.

8. Within the nostalgic outlook that makes some Nigériens long for a return to Kountché's dictatorship, democracy is widely associated with "disorder." Not only has it opened prison doors, allegedly allowing convicted criminals to walk free, but by disrupting social hierarchies, it has emboldened youth and led them to disrespect elders (Bayart, Ellis, and Hibou 1999).

9. References to Tandja's supposed illiteracy commonly peppered fada conversations about "deadwood," bolstering support for the notion—popular among youth—that the country would not be in the "mess" it was if elders ceded power to the younger generation.

10. Tahibou was well aware that by effectively leveraging present excess at harvest time against future deficiencies at "hunger" time, he stood a chance to make a decent profit in contexts of economic uncertainty. He also knew that buying large quantities of beans was a risky proposition, but he did not think he could lose his entire

investment. He had not factored in the pests that can destroy stockpiles of grain in a matter of weeks.

11. Issoufou has been criticized by the opposition for his arrogant and elitist style of governance, known as *guri*.

12. The 1999 constitution limits the president to two terms and bans amending this provision.

REFERENCES

Aboubacar, Sani. 2016. Jeunes et chicha, liaisons dangereuses. *Magazine de L'Afrique*, July 20, http://magazinedelafrique.com/jeunes-chicha-liaison-dangereuse/.

Abraham, R. C. 1946. *Dictionary of the Hausa Language*. London: University of London Press.

Agamben, Giorgio. 1998. *Homo Sacer: Sovereign Power and Bare Life*. Daniel Heller-Roazen, trans. Stanford: Stanford University Press.

Akinyele, R. T. 2001. Ethnic Militancy and National Stability in Nigeria: A Case Study of the Oodua People's Congress. *African Affairs* 100(401):623–40.

Alidou, Ousseina. 2005. *Engaging Modernity: Muslim Women and the Politics of Agency in Postcolonial Niger*. Madison: University of Wisconsin Press.

Allison, Anne. 2013. *Precarious Japan*. Durham: Duke University Press.

Anderson, Ben. 2004. Time-Stilled Space-Slowed: How Boredom Matters. *Geoforum* 35(6):739–54.

Andrewes, Janet. 2005. *Bodywork: Dress as Cultural Tool*. Leiden: Brill.

Appadurai, Arjun. 2000. Spectral Housing and Urban Cleansing: Notes on Millennial Mumbai. *Public Culture* 12(3):627–51.

———. 1996. *Modernity at Large: Cultural Dimensions of Globalization*. Minneapolis: University of Minnesota Press.

Appiah, Kwame Anthony. 2008. *Experiments in Ethics*. Cambridge: Harvard University Press.

Archambault, Julie. 2017. *Mobile Secrets: Youth, Intimacy, and the Politics of Pretense in Mozambique*. Chicago: University of Chicago Press.

Argenti, Nicolas. 2002. Youth in Africa: A Major Resource for Change. In *Young Africa: Realizing the Rights of Children and Youth*, ed. Alex de Waal and Nicolas Argenti, 124–34. Trenton, NJ: Africa World Press.

Augé, Marc. 1995. *Non-places: Introduction to an Anthropology of Supermodernity*. London: Verso.

Barthes, Roland. 1991. *The Responsibility of Forms: Critical Essays on Art, Music and Representation*. Berkeley: University of California Press.

Basso, Keith H. 1996. Wisdom Sits in Places: Notes on a Western Apache Landscape. In *Senses of Place*, ed. Steven Feld and Keith H. Basso, 53–90. Santa Fe, NM: School of American Research Press.

———. 1988. "Speaking with Names": Language and Landscape among the Western Apache. *Cultural Anthropology* 3(2):99–130.

Bastian, Misty L. 2013. Dressing for Success: The Politically Performative Quality of an Igbo Woman's Attire. In *African Dress: Fashion, Agency, Performance*, ed. Karen Tranberg Hansen and D. Soyini Madison, 15–29. New York: Bloomsbury.

Bastide, Roger. 1955. Le principe de coupure et le comportement afro-brésilien. In *Anais do XXXI Congresso internacional de Americanistas*, 493–503. São Paulo: Editora Anhembi.

Baudrillard, Jean. 1993. Kool Killer, or The Insurrection of the Signs. In *Symbolic Exchanges and Death*. Ian Hamilton Grant, trans. Thousand Oaks, CA: Sage.

Bayart, Jean-François. 1979. *L'État au Cameroun*. Paris: Presses de la Fondation Nationale des Sciences Politiques.

Bayart, Jean-François, Stephen Ellis, and Béatrice Hibou. 1999. *The Criminalization of the State in Africa*. Bloomington: Indiana University Press.

Bayart, Jean-François, Achille Mbembe, and Coumi Toulabor. 2008. *Le politique par le bas en Afrique Noire*. Paris: Karthala.

Bayat, Asef. 2010a. *Life as Politics: How Ordinary People Change the Middle East*. Stanford: Stanford University Press.

———. 2010b. Muslim Youth and the Claim of Youthfulness. In *Being Young and Muslim: New Cultural Politics in the Global South and North*, ed. Linda Herrera and Asef Bayat, 27–48. New York: Oxford University Press.

———. 2007. Islamism and the Politics of Fun. *Public Culture* 19(3):433–59.

Bayoumi, Moustafa. 2010. Being Young, Muslim, and American in Brooklyn. In *Being Young and Muslim: New Cultural Politics in the Global South and North*, ed. Linda Herrera and Asef Bayat, 161–74. New York: Oxford University Press.

Bazenguissa-Ganga, Rémy. 1999. Les Ninja, les Cobra, et les Zoulou crèvent l'écran à Brazzaville: Le rôle des médias et la construction des identités de violence politique. *Canadian Journal of African Studies* 33(2–3):329–61.

Beekers, Daan, and Bas von Gool. 2012. From Patronage to Neopatrimonialism: Postcolonial Governance in Sub-Saharan Africa and Beyond. Working Paper 101, African Studies Centre, Leiden, The Netherlands.

Bender, Barbara. 2002. Time and Landscape. *Current Anthropology* 43(S4):S103–S12.

Benjamin, Walter. 2003. *Selected Writings: 1938–1940*. Cambridge: Harvard University Press.

———. 1999. *The Arcades Project*. Howard Eiland and Kevin McLaughlin, trans. Cambridge: Harvard University Press.

Bergson, Henri. 1911. *Matter and Memory*. Nancy M. Paul and W. Scott Palmer, trans. London: George Allen and Unwin.

Berlant, Lauren. 2008. *The Female Complaint: The Unfinished Business of Sentimentality in American Culture*. Durham: Duke University Press.

———. 2000. Intimacy: A Special Issue. In *Intimacy*, ed. Lauren Berlant. Chicago: University of Chicago Press.

Berliner, David. 2005. An Impossible Transmission: Youth Religious Memories in Guinea-Conakry. *American Ethnologist* 32(4):576–92.

Besnier, Niko, and Susan Brownell. 2012. Sport, Modernity, and the Body. *Annual Review of Anthropology* 41:443–59.

Bloch, Ernst. 1995. *The Principle of Hope*. Vol. 1. Cambridge: MIT Press.

Blundo, Giorgio, and Jean-Pierre Olivier de Sardan, eds. 2006. *Everyday Corruption and the State: Citizens and Public Officials in Africa*. London: Zed Books.

Bondaz, Julien. 2013. Le thé des hommes: Sociabilités masculines et culture de la rue au Mali. *Cahiers d'études africaines* 209/210:61–85.

Bourdieu, Pierre. 1984. *Distinction: A Social Critique of the Judgment of Taste*. Richard Nice, trans. Cambridge: Harvard University Press.

———. 1978. Sport and Social Class. *Social Science Information* 17:819–40.

———. 1977. *Outline of a Theory of Practice*. Richard Nice, trans. Cambridge: Cambridge University Press.

Bourgois, Philippe. 1996. *In Search of Respect: Selling Crack in El Barrio*. New York: Cambridge University Press.

Boyer, Florence. 2014. "Faire fada" à Niamey (Niger): Un espace de transgression silencieux? *Carnets de Géographes* 7:1–17.

Brandes, Stanley. 1980. *Metaphors of Masculinity: Sex and Status in Andalusian Folklore*. Philadelphia: University of Pennsylvania Press.

Butler, Judith. 1993. *Bodies That Matter: On the Discursive Limits of Sex*. New York: Routledge.

Casey, Conerly. 2008. "Policing" through Violence: Fear, Vigilantism, and Politics of Islam in Northern Nigeria. In *Global Vigilantes*, ed. David Pratten and Atreyee Sen, 93–124. New York: Columbia University Press.

Casey, Edward S. 1996. How to Get from Space to Place in a Fairly Short Stretch of Time: Phenomenological Prolegomena. In *Senses of Place*, ed. Steven Feld and Keith H. Basso, 13–52. Santa Fe, NM: School for American Research Press.

Certeau, Michel de. 1984. *The Practice of Everyday Life*. Steven F. Randall, trans. Berkeley: University of California Press.

Chalfin, Brenda. 2014. Public Things, Excremental Politics, and the Infrastructure of Bare Life in Ghana's City of Tema. *American Ethnologist* 41(1):92–109.

Charlick, Robert B. 1991. *Niger: Personal Rule and Survival in the Sahel*. Boulder: Westview.

Christiansen, Catrine, Mats Utas, and Henrik E. Vigh. 2006. *Navigating Youth, Generating Adulthood: Social Becoming in African Context*. Uppsala: Nordic Africa Institute.

Cole, Jennifer, and Deborah Durham. 2008. Introduction: Globalization and the Temporality of Children and Youth. In *Figuring the Future: Globalization and the Temporalities of Children and Youth*, ed. Cole and Durham, 3–23. Santa Fe, NM: School for Advanced Research Press.

———, eds. 2007. *Generation and Globalization: Youth, Age, and Family in the New World Economy*. Bloomington: Indiana University Press.

Comaroff, Jean, and John L. Comaroff, eds. 2006. *Law and Disorder in the Postcolony*. Chicago: University of Chicago Press.

———. 2005. Reflections on Youth: From the Past to the Postcolony. In *Makers and Breakers: Children and Youth in Postcolonial Africa*, ed. Alcinda Honwana and Filip De Boeck, 19–30. Trenton, NJ: Africa World Press.

———. 2000. Millennial Capitalism: First Thoughts on a Second Coming. *Public Culture* 12(2):291–343.

———. 1993. Introduction. In *Modernity and Its Malcontents: Ritual and Power in Postcolonial Africa*, ed. Comaroff and Comaroff, xi–xxxvii. Chicago: University of Chicago Press.

Cooper, Barbara M. 2010. Engendering a Hausa Vernacular Christian Practice. In *Being and Becoming Hausa: Interdisciplinary Perspectives*, ed. Anne Haour and Benedetta Rossi, 257–78. Leiden: Brill.

———. 1997. Gender, Movement, and History: Social and Spatial Transformations in

Twentieth-Century Maradi, Niger. *Environment and Planning D: Society and Space* 15(2):195–221.

Cordilia, Anne. 1983. *The Making of an Inmate: Prison as a Way of Life*. Rochester, VT: Shenkman Books.

Cornwall, Andrea. 2016. Women's Empowerment: What Works? *Journal of International Development* 28(3):342–59.

———. 2002. Spending Power: Love, Money, and the Reconfiguration of Gender Relations in Ado-Odo, Southeastern Nigeria. *American Ethnologist* 29(4):963–80.

Cosgrove, Stuart. 1989. The Zoot Suit and Style Warfare. In *Zoot Suits and Second-Hand Dresses: An Anthology of Fashion and Music*, ed. Angela McRobbie, 3–22. New York: Routledge.

Craik, Jennifer. 1994. *The Face of Fashion: Cultural Studies in Fashion*. New York: Routledge.

Dalsgård, Anne Line, et al. 2014. *Ethnographies of Youth and Temporality: Time Objectified*. Temple University Press.

Das, Veena. 2012. Ordinary Ethics. In *A Companion to Moral Anthropology*, ed. Didier Fassin, 133–49. Malden, MA: Wiley-Blackwell.

———. 2010. Engaging the Life of the Other: Love and Everyday Life. In *Ordinary Ethics: Anthropology, Language, and Action*, ed. Michael Lambek, 376–99. New York: Fordham University Press.

Das, Veena, and Deborah Poole, eds. 2004. *Anthropology in the Margins of the State*. Santa Fe, NM: School of American Research Press.

De Boeck, Filip, and Marie-Françoise Plissart. 2004. *Kinshasa: Tales of the Invisible City*. Ghent: Ludion Press.

Debos, Marielle, and Joël Glasman. 2012. Politique des corps habillés: État, pouvoir, et métiers de l'ordre en Afrique. *Politique Africaine* 4(128):5–23.

Deeb, Lara, and Mona Harb. 2013. *Leisurely Islam: Negotiating Geography and Morality in Shi'ite South Beirut*. Princeton: Princeton University Press.

DeLanda, Manuel. 2006. *A New Philosophy of Society: Assemblage Theory and Social Complexity*. London: Continuum.

Diouf, Mamadou. 2003. Engaging Postcolonial Cultures: African Youth and Public Space. *African Studies Review* 46(2):1–12.

———. 1996. Urban Youth and Senegalese Politics. *Public Culture* 8(2):225–50.

Diouf, Mamadou, and Rosalind Fredericks, eds. 2014. *The Arts of Citizenship in African Cities: Infrastructures and Spaces of Belonging*. New York: Palgrave.

Douglas, Mary. 1966. *Purity and Danger: An Analysis of Concepts of Taboo and Pollution*. New York: Routledge.

Durham, Deborah. 2008. Apathy and Agency: The Romance of Agency and Youth in Botswana. In *Figuring the Future: Globalization and the Temporalities of Children and Youth*, ed. Jennifer Cole and Deborah Durham, 151–78. Santa Fe, NM: School for Advanced Research Press.

———. 2004. Disappearing Youth: Youth as a Social Shifter in Botswana. *American Ethnologist* 31(4):589–605.

———. 1999. The Predicament of Dress: Polyvalency and the Ironies of Cultural Identity. *American Ethnologist* 26(2):389–411.

Eco, Umberto. 1986. *Travels in Hyperreality*. Orlando: Harcourt Brace Jovanovich.

Eickelman, Dale F., and James Piscatori. 1996. *Muslim Politics*. Princeton: Princeton University Press.

Entwistle, Joanne, and Elizabeth B. Wilson, eds. 2001. *Body Dressing*. London: Bloomsbury Academics.

Evans-Pritchard, E. E. 1937. *Witchcraft, Oracles, and Magic among the Azande*. Oxford: Clarendon Press.

Ewen, Stuart. 1988. *All Consuming Images: The Politics of Style in Contemporary Culture*. New York: Basic Books.

Ewing, Katherine P. 1990. The Illusion of Wholeness: Culture, Self, and the Experience of Inconsistency. *Ethos* 18(3):251–78.

Farrer, James, and Andrew David Field. 2015. *Shanghai Nightscapes: A Nocturnal Biography of a Global City*. Chicago: University of Chicago Press.

Featherstone, Michael, ed. 2000. *Body Modification*. London: Sage.

Feld, Steven, and Keith H. Basso, eds. 1996. *Senses of Place*. Santa Fe, NM: School of American Research Press.

Felski, Rita. 2000. *Doing Time: Feminist Theory and Postmodern Culture*. New York: New York University Press.

Ferguson, James. 2015. *Give a Man a Fish: Reflections on the New Politics of Distribution*. Durham: Duke University Press.

———. 2006. *Global Shadows: Africa in the Neoliberal World Order*. Durham: Duke University Press.

———. 1999. *Expectations of Modernity: Myths and Meanings of Urban Life on the Zambian Copperbelt*. Berkeley: University of California Press.

Finkelstein, Joanne. 1991. *The Fashioned Self*. Philadelphia: Temple University Press.

Fisher, Daniel. 2013. Intimacy and Self-Abstraction: Radio as New Media in Aboriginal Australia. *Culture, Theory, and Critique* 54(3):372–93.

Foucault, Michel. 1988. Technologies of the Self. In *Technologies of the Self: A Seminar with Michel Foucault*, ed. and trans. Luther Martin, Huck Gutman, and Patrick Hutton, 16–49. Amherst: University of Massachusetts Press.

———. 1985. *The History of Sexuality*, vol. 2, *The Use of Pleasure*. Robert Hurley, trans. New York: Pantheon.

Frake, Charles O. 1996. Pleasant Places, Past Times, and Sheltered Identity in Rural East Anglia. In *Senses of Place*, ed. Steven Feld and Keith H. Basso, 229–57. Santa Fe, NM: School of American Research Place.

Frederiksen, Martin. 2016. *Young Men, Time, and Boredom in the Republic of Georgia*. Philadelphia: Temple University Press.

Freud, Sigmund. 1990. *Beyond the Pleasure Principle*. James Strachey, ed. New York: W. W. Norton.

Fuh, Divine. 2012. The Prestige Economy: Veteran Clubs and Youngmen's Competition in Bamenda, Cameroon. *Urban Forum* 23(4):501–26.

Gal, Susan. 2002. A Semiotics of the Public/Private Distinction. *differences: A Journal of Feminist Cultural Studies* 13(1):77–95.

Gandoulou, Justin-Daniel. 1989. *Dandies à Bacongo: Le culte de l'élégance dans la société congolaise contemporaine*. Paris: L'Harmattan.

Gaudio, Rudolph Pell. 2009. *Allah Made Us: Sexual Outlaws in an Islamic African City*. Malden, MA: Wiley-Blackwell.

Geertz, Clifford. 1972. Deep Play: Notes on the Balinese Cockfight. *Daedalus* 101(1): 1–37.

Geertz, Hildred. 1961. *The Javanese Family: A Study of Kinship and Socialization*. New York: Free Press of Glencoe.

Gill, Rosalind, Karen Henwood, and Carl McLean. 2005. Body Projects and the Regulation of Normative Masculinity. *Body & Society* 11(1):37–62.

Gilroy, Paul. 1993. *The Black Atlantic: Modernity and Double Consciousness*. London: Verso.

Goffman, Erving. 1963. *Behavior in Public Places: Notes on the Social Organization of Gatherings*. New York: Free Press.

———. 1961. *Asylums: Essays on the Social Situation of Mental Patients and Other Inmates*. New York: Doubleday.

Gondola, Ch. Didier. 2009. Tropical Cowboys: Westerns, Violence and Masculinity among the Young Bills of Kinshasa. *Afrique et Histoire* 7:75–98.

Goodstein, Elizabeth. 2005. *Experience Without Qualities: Boredom and Modernity*. Stanford: Stanford University Press.

Göpfert, Mirco. 2012. Security in Niamey: An Anthropological Perspective on Policing and an Act of Terrorism in Niger. *Journal of Modern African Studies* 50(1):53–74.

Guillon, Jean-Michel, and Bernard Hernandez. 1968. Dogondoutchi, petit centre urbain du Niger. *Revue de Géographie Alpine* 56(2):297–358.

Gupta, Akhil. 1995. Blurred Boundaries: The Discourse of Corruption, the Culture of Politics, and the Imagined State. *American Ethnologist* 22(2):375–402.

Gutmann, Matthew C. 1997. Trafficking in Men: The Anthropology of Masculinity. *Annual Review of Anthropology* 26:385–409.

———. 1996. *The Meanings of Macho: Being a Man in Mexico City*. Berkeley: University of California Press.

Guyer, Jane I. 2007. Prophecy and the Near Future: Thoughts on Macroeconomic, Evangelical and Punctuated Time. *American Ethnologist* 34(3):409–21.

———. 1995. Wealth in People, Wealth in Things: Introduction. *Journal of African History* 36:83–90.

Hamidou, Issaka Maga, and Sani Ali. 2005. Impacts sectoriels de la croissance démographique dans un contexte de stratégie de réduction de la pauvreté. Niamey: Ministère de la Population et de l'Action Sociale.

Hansen, Karen Tranberg. 2010. Secondhand Clothing and Fashion in Africa. In *Contemporary African Fashion*, ed. Suzanne Gott and Kristyne Lougran, 39–52. Bloomington: Indiana University Press.

———. 2009. Youth, Gender, and Secondhand Clothing in Lusaka, Zambia: Local and Global Styles. In *The Fabric of Cultures: Fashion, Identity, and Globalization*, ed. Eugenia Paulicelli and Hazel Clark, 112–27. New York: Routledge.

———, ed. 2008. *Youth and the City in the Global South*. Bloomington: Indiana University Press.

———. 2005. "Getting Stuck in the Compound": Some Odds against Social Adulthood in Lusaka, Zambia. *Africa Today* 51(4):3–16.

———. 2004. Dressing Dangerously: Miniskirts, Gender Relations, and Sexuality in Zambia. In *Fashioning Africa: Power and the Politics of Dress*, ed. Jean Allman, 166–85. Bloomington: Indiana University Press.

Hansen, Thomas Blom. 2012. *Melancholia of Freedom: Social Life in an Indian Township in South Africa*. Princeton: Princeton University Press.

Harvey, David. 2008. The Right to the City. *New Left Review* 53:23–40.

Hassane, H. 2003. Tuer le temps dans les fadas: chômage, mode d'emploi. *Tel Quel*, May, 4.

Havard, Jean-François. 2001. Ethos "Bul Faale" et nouvelles figures de la réussite au Sénégal. *Politique Africaine* 82:63–77.

Hebdidge, Dick. 1979. *Subculture: The Meaning of Style*. New York: Methuen.

Hecht, Tobias. 2008. Globalization from Way Below: Brazilian Streets, a Youth, and World Society. In *Figuring the Future: Globalization and the Temporalities of Children and Youth*, ed. Jennifer Cole and Deborah Durham, 223–43. Santa Fe, NM: School for Advanced Research Press.

Heidegger, Martin. 1995. *The Fundamental Concepts of Metaphysics: World, Finitude, Solitude*. William McNeill and Nicholas Walker, trans. Bloomington: Indiana University Press.

———. 1977. Building Dwelling Thinking. In *Martin Heidegger: Basic Writings*, ed. David Farrell Krell, 319–39. New York: Harper and Row.

Herrera, Linda, and Asef Bayat, eds. 2010. *Being Young and Muslim: New Cultural Politics in the Global South and North*. New York: Oxford University Press.

Herzfeld, Michael. 2005. *Cultural Intimacy: Social Poetics and the Nation-State*. 2nd ed. New York: Routledge.

———. 1988. *The Poetics of Manhood: Contest and Identity in a Cretan Mountain Village*. Princeton: Princeton University Press.

Heuzé, Gérard. 1996. *Workers of Another World: Miners, the Countryside and Coalfields in Dhanbad*. Delhi: Oxford University Press.

Honwana, Alcinda. 2015. "Enough Is Enough!": Youth Protests and Political Change in Africa. In *Collective Mobilisations in Africa*, ed. Kadya Tall, Marie-Emmanuelle Pommerolle, and Michel Cahen, 45–66. Leiden: Brill.

———. 2012. *The Time of Youth: Work, Social Change, and Politics in Africa*. Sterling, VA: Kumarian Press.

Honwana, Alcinda, and Filip De Boeck, eds. 2005. *Makers and Breakers: Children and Youth in Postcolonial Africa*. Trenton, NJ: Africa World Press.

Hornberger, Julia. 2008. Nocturnal Johannesburg. In *Johannesburg: Elusive Metropolis*, ed. Sarah Nuttall and Achille Mbembe, 285–96. Durham: Duke University Press.

Humphrey, Caroline. 2012. Hospitality and Tone: Holding Patterns for Strangeness in Rural Mongolia. *Journal of the Royal Anthropological Institute* 16(1):S63–S73.

Ingold, Tim. 2007. Materials Against Materiality. *Archaeological Dialogues* 14(1):1–16.

———. 2000. *The Perception of the Environment: Essays on Livelihood, Dwelling, and Skill*. New York: Routledge.

Institut National de la Statistique. 2010. *Annuaire Statistique*. Niamey: Ministère de l'économie et des finances.

Issaka, Hamadou. 2010. Mise en carte et gestion territoriale des risques en milieu sahélien à travers l'exemple de Niamey (Niger). PhD diss., University of Strasbourg.

Issaley, Nana Aïchatou, and Jean-Pierre Olivier de Sardan. 2015. Les élections locales à Namaro en 2004. In *Élections au village: Une ethnographie de la culture électorale au Niger*, ed. Jean-Pierre Olivier de Sardan, 255–72. Paris: Karthala.

Jackson, Michael. 1998. *Minima Ethnographica: Intersubjectivity and the Anthropological Project*. Chicago: University of Chicago Press.

Janson, Marloes. 2014. *Islam, Youth, and Modernity in the Gambia: The Tablighi Jama'at*. Cambridge: Cambridge University Press.

Jauregui, Beatrice. 2014. Provisional Agency in India: *Jugaad* and Legitimation of Corruption. *American Ethnologist* 41(1):76–91.

Jeffrey, Craig. 2010. *Timepass: Youth, Class, and the Politics of Waiting in India*. Stanford: Stanford University Press.

———. 2008. Generation Nowhere: Rethinking Youth through the Lens of Un/underemployed Young Men. *Progress in Human Geography* 32(6):739–58.

Jeffrey, Craig, and Jane Dyson. 2013. Zig Zag Capitalism: Youth Entrepreneurship in the Contemporary Global South. *Geoforum* 49:R1–R3.

Jervis, Lori L., et al. 2003. Boredom, "Trouble," and the Realities of Postcolonial Reservation Life. *Ethos* 31(1):38–58.

Johnson-Hanks, Jennifer. 2002. On the Limits of Life Stages in Ethnography: Towards a Theory of Vital Conjectures. *American Anthropologist* 104(3):865–80.

Jones, Carla. 2010. Materializing Piety: Gendered Anxieties about Faithful Consumption in Contemporary Urban Indonesia. *American Ethnologist* 37(4):617–31.

Jones, Jeremy. 2014. "No Move to Make": The Zimbabwe Crisis, Displacement-in-Place and the Erosion of "Proper Places." In *Displacement Economies in Africa: Paradoxes of Crisis and Creativity*, ed. Amanda Hammar, 206–29. New York: Zed Books.

Keane, Webb. 2016. *Ethical Life: Its Natural and Social Histories*. Princeton: Princeton University Press.

———. 2010. Minds, Surfaces, and Reasons in the Anthropology of Ethics. In *Ordinary Ethics: Anthropology, Language, and Action*, ed. Michael Lambek, 64–83. New York: Fordham University Press.

———. 2007. *Christian Moderns: Freedom and Fetish in the Mission Encounter*. Berkeley: University of California Press.

———. 2005. Signs Are Not the Garb of Meaning: On the Social Analysis of Material Things. In *Materiality*, ed. Daniel Miller, 182–205. Durham: Duke University Press.

Khosravi, Shahram. 2007. *Young and Defiant in Tehran*. Philadelphia: University of Pennsylvania Press.

Kieffer, Julien. 2006. Les jeunes des "grins" de thé et la campagne électorale à Ougadougou. *Politique Africaine* 101:63–82.

Kim, Annette Miae. 2015. *Sidewalk City: Remapping Public Space in Ho Chi Minh City*. Chicago: University of Chicago Press.

Klein, Alan. 1993. *Little Big Men: Bodybuilding Subculture and Gender Construction*. Albany: SUNY Press.

Kohlhagen, Dominik. 2006. Frime, escroquerie et cosmopolitisme: Le succès du "coupé-décalé" en Afrique et ailleurs. *Politique Africaine* 100:92–105.

Kreil, Aymon. 2016. Territories of Desire: A Geography of Competing Intimacies in Cairo. *Journal of Middle East Women's Studies* 12(2):166–80.

Krims, Adam. 2000. *Rap Music and the Poetics of Identity*. Cambridge: Cambridge University Press.

Kristeva, Julia. 1984. *Revolution in Poetic Language*. Margaret Waller, trans. New York: Columbia University Press.

Kuhn, Reinhard C. 1976. *The Demon of Noontide: Ennui in Western Literature*. Princeton: Princeton University Press.

Lacan, Jacques. 1998. *The Seminar of Jacques Lacan. On Feminine Sexuality: The Limits of Love and Knowledge, Encore 1972–3*. Jacques-Alain Miller, ed. Bruce Fink, trans. New York: W. W. Norton & Company.

Lacey, W. K. 1968. *The Family in Classical Greece*. Ithaca, NY: Cornell University Press.

Laidlaw, James. 2014. *The Subject of Virtue: An Anthropology of Ethics and Freedom*. Cambridge: Cambridge University Press.

Lambek, Michael. 2010. Introduction. In *Ordinary Ethics: Anthropology, Language, and Action*, ed. Lambek, 1–36. New York: Fordham University Press.

Larkin, Brian. 1997. Indian Films and Nigerian Lovers: Media and the Creation of Parallel Modernities. *Africa* 67(3):406–40.

Last, Murray. 2008. The Search for Security in Muslim Northern Nigeria. *Africa* 78(1): 41–63.

Leach, Edmund. R. 1968. *Rethinking Anthropology*. London: Athlone Press.

LeBlanc, Marie-Nathalie. 2000. Versioning Womanhood and Muslimhood: "Fashion" and the Life Course in Contemporary Bouaké, Côte d'Ivoire. *Africa* 70(3):443–81.

Lefebvre, Henri. 2004. *Rhythmanalysis: Space, Time and Everyday Life*. Gerald Moore and Stuart Elden, trans. New York: Continuum.

———. 1996. *Writings on Cities*. Eleonore Kofman and Elizabeth Lebas, trans. and eds. Malden, MA: Blackwell.

———. 1991. *The Production of Space*. Donald Nicholson-Smith, trans. Malden, MA: Blackwell.

———. 1968a. *Le droit à la ville*. Paris: Anthropos.

———. 1968b. L'irruption de Nanterre au sommet. *L'Homme et la société* 8(1):49–99.

Le Monde. 2009. Le corps incarcéré. June 22. http://www.lemonde.fr/societe/visuel/2009/06/22/le-corps-incarcere_1209087_3224.html#xtor=EPR-32280246-%5Bdocu_prisons_relance%5D-20090630.

Le Sahel. 2012. Le Phénomène des "fada" et "palais," du mythe à la réalité: Les raisons du phénomène et les solutions préconisées. http://www.lesahel.org/index.php/component/k2/item/982-le-phenomene-des-fada-et-palais-du-mythe-a-la-realite—les-raisons-du-phenomene-et-les-solutions-preconisees. Accessed February 2, 2014.

Levy, Claire. 2001. Rap in Bulgaria: Between Fashion and Reality. In *Global Noise: Rap and Hip-Hop outside the USA*, ed. Tony Mitchell, 134–48. Middletown: Wesleyan University Press.

Liechty, Mark. 2002. *Suitably Modern: Making Middle-Class Culture in a New Consumer Society*. Princeton: Princeton University Press.

Loimeier, Roman. 2005. The Baraza: A Grassroots Institution. *ISIM Review*, 26–27.

Lund, Christian. 2009. Les dynamiques politiques locales face à une démocratie fragile. In *Les pouvoirs locaux au Niger*. Jean-Pierre Olivier de Sardan and Mahaman Tidjani Alou, eds. Paris: Karthala.

———. 2006. Twilight Institutions: An Introduction. *Development and Change* 37(4): 673–84.

———. 2001. Precarious Democratization and Local Dynamics in Niger: Micro-politics in Zinder. *Development and Change* 32(5):845–69.

Luxereau, Anne. 1998. "Avant Kountché, si tu mangeais du *wake*, tu n'étais rien": Changement des comportements alimentaires en pays hausa (Niger, région de Maradi). *Techniques & Cultures* 31–32:293–305.

Maazou, Souleymane Saddi. 2007. Le niébé, aliment vedette des Nigériens. *Le Républicain*, May 11, 7.

Mahmood, Saba. 2005. *Politics of Piety: The Islamic Revival and the Feminist Subject*. Princeton: Princeton University Press.

Mains, Daniel. 2012. *Hope Is Cut: Youth, Unemployment, and the Future in Urban Ethiopia*. Philadelphia: Temple University Press.

Maira, Sunaina, and Elisabeth Soep, eds. 2005. *Youthscapes: The Popular, the National, the Global*. Philadelphia: University of Pennsylvania Press.

Makama Bawa, Oumarou. 2015. Sayi kaayi! ou comment se faire élire au Niger: Analyse des stratégies électorales d'un candidat aux législatives de 2009. In *Élections au village: Une ethnographie de la culture électorale au Niger*, ed. Jean-Pierre Olivier de Sardan, 75–106. Paris: Karthala.

Makhulu, Anne-Maria, Beth A. Buggenhagen, and Stephen Jackson. 2010. Introduction. In *Hard Work, Hard Times: Global Volatility and African Subjectivities*, ed. Makhulu, Buggenhagen and Jackson, 1–27. Berkeley: University of California Press.

Malpas, Jeff. 2008. *Heidegger's Topology: Being, Place, World*. Cambridge: MIT Press.

Mannheim, Karl. 1952. *Essays on the Sociology of Knowledge*. Paul Kecskemeti, ed. London: Routledge & Kegan Paul.

Marchand, Trevor H. J. 2009. *The Masons of Djenne*. Bloomington: Indiana University Press.

Marsden, Magnus. 2005. *Living Islam: Muslim Religious Experience in Pakistan's North-West Frontier*. New York: Cambridge University Press.

Masquelier, Adeline. 2009a. Lessons from *Rubí*: Love, Poverty, and the Educational Value of Televised Dramas in Niger. In *Love in Africa*, ed. Jennifer Cole and Lynn M. Thomas, 204–28. Chicago: University of Chicago Press.

———. 2009b. *Women and Islamic Revival in a West African Town*. Bloomington: Indiana University Press.

———. 2007. Negotiating Futures: Youth, Islam, and the State in Niger. In *Islam and Muslim Politics in Africa*, ed. Benjamin F. Soares and René Otayek, 243–62. New York: Palgrave.

———. 2005. The Scorpion's Sting: Youth, Marriage, and the Struggle for Social Maturity in Niger. *Journal of the Royal Anthropological Institute* 11(1):59–83.

Massey, Doreen. 2003. Some Times of Space. In *Olafur Eliasson: The Weather Project*, ed. Susan May, 107–18. London: Tate.

———. 1998. The Spatial Construction of Youth Cultures. In *Cool Places: Geographies of Youth Cultures*, ed. Tracey Skelton and Gill Valentine, 121–29. London: Routledge.

———. 1994. *Space, Place, and Gender*. Minneapolis: University of Minnesota Press.

———. 1991. A Global Sense of Place. *Marxism Today* 35(6):24–29.

Mattingly, Cheryl. 2014. *Moral Laboratories: Family Peril and the Struggle for the Good Life*. Berkeley: University of California Press.

Mauss, Marcel. 1973. Techniques of the Body. *Economy and Society* 2(1):70–89.

Mazzocchetti, Jacinthe. 2009. *Être étudiant à Ouagadougou: Itinérances, imaginaire et précarité*. Paris: Karthala.

Mbembe, Achille. 2002. African Modes of Self-Writing. *Public Culture* 14(1):239–73.

———. 2001. *On the Postcolony*. Berkeley: University of California Press.

Mbembe, Achille, and Sarah Nuttall. 2008. Introduction: Afropolis. In *Johannesburg: The Elusive Metropolis*, ed. Nuttall and Mbembe, 1–33. Durham: Duke University Press.

McCullough, Aoife, Abdoutan Harouna, and Hamani Oumarou. 2016. Économie politique de l'engagement des électeurs au Niger. ODI Briefing. London: Overseas Development Institute. https://www.odi.org/sites/odi.org.uk/files/odi-assets/publications -opinion-files/10305.pdf.

McGovern, Mike. 2010. This Is Play: Popular Culture and Politics in Côte d'Ivoire. In *Hard Work, Hard Times: Global Volatility and African Subjectivities*, ed. Anne-Maria Makhulu, Beth A. Buggenhagen, and Stephen Jackson, 69–90. Berkeley: University of California Press.

Meinert, Lotte, and Nanna Schneidermann. 2014. Making a Name: Young Musicians in Uganda Working on the Future. In *Ethnographies of Youth and Temporality*, ed. Anne Line Dalsgård et al., 153–74. Philadelphia: Temple University Press.

Meiu, George Paul. 2015. "Beach-Boy Elders" and "Young Big-Men": Subverting the Temporalities of Ageing in Kenya's Ethno-Erotic Economies. *Ethnos* 80(4):472–96.

Miller, Daniel. 2005. Introduction. In *Clothing as Material Culture*, ed. Susanne Küchler and Daniel Miller, 1–19. New York: Berg.

Mitchell, Tony. 2001. *Global Noise: Rap and Hip-Hop outside the USA*. Middletown: Wesleyan University Press.

Miyazaki, Hiro. 2005. From Sugar to "Swords": Hope and the Extensibility of the Gift in Fiji. *Journal of the Royal Anthropological Institute* 11(2):277–95.

Moore, Henrietta L. 2011. *Still Life: Hopes, Desires, and Satisfactions*. Cambridge, UK: Polity.

Morrell, Robert. 2001. The Times of Change: Men and Masculinity in South Africa. In *Changing Men in Southern Africa*, ed. Morrell, 3–37. New York: Zed Books.

Motcho, Kokou Henri. 2004. Croissance urbaine et insécurité dans la ville de Niamey. *Geographica Helvetica* 59(3):199–207.

Mulvey, Laura. 1975. Visual Pleasure and Narrative Cinema. *Screen* 16(3):6–18.

Munn, Nancy D. 2013. The "Becoming-Past" of Places: Spacetime and Memory in Nineteenth-Century Pre–Civil War New York. *HAU: Journal of Ethnographic Theory* 3(2):359–80.

———. 1992. The Cultural Anthropology of Time: A Critical Essay. *Annual Review of Anthropology* 21:93–123.

———. 1986. *The Fame of Gawa: A Symbolic Study of Value Transformation in a Massim (Papua New Guinea) Society*. Durham: Duke University Press.

Musharbash, Yasmine. 2007. Boredom, Time, and Modernity: An Example from Aboriginal Australia. *American Anthropologist* 109(2):307–17.

Newell, Sasha. 2012. *The Modernity Bluff: Crime, Consumption, and Citizenship*. Chicago: University of Chicago Press.

Nicolas, Guy. 1975. *Dynamique sociale et appréhension du monde au sein d'une société hausa*. Paris: Institut d'Ethnologie.

Olivier de Sardan, Jean-Pierre. 1999. A Moral Economy of Corruption in Africa? *Journal of Modern African Studies* 37(1):25–52.

O'Neill, Bruce. 2017. *The Space of Boredom: Homelessness in the Slowing Global Order*. Durham: Duke University Press.

Parikh, Shanti. 2015. *Regulating Romance: Youth Love Letters, Moral Anxiety, and Intervention in Uganda's Time of AIDS*. Nashville: Vanderbilt University Press.

Peteet, Julie. 1996. The Writing on the Walls: The Graffiti of the Intifada. *Cultural Anthropology* 11(2):139–59.

Phillips, Susan A. 1999. *Wallbangin': Graffiti and Gangs in L.A.* Chicago: University of Chicago Press.

Pieterse, Edgard. 2010. Cityness and African Urban Development. *Urban Forum* 21(3): 205–19.

Pratten, David. 2008a. Introduction: The Politics of Protection: Perspectives on Vigilantism in Nigeria. *Africa* 78(1):1–15.

———. 2008b. "The Thief Eats His Shame": Practice and Power in Nigerian Vigilantism. *Africa* 78(1):64–83.

———. 2006. The Politics of Vigilance in Southeastern Nigeria. *Development and Change* 37:707–34.

Pype, Katrien. 2007. Fighting Boys, Strong Men and Gorillas: Notes on the Imagination of Masculinities in Kinshasa. *Africa* 77(2):250–71.

Quayson, Atto. 2014. *Oxford Street, Accra: City Life and the Itineraries of Transnationalism*. Durham: Duke University Press.

Ralph, Michael. 2008. Killing Time. *Social Text* 26(4[97]):1–29.

Rancière, Jacques. 1999. *Disagreement: Politics and Philosophy*. Julie Rose, trans. Minneapolis: University of Minnesota Press.

Raposa, Michael L. 1999. *Boredom and the Religious Imagination*. Charlottesville: University of Virginia Press.

Ras-Idris. 2005. Studio Kountché. *Fofo Magazine*, January 2. http://www.fofomag.com/Index.asp?affiche=News_display.asp&ArticleID=279.

Reiter, Rayna R. 1975. Men and Women in the South of France: Public and Private Domains. In *Toward an Anthropology of Women*, ed. Reiter, 252–82. New York: Monthly Review Press.

Reno, William. 2002. The Politics of Insurgency in Collapsing States. *Development and Change* 33(5):837–58.

Richard, Analiese, and Daromir Rudnyckyj. 2009. Economies of Affect. *Journal of the Royal Anthropological Institute*, n.s., 15:57–77.

Ricoeur, Paul. 1992. *Oneself as Another*. Kathleen Blamey, trans. Chicago: University of Chicago Press.

Robbins, Joel. 2013. Beyond the Suffering Subject: Toward an Anthropology of the Good. *Journal of the Royal Anthropological Institute* 19(3):447–62.

Roitman, Janet. 2014. *Anti-crisis*. Durham: Duke University Press.

Rosaldo, Michelle. 1980. *Knowledge and Passion: Ilongot Notions of Self and Social Life*. Cambridge: Cambridge University Press.

Roth, Claudia. 2008. "Shameful!" The Inverted Intergenerational Contract in Bobo-Dioulasso, Burkina Fasso. In *Generations in Africa: Connections and Conflicts*, ed. Alber Erdmute, Sjaak van der Geest, and Susan Reynolds Whyte, 47–70. Berlin: Lit Verlag.

Ruszniewski, Jean-Yves, and Saley Boubé Bali. 2005. *Kokowa: La lutte traditionnelle au Niger*. Saint-Maur-des-Fossés: Éditions Sépia.

Sahlins, Marshall. 2013. *What Kinship Is—and Is Not*. Chicago: University of Chicago Press.

Scherz, China. 2014. *Having People, Having Heart: Charity, Sustainable Development, and Problems of Dependence in Uganda*. Chicago: University of Chicago Press.

Schielke, Samuli. 2010. Being Good in Ramadan: Ambivalence, Fragmentation, and the Moral Self in the Lives of Young Egyptians. In *Islam, Politics, Anthropology*, ed. Filippo Osella and Benjamin Soares, 23–38. Malden, MA: Wiley-Blackwell.

———. 2009. Ambivalent Commitments: Troubles of Morality, Religiosity and Aspiration among Young Egyptians. *Journal of Religion in Africa* 39(2):158–85.

Schritt, Jannik. 2015. The "Protests Against Charlie Hebdo" in Niger: A Background Analysis. *Africa Spectrum* 1:49–64.

Seidou, M. S. 2008. Le dada des "fadas." *Le Sahel*, August 14, 5.

Sen, Atreyee, and David Pratten. 2008. Global Vigilantes: Perspectives on Justice and Violence. In *Global Vigilantes*, ed. Pratten and Sen, 1–24. New York: Columbia University Press.

Sharp, Lesley A. 2002. *The Sacrificed Generation: Youth, History, and the Colonized Mind in Madagascar*. Berkeley: University of California Press.

Sherif, Elisabeth. 2015. Zoom sur le premier parti du Niger. *ActuNiger*, May 9. http://www.actuniger.com/tribune-opinions/10040-zoom-sur-le-premier-parti-du-niger.html.

Shipley, Jesse Weaver. 2013. *Living the Hip Life: Celebrity and Entrepreneurship in Ghanaian Popular Music*. Durham: Duke University Press.

———. 2010. Self-Sovereignty and Creativity in Ghanaian Public Culture. In *Hard Work, Hard Times: Global Volatility and African Subjectivities*, ed. Anne-Maria Makhulu, Beth A. Buggenhagen, and Stephen Jackson, 91–112. Berkeley: University of California Press.

Simon, Gregory. 2009. The Soul Freed of Cares? Islamic Prayer, Subjectivity, and the Contradictions of Moral Selfhood in Minangkabau, Indonesia. *American Ethnologist* 36(2):258–75.

Simone, AbdouMaliq. 2006. Pirate Towns: Reworking Social and Symbolic Infrastructures in Johannesburg and Dovala. *Urban Studies* 43(2):257–70.

———. 2004. People as Infrastructure: Intersecting Fragments in Johannesburg. *Public Culture* 16(3):407–29.

Simone, AbdouMaliq, and Edgar Pieterse. 2017. *New Urban Worlds: Inhabiting Dissonant Times*. Cambridge, UK: Polity.

Singerman, Diane. 2007. The Economic Imperatives of Marriage: Emerging Practices and Identities among Youth in the Middle East. Working Paper 6, Wolfensohn Center for Development, Washington, DC, and Dubai School of Government.

Smith, Daniel Jordan. 2017. *To Be a Man Is Not a One-Day Job: Masculinity, Money, and Intimacy in Nigeria*. Chicago: University of Chicago Press.

———. 2008. *A Culture of Corruption: Everyday Deception and Popular Discontent in Nigeria*. Princeton: Princeton University Press

———. 2004. The Bakassi Boys: Vigilantism, Violence, and Political Imagination in Nigeria. *Current Anthropology* 19(3):429–58.

Sommers, Marc. 2012. *Stuck: Rwandan Youth and the Struggle for Adulthood*. Athens: University of Georgia Press.

Sontag, Susan. 1987. The Pleasure of the Image. *Arts in America* 75(11):122–31.

Sounaye, Abdoulaye. 2012. God Made Me a Preacher: Youth and Their Appropriation of the Islamic Sermon in Niamey, Niger. PhD diss., Northwestern University.

———. 2011. La "discothèque" islamique: CD et DVD au cœur de la réislamisation nigérienne. *Ethnographiques.org*, no. 22 (May). http://www.ethnographiques.org/2011/Sounaye.

———. 2009. Islam, État et société: À la recherche d'une éthique publique au Niger. In *Islam, État et société en Afrique*, ed. René Otayek and Benjamin Soares, 327–52. Paris: Karthala.

Stambach, Amy. 2000. *Lessons from Kilimanjaro: Schooling, Community, and Gender in East Africa*. New York: Routledge.

Stephens, Sharon, ed. 1995. *Children and the Politics of Culture*. Princeton: Princeton University Press.

Stewart, Kathleen C. 1996. An Occupied Place. In *Senses of Place*, ed. Steven Feld and Keith H. Basso, 137–66. Santa Fe, NM: School of American Research Place.

Strathern, Marilyn. 1988. *The Gender of the Gift: Problems with Women and Problems with Society in Melanesia*. Berkeley: University of California Press.

Swedenburg, Ted. 2001. Islamic Hip-Hop vs. Islamophobia. In *Global Noise: Rap and Hip-Hop outside the USA*, ed. Tony Mitchell, 57–85. Middletown: Wesleyan University Press.

Thompson, John B. 1991. Editor's introduction. In *Language and Symbolic Power*, by Pierre Bourdieu. Malden, MA: Polity Press.

Tsing, Anna. 1993. *In the Realm of the Diamond Queen*. Princeton: Princeton University Press.

Turner, Bryan. 1984. *The Body and Society: Explorations in Society and Theory*. New York: Sage Publications.

Turner, Terence. 1980. The Social Skin. In *Not Work Alone: A Cross-cultural View of Activities Superfluous to Survival*, ed. Jeremy Cherfas and Roger Lewin, 27–47. New York: Cambridge University Press.

Turner, Victor. 1967. *The Forest of Symbols: Aspects of Ndembu Ritual*. Ithaca, NY: Cornell University Press.

Veblen, Thorstein. 1994. *The Theory of the Leisure Class*. Mineola, NY: Dover Thrift Editions.

Vergote, Antoine. 1996. *In Search of a Philosophical Anthropology*. M. S. Muldoon, trans. Leuven: Leuven University Press.

Vigh, Henrik. 2006. *Navigating Terrains of War: Youth and Soldiering in Guinea-Bissau*. New York: Berghahn.

Wacquant, Loïc. 2004. *Body and Soul: Notebooks of an Apprentice Boxer*. Oxford: Oxford University Press.

———. 1998. The Prizefighter's Three Bodies. *Ethnos* 63(3):325–52.

Wagner, Roy. 1986. *Asiwinarong: Ethos, Image, and Social Power among the Usen Barok of New Ireland*. Princeton: Princeton University Press.

Wahidin, Azrini. 2004. Reclaiming Agency: Managing Aging Bodies in Prison. In *Old Age and Agency*, ed. Emmanuelle Tulle, 69–86. New York: Nova.

Warner, Michael. 2002. *Publics and Counterpublics*. New York: Zone Books.

Wedeen, Lisa. 2008. *Peripheral Visions: Publics, Power, and Performance in Yemen*. Chicago: University of Chicago Press.

Weiner, Annette. 1976. *Women of Value, Men of Renown: New Perspectives in Trobriand Exchange*. Austin: University of Texas Press.

Weiss, Brad. 2009. *Street Dreams and Hip Hop Barbershops: Global Fantasy in Urban Tanzania*. Bloomington: Indiana University Press.

———. 2004. Introduction: Contentious Futures: Past and Present. In *Producing African Futures: Ritual and Reproduction in a Neoliberal Age*, ed. Weiss, 1–20. Leiden: Brill.

Williams, Raymond. 1977. *Marxism and Literature*. Oxford: Oxford University Press.

Winegar, Jessica. 2012. The Privilege of Revolution: Gender, Class, Space, and Affect in Egypt. *American Ethnologist* 39(1):67–70.

Yahaya, Ibrahim Y. 1988. *Hausa a rubuce: Tarihin rubuce rubuce cikin Hausa*. Zaria, Nigeria: Northern Nigeria Publishing Company.

Youngstedt, Scott M. 2013. *Surviving with Dignity: Hausa Communities of Niamey, Niger*. New York: Lexington Books.

Žižek, Slavoj. 1989. *The Sublime Object of Ideology*. London: Verso.

INDEX